Praise for *Quantum Love*

"Laura Berman's wake-up call, breast cancer, led her to a truly quantum understanding of health, healing, and loving. In Quantum Love *she lays out a series of deep commitments to self-love that have the power to transform your health and your relationships. This is the real deal. Bravo Laura!"*

— **Christiane Northrup, M.D.**, *New York Times* best-selling author of *Goddesses Never Age: The Secret Prescription for Radiance, Vitality, and Well-Being*

"Dr. Laura Berman is like the best girlfriend we'd all love to have who just happens to know a lot more about love, sex, and relationships than we do! She is thinking about love in a whole new way. Quantum Love *will bring your relationship to a whole new level."*

— **Eva Longoria**, actress, producer, director, philanthropist

"Simply put, Laura Berman is the best relationship expert in the field."

— **Steve Harvey**, Emmy award–winning television and radio personality and best-selling author

"Laura Berman gets to the root of human essence when it comes to loving and being loved. Quantum Love *has helped me navigate my own journey to being the best version of myself I can be and breaking through into a place of light and love."*

— **Cat Cora**, celebrity chef and founder of Chefs for Humanity

"This beautifully written book skillfully illuminates both the art of love and the science of love. Inspiring, enlightening, and easy to understand, Quantum Love *will transform how you feel and express your love into a deeper and more profound experience. A must read."*

— **Arielle Ford**, author of *Turn Your Mate into Your Soulmate*

QUANTUM LOVE

ALSO BY LAURA BERMAN

The Book of Love

For Women Only

It's Not Him, It's You

Loving Sex

The Passion Prescription

Real Sex for Real Women

Secrets of the Sexually Satisfied Woman

Talking to Your Kids about Sex

QUANTUM LOVE

Use Your Body's Atomic Energy to Create the Relationship You Desire

Laura Berman, Ph.D.

HAY HOUSE, INC.
Carlsbad, California • New York City
London • Sydney • Johannesburg
Vancouver • Hong Kong • New Delhi

Published and distributed in the United States by: Hay House, Inc.: www.hayhouse.com® • *Published and distributed in Australia by:* Hay House Australia Pty. Ltd.: www.hayhouse.com.au • *Published and distributed in the United Kingdom by:* Hay House UK, Ltd.: www.hayhouse.co.uk • *Published and distributed in the Republic of South Africa by:* Hay House SA (Pty), Ltd.: www.hayhouse.co.za • *Distributed in Canada by:* Raincoast Books: www.raincoast.com • *Published in India by:* Hay House Publishers India: www.hayhouse.co.in

Cover design: Amy Rose Grigoriou • *Interior design:* Nick C. Welch
Illustration of the chakra system: Courtesy of Bruce Lipton
Illustration of the wHolyShift: Thanks to Jacqueline Lesser Faust.
Visit www.THEwHolyShift.com

Library of Congress Cataloging-in-Publication Data

Names: Berman, Laura.
Title: Quantum love : use your body's atomic energy to create the relationship you desire / Laura Berman.
Description: 1st Edition. | Carlsbad : Hay House, Inc., 2016.
Identifiers: LCCN 2015039437 | ISBN 9781401948832 (hardback)
Subjects: LCSH: Intimacy (Psychology) | Love. | Sex instruction for women. | Man-woman relationships. | BISAC: FAMILY & RELATIONSHIPS / Love & Romance.
| SELF-HELP / General.
Classification: LCC BF575.I5 B47 2016 | DDC 306.7--dc23 LC record available at http://lccn.loc.gov/2015039437

Hardcover ISBN: 978-1-4019-4883-2

10 9 8 7 6 5 4 3 2 1
1st edition, February 2016

Printed in the United States of America

This book is dedicated to YOU:
that inner, essential self who always
and unconditionally holds you
in Quantum Love

CONTENTS

A WELCOME NOTE

Dearest Reader,

Are you ready to fall into Quantum Love?

I know it may be a term that on first listen sounds like a band from the 1980s or something you tuned out during high school physics. Well, let me assure you, this is neither a hair metal band nor a boring lecture. Quantum Love is a term I use to describe love that is fulfilling, unconditional, passionate, life affirming, rewarding, and erotic. *Is that all?* you might ask. Nope! It's just the beginning. I believe Quantum Love is why we are all on this planet in the first place. It is what drives us and connects us. It is what inspires us and what will heal us, if we will only let it.

If you have picked up this book because you are broken-hearted, I see you. I hear you. You have come to the right place. If you're here because you think your partner doesn't love you anymore, or you imagine you can't let your mate see your "ugly body" naked; if you're tired of having the same arguments; if you feel like you don't get kissed or romanced enough, or you think you will never meet Mr. or Mrs. Right; if you are lonely, grief stricken, ashamed, scared, or angry, this is the right book for you. And if you're happy with your relationship but curious about how much better it can get, you've come to the right place.

Quantum Love is our inalienable birthright. Yet most of us spend our entire lives totally disconnected from it. In fact, I was in that very same boat just a few years ago. I had spent 25 years working with couples and helping them achieve better love lives. It was fulfilling, meaningful, and important work. Then my seemingly perfect life began to give way underneath me, and I finally reached out and took the plunge into the unknown. There

I began a journey of discovery, wading into an entirely new and deep pool of wisdom composed of science, philosophy, physics, and even metaphysics. It would add a powerful new layer to my work, not to mention the rest of my life. I've written this book to share what I've learned with you.

Let me explain the format of this book a bit. It is divided into two different kinds of chapters, essentially moving you from theory into practice. There are the regular theory chapters, which explain in depth what Quantum Love is, how it works, why it works, and what it can do for you, your partner, and your relationship from an emotional, physical, and spiritual perspective. These chapters are interwoven with Commitment chapters, which are the practice chapters. Here I will be asking you to make key commitments to do the things that will bring you closer to Quantum Love, and I will teach you practical ways to apply what you are learning to create Quantum Love in your life. There will be places where I'll ask you to do a written exercise or record some key steps on your Quantum Love path, so you may want to get a blank book or notebook and make it your Quantum Love Journal—or you can go online to www.drlauraberman.com/quantumlove and download an electronic version of a Quantum Love Journal to accompany you on the journey. Some core exercises will be presented to you in the chapters themselves. Others will be available to you in the Appendix. And you'll find even more tools and exercises online at www.drlauraberman.com/quantumlove.

There are a few things I want to note before we move forward. First, Quantum Love is for *everyone* and *all* types of relationships: gay, straight, or somewhere in between. Romantic love is romantic love, and it is beautiful and fulfilling in all its forms.

Also, please know singles are welcome! You can use this book to create and practice Quantum Love in your life regardless of your relationship status. Most of what I will be discussing, and the advice and exercises I will offer, will be in the context of relationships. When you build Quantum Love in your own life, it will definitely help you to attract the perfect mate for you. What's more, all of the techniques you will learn in this book will help you build a lasting, rich, deep, and satisfying love when it comes.

All of the models and tools I have created for Quantum Love were built from the wisdom of sages and thought leaders who came before us, many thousands of years ago and counting. I am going to "prove" with science and research as much as I can about how and why Quantum Love works. But there will sometimes be a gap between what I can prove to you with empirical data and what I can tell you I fully believe to be true based on how it has worked in my own life and in the lives of the countless individuals whom I have counseled. All names and identifying information in the cases I outline in this book have been changed. Trust and respect are vital in all relationships, including (and especially) the relationships of people who have come into my life looking for help.

Make no mistake: moving into Quantum Love is a journey. It will require you to open yourself to new ideas, to challenge long-held beliefs, and to take responsibility for the reality you have created and the new, much better one you can build. It may not be easy, but believe me when I tell you that it will be worth it. You are fully worthy of the love that you want. It is waiting for you. It's time to take the first step forward down a new path, the path of Quantum Love.

Quantum Love is a transformation. Once you learn to put the powerful energy of your mind, body, and spirit to work for you, your life and your relationship won't be the same. Quantum Love is also a reclamation. You were born in a perfect state of love, and while your experience may have moved you away from the truth and wisdom of this essential self, it is still there unchanged, bright and perfect. You simply need to move back into it. *Quantum Love* will show you how.

CHAPTER 1

What Is Quantum Love, Anyway?

Lovers don't finally meet somewhere.
They're in each other all along.

— Rumi

Simply put, Quantum Love is the love that results when you consciously take ownership of the energy in your body, heart, and mind and use it to serve your relationship. It's taking quantum physics—the science of how energy works—and applying it to your love life in a way that reveals your hidden power to create exactly the relationship you want.

You may believe that the best part of love was right at the very beginning of your relationship: the dopamine-drenched, can't-eat-can't-sleep, head-over-heels honeymoon phase. Once the butterflies in the stomach subside, you settle in for the long haul, either feeling calmer and more connected or, like most people, worrying that something is missing or lost.

You may have already tried everything from couple's counseling to the Kama Sutra. Maybe, in an attempt to bring back the excitement and drama, you get stuck on the sickening merry-go-round of explosive fights and injurious mind games. Or perhaps you simply settle for what you think is the best you can hope for:

lackluster sex, repetitive fights, and a gnawing feeling of boredom and dissatisfaction.

You've probably been thinking there are only two options: somehow recapturing that early magic or throwing your hands up in defeat. But the truth is, there's a better, more fulfilling alternative—a higher level of love beckoning you to move forward, not backward. It's Quantum Love.

Thanks to tremendous advancements in the field of quantum physics, the study of our life and our world at the tiniest, most fundamental level, we now know that at our molecular core, each of us is simply a vessel of energy. A range of fascinating studies, many of which I will share in this book, have made clear that the reality in which we exist is actually created *by us* through the expectations we have of it. This is especially true in our most important relationships. Quantum physics has established that the observer (you) and whatever is being observed (your partner and your relationship) are energetically linked and that you can influence what you observe in any way you choose. In essence, the science of quantum physics has demonstrated that every possible reality is available to us at every millisecond, but it is our *personal perspective*—our expectation of what our reality will be—that brings it into being!

In the following pages, I will teach you what's already *actually* happening in your internal world and then explain how you can consciously use it to create passion, excitement, and connection you never imagined possible. You can't go back to the honeymoon phase. And if you're really honest with yourself, you know you don't want to trade the comfort, trust, and familiarity of a long-term relationship for the excitement of something brand-new. You want it all: a love that feels intense and fulfilling, satisfying your needs and desires on every level, but also a love that reaches new heights of intimacy and connects you to a fuller sense of purpose.

Does this sound too good to be true?

It's not. It's completely within your power. As a sex and relationship expert, I help couples get there all the time. And if you're willing, you and your mate can get there too, transforming your relationship into the manifestation of your deepest desires.

Why in the World Am *I* Writing *This* Book?

If you have read my work or followed my television appearances in the past, this topic might seem like a bit of a departure for me. What could lead a sex and relationship therapist to suddenly delve into the world of energy and matter? And how the heck does that apply to relationships?

It certainly wasn't something anyone in my work or personal life expected, and it wasn't anything I had ever studied in the past. I had a general idea of how the universe worked, and it made sense to me. But I have since shifted and widened my perspective, in large part because I had no other choice.

It wasn't until I reached 41 years old that I began questioning everything I thought I knew. When my mother passed away from cancer quite suddenly, it caused a seismic shift in my universe. For the first time in my adult life, I felt uncertain, overwhelmed, and lost. I experienced a pain I didn't know it was possible to feel, as if a piece of me had been ripped away. I wasn't sure who I was anymore, or how to move through the grief in an effective way. I had certainly counseled many through this process and experienced loss many times myself before then. But the connection I'd had with my mother was deeper than almost anything else in my life.

Then, less than a year after I lost her, I was diagnosed with breast cancer—in the same breast where my mother's cancer had originated. Never before had I needed my mother's love and guidance more, and never before had I faced my own mortality in such a stark and vulnerable way. My mother was gone; now would I be next? Would my own young children be forced to face the pain and grief I was barely able to handle as an adult?

Needless to say, the cancer sent shock waves through my family. My husband, Sam, and my sons, Ethan, Sammy, and Jackson, all dealt with it differently. Sam tried to be my rock, but I knew the terror and helplessness he felt. He was so used to always being in control, successful, and on top of things. Now here he was, unable to fix the worst problem he had ever confronted. Meanwhile, my kids were frightened and anxious, and they acted out as they struggled to confront the terrifying prospect of losing Mommy. As for me, I was left feeling depressed, disconnected, and even angry. Why was this happening? I lived a healthy lifestyle. I did yoga, didn't smoke, and rarely touched alcohol. Why was my body betraying me after I took such pains to care for it? Why was the world so uncertain and so unkind? How could I feel safe and secure when it felt like I was living on a fault line?

Soon my questions became more than just inner rhetorical laments. I am a born-and-bred reader and researcher, so I became the Nancy Drew of existential crises. I wanted to understand what I was going through and learn how to support my body and mind (not to mention my family) through the harrowing time ahead. I wanted to maximize my chances of survival and the time I had with my loved ones. Armed with nothing but my Kindle and an inquisitive mind, I was bound and determined to look life and death in the face and get some answers.

I suppose I was hoping that if I understood the secret to how life worked, I could make more sense of my grief and fear. I was right, but I didn't realize the way in which my search would change the trajectory of my life and my career. Looking back, I can't help but feel a rush of gratitude. It was the bleakest time of my life, but it was also the most enriching, powerful, and transformative.

I have taken to calling my life's crises AFGEs (shorthand for Another F#!&ing Growth Experience), because losing my mom and living through cancer taught me that with our greatest pains can come our greatest gifts. Were it not for the intense pain and loss I was experiencing, I would have kept going as I was going. My life, which was wonderful, would have remained the same, but I wouldn't have reached the state of clarity, knowing, and wonder that I have reached since. Pain is a wonderful teacher and a fierce motivator. It drove me to learn the lessons that have changed my life, my relationships, and the way I work with the individuals and couples I treat.

First, I started exploring how to survive and thrive through cancer. I wanted to hear from other survivors and learn from their wisdom and strength. But when I followed the bread crumbs of what I was reading and where it was leading, I realized these authors had more than just war stories and lists of superfoods to share with me. The books traveled beyond nutrition and an anti-cancer diet to research on neuroscience, biofeedback, and how deeply connected our minds and bodies really are. The more I learned, the more it made sense to me, and I began to apply the science behind it to my own self-care.

Then things got really interesting.

It was through my exploration of writings on the power of the mind that I stumbled back onto *The Secret*. Most of us have heard of Rhonda Byrne's 2006 bestseller about the Law of Attraction. After all, it sat on the bestseller list for 146 consecutive weeks. Through the success and popularity of Byrne's book, the Law of Attraction became part of the mainstream lexicon, albeit often accompanied by a roll of the eyes. There was even a *Saturday Night Live* skit about it. The Law of Attraction teaches that "like attracts like." In other words, positive thoughts attract positive occurrences and negative thoughts attract negative occurrences. Byrne best sums it up with this description: "Thoughts are magnetic, and thoughts have a frequency. As you think thoughts, they are sent out into the universe, and they magnetically attract all like things that are on the same frequency. Everything sent out returns to the source—you."

Like many others, I sort of got the idea. I played around the edges of it but never effectively put it into practice. I wanted to believe it but didn't completely buy it. Sure, positive thought was great, and I could understand the physical benefits, but I couldn't wrap my mind around what the Law of Attraction actually *was*. My doubt came through in questions that I couldn't find answers to: *What is the mechanism for it? And what does it say about me that I am attracting all these losses and illnesses into my life?*

I am a scientist at heart; I depend on data and research in order for something to feel real to me. This is part of the reason why I was struggling so much with *The Secret*. I needed less "feely" and more "factual." So I kicked into science mode and started to dig deeper. *Who says this really works, and why does it work? Is there any science behind this "new thought" of the Law of Attraction?* Instead of staying frustrated by my questions, I decided to find cold, hard answers.

It was in this state of questioning that I first came across quantum physics. In my studies, I came to realize that the lessons of quantum physics could be applied not only in science but throughout the entirety of human existence. I discovered that, in essence, quantum physics *is* the science behind the Law of Attraction. Now it all started to make sense. As I learned about the quantifiable lessons beneath this amazing metaphysical idea, it became more real and tangible to me. I started to play with the information and put it into practice in my own life, and soon I could feel the astonishing impact of this new understanding. I was flabbergasted by what I discovered about my own body's energy and how it affected those around me in material ways.

I began using the lessons I learned to help couples who came to me for therapy, and I was amazed by the positive results. I used what I learned to help my kids deal with anxiety and stress. I applied the principles in my relationship with my husband, and I saw our bond almost immediately begin to deepen and mature. Like a ripple in a pond, the change spread out throughout the whole of my existence. And I knew I had something important to share with the world.

I'm Coming Out

Here's the truth: in addition to being a researcher, therapist, and scientist, after my study of the quantum world I now have a much clearer and firmer belief in God. I know that word is loaded for many people. But the God I believe in is universal, encompassed in all religions and beliefs. To me, "God" is not a religious, institutional, or external concept. Whether you call God Jesus Christ, Allah, Krishna, Gaia, some other name, or no name at all,

I think almost everyone who believes in God can agree that God at his/her source is nothing more than pure, beautiful *Love.*

So when I refer to God, I am really talking about the energy of Love, vibrating at the very highest frequency. I do not think that God is somewhere out there in the distance, a million miles away. Rather, I think we are all God and God is in us. I believe that each of us is a gorgeous, unique, and magical expression and creation of that all-knowing, all-encompassing, perfectly designed Love. If God is the sun, we are the millions of rays that shoot out of it. Even though we appear separate, we are actually all made of the same thing, and we all come from the same source.

Does religion play a role in this book? No. Whether you are Jewish, Muslim, Christian, Wiccan, atheist, or agnostic, the principles within this book can be applied to your life. And the following pages will be much less esoteric, I promise. But I do want you to know that ideas such as these will inevitably pop up, as there is no denying that our world is charged with a power that is indefinable and mysterious. Science can take us only so far, and after that, faith has to take us a little farther. So although this isn't a religious book, it involves some spiritual precepts to the extent that life itself does, and therefore I cannot separate these ideas from the discussion entirely.

Historically, clinicians and scientists aren't supposed to be into the more esoteric, at least not publicly. If it can't be pinned down in black and white and proven empirically, then we aren't supposed to even consider it. So I do have some doubt and fear about "coming out" about my beliefs. But I am taking the leap because I believe what I have learned is too important to keep hidden. Go ahead and be skeptical—even slightly annoyed if you wish. But please don't be discouraged! If you just hang in there, I promise you will learn invaluable lessons, no matter what you believe.

A Note on the Real You

This is a book about your relationship and how to create fulfillment, connection, and bliss within it. But I want to spend a moment on the most crucial piece of this puzzle: *you.*

Who are you? It sounds like a simple question. You might answer, "I am a mother" or "I am a teacher" or "I am an engineer" or "I am a stay-at-home dad." Or you might get more detailed and say, "I am a Christian" or "I am a Jew" or "I am Egyptian" or "I am Brazilian." Maybe you would tell me, "I am a sports fanatic" or "I love chocolate" or "I am a cancer survivor" or "I am a kick-ass golfer" or "I love Bruce Springsteen." In short, you would tell me about all the things that make up who you are, whether about your past, your family, your job, your interests, or your beliefs.

Except here's the thing: none of that is really *you.* That stuff merely makes up your identity. It's the information I could find on your Facebook or LinkedIn page. It's the stuff you might share on a first date or with a new acquaintance. But I am here to tell you that *none of that* is the *real* you.

The real you could never be boiled down to a social media profile. It could never be distilled on a first date. The real you is eternal, unchangeable, formless. The real you is the light inside of you that is always on, the life source that is buried deep within you and watching all of life unfold without ever changing, aging, wavering, or decaying. I call the real you the *essential self.* And your essential self (rather than your ego self) is the one who will create Quantum Love.

In his amazing book *The Untethered Soul,* Michael Singer writes, "There is nothing more important to true growth than realizing that you are not the voice of the mind—you are the one who hears it." In other words, your essential self isn't the part of your brain that's reading these words. It's not even the part that's thinking about these words. Nor is it the part thinking about making dinner, or the part worried about work, or the part keeping an eye on your nearby child. No, the real you is doing nothing but observing. The real *you* is the you who *hears* the thought, not the one who *has* the thought. The real you is the you that has been inside of you since the day you were created, the you that was there on your 4th birthday and on your 40th.

Why is it so important to realize that this is the real you? Because once you realize that you are not just the mother, the teacher, the Christian, the golfer, or the chocolate addict—that you are just *you*, eternally and unquestionably and unchangeably—suddenly it is easier to let go. You aren't as threatened by life, whether it's an unkind word, an argument, a loss of a job, a change in finances, or a problem with your children. All of that stuff is important, yes, but ultimately it cannot impact or detract from the real you. The real you will remain as impervious and entire as a star in the night sky.

Physicists say that energy can be neither created nor destroyed. And quantum physics tells us that you are nothing but energy. So it stands to reason that you too can be neither created nor destroyed. The real you cannot be negatively impacted by anything in the world. It cannot be added to or subtracted from, improved, or altered in any way. You exist, you are entire, and you don't have to do anything to make yourself more real or more lovable. What an amazing discovery!

What does all this information have to do with your love life and your relationship? And how can you apply the principles of quantum physics to your life in real, sustainable, and powerful ways? Allow me to show you. Remember, it's okay to have questions and doubts as you read on. In fact, I would be surprised if you didn't! Accept those doubts. Love those doubts. Let the questions exist without trying to force answers upon yourself.

This journey will empower you and your partner to take the physical and emotional intimacy between you to a whole new level. My guess is it will be something that you have never experienced before—in a good way. In the following chapters, you will learn about your body's energy, what the unique frequency of your own energy is, and how to consciously experience the perfect harmony that already exists between your frequency and your partner's. That doesn't mean there won't be hurdles or you won't get stuck. Rather, you will be so finely in tune with yourself and your partner that you'll know how to *stay* in tune and turn every crisis into a welcome opportunity to grow together—psychically, emotionally, and sexually.

I am not a spiritual guru or a quantum physicist. I am a clinician, a scientist, and a happily married woman. Through my own journey, research, and practice, I have found a formula that can help you discover Quantum Love within yourself and your partner. Using personal and professional anecdotes, case studies, and the newest metaphysical and scientific research, I will teach you how to create Quantum Love in your life. You will learn to make fundamental shifts that resonate with the profoundly spiritual but make perfectly sound, scientific sense.

I am so excited that you are on this journey with me, and I can't wait to begin!

CHAPTER 2

Meet Your Inner Quantum Physicist

Stop acting so small.
You are the universe in ecstatic motion.

— Rumi

Have you ever envisioned something you wanted to happen—and then it happened? Met someone and felt immediately as though you'd known him or her all your life? Sensed that something was wrong with a friend or loved one and later got a call that this person was in the hospital? That's quantum physics at work in your life.

Now, have you ever found yourself thinking about your partner, and then he or she called? Held someone in your arms and felt a spiritual and emotional connection that surpassed words? Felt your mood change when your partner walked into the house? Known what your partner was thinking without being told? That is quantum physics at work *in your relationship.*

As you will soon learn, we are all made of pure energy. That energy makes up our physical bodies as well as our thoughts and emotions, and it is in constant vibration at varying speeds, or frequencies. The energy of our bodies, thoughts, and emotions is unbelievably powerful, and it attracts things into our consciousness that are vibrating at the same frequency, like tuning forks that come together to sound a single note. In other words, if we become aware of something through any one of our five senses, then it means that its frequency is in harmony with the vibrations we are putting out into the world.

So what does this mean for our love lives? Everything! Your mate is in your life because your personal vibrations have pulled you into each other's world. He or she is ultimately in harmony with you (even if it doesn't always feel that way). Each of you has the power to affect the other's energy—and by virtue of affecting each other's energy, you actually affect each other's physical, mental, and emotional frequency. Quantum Love is a state in which you and your partner are in energetic harmony together in your optimal energetic state, as a couple and individually. As the book goes on, I'll give you the tools you need to consciously and intentionally get into that state—and stay there. But first we're going to learn more about the science that makes these tools work.

What in the World IS Quantum Physics?

If you are like most people, your brain starts to spin when you hear the term *quantum physics*. This is probably especially true if you aren't a left-brain person, have never excelled at math or science, or would never dream of settling in to watch an episode of *Nova*.

I used to feel the same way. Quantum physics seemed like an exclusive field, one that required advanced degrees and a stunning intellect to even join the conversation. It just sounded, well, *hard*. I never anticipated that its principles would be relatively simple. The basic lessons of the field can be understood and applied by everyone, even those of us who passed high school science by the skin of our teeth. All we have to do is be open to new possibilities.

In fact, the true difficulty of understanding quantum theory doesn't stem from complex abstractions or scientific jargon; it comes from the fact that these concepts fly in the face of everything we think we know about our universe. Just as people in the Middle Ages used to think the world was flat and the sun revolved around the earth, it wasn't too long ago that people in our own time had very flawed ideas about what made the world work.

In the past, classical physics told us that we were the result of our physical actions and experiences. The same was true of everything around us—everything we touched, saw, and experienced was the result of external forces. We looked to the elements—air, earth, fire, and water—as the natural forces that shaped the world we know. Quantum physicists, however, are looking *deeper.* They are studying the smallest particles in the universe, the foundation of everything in this world *and in us,* and have discovered that the universe may not work as we previously thought.

This new understanding of how our world works and our role within it has huge implications for our relationships. Quantum physics leads us to question not just who we are but *why* we are and *how* we are, and what that means for our future, our life, and especially our relationships.

This Will Only Hurt a Little: Opening Up to the Principles of Quantum Theory

Quantum physics is undeniably complex, so I am going to focus only on the fundamental principles that I believe are the foundation for changing your relationship. So don't worry, no advanced degree required!

Also, I want to be clear. I love designing and implementing scientific research, but I am not a quantum physicist. When I began this journey, I was intimidated because I feared the subject would be too hard for me to understand. For that reason, I will seek to put things in laymen's terms as much as possible. I apologize to all the quantum physicists out there if my explanations seem too simplified! Accessibility is my goal, as I believe that everyone can benefit from these transformational ideas.

For now, all you need is an open mind and the willingness to look at life through a new lens. I am going to ask you to view the world, and your reality, in a way that will seem kind of strange.

Remember, for thousands and thousands of years, humans have thought they "knew" everything there was to know about life on earth—until a new generation came along and proved the past generation's knowledge wrong or incomplete. The same will certainly happen with our generation's beliefs. So don't be afraid to consider and even challenge your long-held thoughts.

Remember, it's okay if you aren't 100 percent on board with these ideas. You don't have to be. Just be willing to think about them, play with them, and step back and view your life with an open, searching mind.

Quantum Physics Principle #1: Everything Is Energy

You are pure potential. I don't just mean this in the literal sense that you have the potential to change your job, lose weight, or write a bestseller. You do have the potential to do all of those things, and that is a very powerful and life-altering truth to believe and accept. But even more than that, on an even deeper level, you are *pure energy*. Energy that cannot die or be tarnished or destroyed.

This same energy connects you to everything and everyone around you. You are made up of the same energy as your partner, your neighbor, a woman across the world, the stars, even the wind itself! The boundaries that you perceive between yourself and the world around you don't exist on a quantum level. You aren't a single, solitary puddle. You are a wave in a vast ocean of intelligence, power, and wisdom.

You might think: *It's great that we are all beings packed with potential energy, but what does that really mean? And if I have so much energy within me, why am I so dead tired at the end of the day?* When I use the term *energy* in this book (and when quantum physicists use the term), it's not meant in the way that you are probably used to hearing it, as in "Kids have tons of energy" or "Eating lean protein is a good way to increase your energy."

Instead, I am referring to the life source itself, the ocean of pure existence within us and around us at every moment.

The energy inside us and in every piece of the world around us is constantly moving. Picture it as billions of dancing, wiggling strings of energy. Each string has a unique vibration and movement and acts like a magnet, attracting strings with comparable frequencies and vibrations. This attraction can expand across all space and time (because space and time don't exist at the quantum level). As those energy strings get attracted to one another, they clump together. When enough energy clumps together, it creates a form we can actually see. This is called mass.

If the term *mass* is giving you unpleasant flashbacks to high school science class, don't worry. Mass is actually very simple to define. Mass is energy (and conversely, energy is mass). They are the same thing, just in different forms. Think of it this way: mass is energy that has a form we can touch or see, whereas energy is potential mass that has yet to be formed.

Think about what this means about you, your body, and your mind. Your body, and every piece that makes up your body, is mass. It is your energy in physical form. Your thoughts are energy too, but they are formless. They do not have mass; they simply exist as energy. Your feelings can be both. We can't see our actual emotions, but we can certainly see them manifested in our smiles or frowns, laughter or tears. All of that is energy—*your energy*.

Our energy isn't locked inside of us either. It is constantly flying out into the universe and can impact our world and the people around us in very tangible ways. This occurs because of the power of our shared connection.

Quantum Physics Principle #2: We Are All Connected

The Mayans had a traditional greeting, *"In Lak'ech."* It translates to "I am another yourself." What a simple yet powerful thought! While ancient Mayans probably didn't have a clue about quantum physics, this saying perfectly encapsulates one of its basic principles: *You are not alone.* Famed psychiatrist and psychotherapist Carl Jung put it similarly, if a little less succinctly, when he wrote, "We meet ourselves time and again in a thousand disguises on the path of life." In other words, even though you might feel separate from the world around you, even isolated at times, you are actually connected to everything and every person around you, and every person you interact with has the potential to teach you something.

Accepting a philosophy of unity isn't easy in our culture, especially where individualism and autonomy are highly regarded (as they are particularly among Americans). However, the truth is that unity is what has allowed humanity to thrive. When humankind was new on this planet, our survival hinged on our togetherness. We couldn't survive without our fellow humans any more than we could have survived without oxygen or fresh water. We needed one another for protection, companionship, and the continuation of the species. Back then our circumstances mirrored the lack of separation between us that exists at the quantum level. However, as time rolled by, subsequent societies became less and less dependent on one another. We went from living in a cave or traveling together in nomadic tribes, to living in separate huts, to living in separate communities, to living in separate apartments, to living in large homes where we are separated from our own families by thousands of miles. Little by little the ability to be separate—the pleasure of being alone and of defining ourselves as individuals—became not just the cultural norm, it became a prize.

As comforting as principles of individualism might be to our ego (and as closely tied as they are to our core belief systems), many of today's thought leaders are now challenging this commonly held belief that people are separate from one another. In fact, they are challenging the belief that people are separate from anything at all.

In quantum physics, the principle that everything is connected is known as "non-locality." It holds that one energy particle can influence another energy particle, even when the particles do not touch in any way and even when they are separated by billons of miles. Quantum ideas such as this may be the science behind human connection.

The Evolution of Human Connection at an Energetic Level

In 1964, Irish physicist John Stewart Bell published a short article in which he posited that tiny particles, such as electrons, could display instantaneous coordination (i.e., the movement of one could cause the other to move at the exact same time) even when separated by miles and miles. Albert Einstein wasn't impressed by the idea, which he called "spooky action at a distance." Yet testing has since suggested a phenomenon physicists refer to as "quantum entanglement."[1]

Austrian physicist Erwin Schrödinger was one of the first to broach this idea of entanglement with his realization that different particles can behave as if they are the same thing, even if they are separated by space or time. In fact, this connection can still exist even if one of the particles no longer exists.[2]

The thought of it is enough to make you go cross-eyed! But think of it this way: we know that energy cannot be created or destroyed—it simply *is*. The *form* of that energy can change, though. So no matter where energy particles are, or what form they take, if two particles are entangled, they are the same. It doesn't matter if one is located on the moon and one is located in Miami—if one of them spins, the other one will spin as a result. And because energy is in everything and everyone and exists in countless forms, it's safe to say that the energy particles of which we are made have infinite entanglements across time and space. This kind of connectedness and coordination means that "oneness" is real. Thanks to entanglement, we are all *one* on the quantum level. We aren't all separate beings floating unconnected in space. We are each made up of millions of molecules that all share the same history and future. What a concept!

It's even more amazing when you apply the concept of entanglement to couples. The strength of the energetic entanglement between partners can be so intense that two bodies can behave as though they are the same being in surprising ways.

Researchers at the University of Washington were interested in seeing just how linked lovers were, and so they asked couples to undergo a test. They took one partner into a room and sent the other partner to another part of the building. Then they shone a light into the eye of the first partner while studying the ocular and brain reactions of the second. They found that the ocular center of the second partner's brain reacted when the first partner was exposed to the light, even though they were widely separated and had no idea what was happening in the other room![3]

The old rules of physics could never begin to explain such a shocking and moving reaction. However, quantum physics has a simple explanation: we are all connected, and we are all influencing the world around us at every moment. Our ability to influence through energetic connection is called *coherence.*

How We Influence Energy in Our Partners and Our Selves: Coherence and Entrainment

Coherence is a calm, peaceful, loving state of alignment within yourself that occurs when your heart is open—a state that I will show you how to reach a little bit later in this book. When you are in a state of coherence, your heart and your mind are working together in perfect harmony. There is no turmoil within you, just flow as your systems come into optimal alignment. When you are in coherence, your systems are aligned and vibrating at a high frequency.

As you will learn in the following chapters, a high frequency is key to getting on the path to Quantum Love. It corresponds to higher and happier states of consciousness, like joy, love, and gratitude. A coherent energetic state is great for your body too. It can support your immune system, reduce stress, and keep you feeling really good. And, finally, when you are in a coherent energetic state, you are positively impacting your partner and your relationship. One of the key points of this book is the lesson that *you* have the power to create or reshape the landscape of your relationship any way you desire, simply by creating the change in yourself first. When you are in an openhearted, coherent state, you are moving into Quantum Love, and by virtue of quantum physics, you move your partner and your relationship into Quantum Love as well. There's an art to getting into coherence. I will be teaching you how to get there in Chapter 4 ("Commitment #1—I Will Take Responsibility for the Energy I Bring into My Relationship").

When you are physiologically and energetically in coherence, there's a level of clarity and wisdom available to you that isn't available when you're not in coherence. Most of the time, when we're trying to find the solution to a problem, we feel anxious or upset, and it's difficult to find solutions from that place. Getting into coherence gives you access to the wisdom of your essential self. It can also positively influence your partner's energy through a process called *entrainment*.

The principle of entanglement helps us understand that we are all connected. Entrainment is one result of entanglement, a form of coherence in which one system's energetic state can actually influence another system. It can exist within just ourselves, as when our heart rate increases and our breathing rate speeds up, too, or it can extend beyond us and influence our partner.

Entrainment in Action

My husband and I were in the midst of a fight.

"I already told you about this. You *knew*. And *still* . . ."

I could feel myself going into defensive mode. It was a reflex that happened all too often when I felt challenged or frustrated. Sam was telling me his side of the story, but his words fell away as I began thinking of all the things I was going to say back to him. I wasn't even listening to what he was saying anymore; I was simply waiting for my turn to talk.

This was my usual M.O. I have never been someone who will stand down from an argument. Like most of my postfeminist peers, I like to say I nursed through a burning bra. My mom taught me to never let a man (or anyone, for that matter) control me and to always stand my ground. I grew up with the idea that not fighting back was equivalent to cowering. The ability to argue my case, on the other hand, was a sign of strength. These were lessons I had taught my own kids as well. It was a long-standing pattern in my life and family, one that many people share.

The energy between Sam and me was sharp, tense. It was palpable in the tone of our voices, our body language, and the words we were choosing to use—and it certainly wasn't helping the situation. But this time, I consciously decided not to drop into my usual pattern. I tuned in to my body's energy and felt the tightness in my chest and back. As I became aware of how that energy was adding to my tension, making me physically uncomfortable and beefing up my defenses, I realized neither of us would feel better until we shifted out of that detrimental state.

I decided that, just this once, as an experiment, I would shift out of defense mode by simply relaxing into a state of pure, unconditional love for my husband. I always feel it for him, even when I'm angry with him, even when it's buried under a pile of resentment and defensiveness. Without reaching for him physically or changing my expression in any way, I reached for him emotionally. I thought about how much I loved him and how this argument was a blip on the huge screen of our relationship and its story. I opened my heart to him. And I let him keep talking.

A strange thing happened.

Sam suddenly looked slightly confused. Then he said, "I forgot what I was saying." You have to understand that one of the many things I find attractive about my husband is his razor-sharp mind. He could argue before the Supreme Court if he wanted to. So for him to lose his train of thought was unprecedented in itself. Then his body visibly relaxed. His face softened and his shoulders came down from his ears. It was as though my loving energy had dispelled all the anger and tension inside of him, even though he didn't realize what was happening.

In quantum physics, the connection between Sam and me that made this shift possible is a form of coherence called entrainment. When I entered into an openhearted state, I achieved coherence within myself, and because Sam and I are energetically entangled, his physical state entrained with mine. Our energies came into vibrational harmony and allowed us to connect with our highest selves. Our anger and physical tension fell away as we came together in loving connection.

Coherence and entrainment show how deep and meaningful human relationships really are. You are not connected to your partner simply because you share a home or the same last name. Nor is your connection entirely physical or even entirely mental. There is something much deeper inside all of us that is connecting us to one another.

Coherence, it turns out, is a key to creating the life and the relationship you want. You and your partner are plugged into each other at your most fundamental level. You are constantly sending and receiving messages to each other, even when you are not aware you are doing so, and even when you aren't in the same room. If your partner is emitting a negative energy, it is going to negatively affect your own frame of mind, and if it goes unaddressed and unresolved, it may damage the relationship.

Imagine, in my argument with Sam, if instead of moving into a state of loving coherence I had switched into a state of intense anger. That energy would certainly have come across to him, and he would have likely responded with angry energy of his own. You and your partner naturally entrain to each other's energy levels, whether you realize it or not. But all too often, those energy levels are negative and unproductive. When you learn to control your energy and harness it effectively, you can make your connection with your partner deeper and stronger. This ability is not bound by anything physical, nor is it held within the lines of time and space. The influence of our energy can travel anywhere and manifest itself in tangible ways.

This connection gives us an amazing capacity for creating Quantum Love in our lives.

Quantum Physics Principle #3: You Create Your Reality

If I asked you, "What is real?" you might find it a very simple question to answer. You might say, "I am real, you are real, this table is real, this room is real. The plant in the corner is real, the tea in our cups is real, and the cat on the sofa is real. Everything we see, hear, feel, smell, and touch is real. The rest is just our imaginations and our memories."

But is it? Allow me to illustrate with a very interesting thought experiment created by Erwin Schrödinger in 1935. Schrödinger asked people to picture a cat in a box. With the cat is a flask of poison and a radioactive material. If the radioactive material becomes destabilized, it will cause the flask of poison to break. This, in turn, will kill the cat. (Poor kitty! Don't worry. This is all hypothetical.)

Schrödinger then posed the question: Is the cat alive or dead? Since we're all outside the box, the only way to be sure would be to open the box and observe: "Yes, the flask broke; the cat is dead" or "No, the flask didn't break; the cat is still alive." However, if we do not open the box, Schrödinger says, the cat is both alive *and* dead. Because both possibilities exist and neither outcome has been eliminated, both options are still on the table.[4]

So it is with our reality. We can only say, "Yes, the cat is alive" by checking the box to make sure. If we don't check the box, the potential for both life and death remains. So will the cat live to meow another day? That's up to you.

So let me ask you again, "What is real?" The answer is: *whatever we decide.* We choose our reality. We are in charge. We decide.

Your personal vibrations will dictate the world you create. If you are angry, you are likely to create more scenarios to sustain your anger as the energy of that emotion attracts the things that are vibrating in harmony with it. Whatever is in your material world embodies your personal vibration in some way. In other words, whatever your stories are, your energy is probably working to prove them right.

Observing the World Changes the World

What if I told you that in every moment the universe is being created for you, by you, right before your very eyes? It sounds crazy, but it's true.

Everything in our physical world is made up of atoms. But what are atoms? Scientists have found that atoms are actually nothing more than 99.99999999999 percent empty space. However, it isn't actually empty, a void filled with nothing. It is a space filled with potential, with energy, and with information. It is a pool of possibility waiting to form and take shape for us. It is the quantum field.

Scientists have even found that matter exists only when it is observed. Atoms take shape when we put our attention on them. Otherwise they return to their original state of pure energy and potential. Quite literally, the universe is being created *for* us, and as quantum physics shows, the universe is also being created *by* us, because our expectations and our beliefs about the world have the power to shape what we see or determine whether we see it at all.

Historically, we used to believe in an observer-observed paradigm. There was a world, and a person observing the world. The two were not connected in any way. Scientists used to believe that they could study subjects and perform research without influencing the outcome of their experiments whatsoever. This meant their findings were completely inviolable and reliable.

We now know that is patently untrue. It isn't true for individuals (people who are being studied are always affected by this knowledge, hence the need for control groups and placebos), and it isn't true even for nonhuman study subjects. This extends to the quantum level as well; the distinction between observer and observed isn't even true for electrons at the subatomic level.

Physicist Fred Alan Wolf has stated that the universe doesn't exist without a perceiver of the universe. It might sound hard to believe, but research in the field of quantum physics backs up his assertion. The best example of this is a study known as the double-slit experiment, first performed at the Weizmann Institute of Science and replicated hundreds, if not thousands, of times around the world.

Scientists at Weizmann built a tiny, barrier-like device with two openings. They then shot particles (little bits of matter) at the device and examined how the particles exited the device from the other side. Not surprisingly, the particles went through the two openings and left a neat, orderly pattern as proof of their trajectory. Next, the researchers sent waves through the device. They found that the waves interfered with each other and created an "interference pattern" as they exited the device. Again, this made sense to the physicists, as the waves were overlapping (as they do in nature) and hence were unable to behave like particles.

Next they sent electrons through the device, expecting the electrons to behave like particles and create a neat, orderly pattern. (An electron is a subatomic particle with a negative charge.) Instead, the electrons left no discernible, predictable pattern. But how could this be? At first, the researchers wondered if the electrons were possibly interfering with one another, just as the waves were, so they decided to send just one electron at a time through the barrier. They found that the electron still created an interference pattern—as though it were interfering with itself!

Eager to learn more, the physicists decided to create a device that could measure (or observe) exactly what the electron was doing when it passed through. They were once again shocked to discover that when the electron was being observed, it *stopped* behaving as a wave. It started behaving as a particle and leaving a particle-like pattern rather than an interference pattern. The physicists were amazed, as their findings showed that the very act of observation literally changed how this tiny electron chose to behave, as if the electron were aware it was being watched and decided to change form because of it![5]

So what does this really mean? I and many other scientists and teachers believe it means that we actually create our own reality in our life and in our relationships. Sure, we all know that we create our *perception* of reality. We also tend to agree that how we choose to interpret different events intellectually and emotionally creates our life experience. We are going to get into that in the following chapters. But what I'm talking about here is the idea that is the science behind the Law of Attraction and *The Secret*. We are creating our reality every millisecond. Even tiny, tiny bits of matter are literally responding to our gaze and acting differently because of it. We are the architects of the world we see around us each day.

In fact, we control our realities to such a degree that we are essentially choosing one reality while ignoring all other possibilities. And we are doing this every millisecond. Even though we think things "just happen" or the world "just is," the truth is, you could have chosen from a host of different options. You could have chosen a completely different reality . . . just as you can choose right now.

There Are Infinite Realities

Millions of women are diagnosed with breast cancer. However, the way I experienced breast cancer wasn't the same as the way other women did, even those who had nearly the exact same diagnosis and treatment. We each filtered our experience through our own belief systems and our expectations, as did our family members and friends. Each of my sons felt differently about my diagnosis and reacted in different ways, as did my husband. In other words, we all experienced a different reality.

Whether we realize it or not, this is quantum physics at work. If realities were set in stone, each member of my family would have experienced my cancer diagnosis in the same way. That simply isn't the case. There is an amazing freedom that comes with this realization: your reality is malleable and you have the power to control it.

There has been a great body of research that has helped to illuminate just how influential human thought can be on the material world. Dr. Masaru Emoto was a Japanese researcher who spent much of his career focusing on the study of water and the molecular changes that occur within water as droplets crystallize. Dr. Emoto wanted to discover if outside forces could change the way that water crystals take shape. Essentially, he wanted to discover if human consciousness, human intention, could actually *change* the molecular structure of water. Would the water *react* to the energy of human thoughts and feelings?

In order to research this, Dr. Emoto photographed water molecules after they crystallized. But before they did, he channeled different energy to each droplet. For some droplets he played Beethoven; for others, Metallica. For some droplets he channeled emotions like anger or images of people like Adolf Hitler. For others he thought of peace or people like Mother Teresa and channeled the positive energy those images created. Amazingly, his photographs show that the water actually seemed to respond differently to positive and negative thoughts and harmonious or cacophonous music. Water that received the focus of "gratitude" and "peace" formed into beautiful, almost symmetrical shapes. Water that received the energy of anger, betrayal, and murder turned into irregular, black, and rugged-looking crystals.[6]

Now consider this: Human beings are primarily made up of water. Think of what the negative and positive intentions and emotions did to the water droplets. Imagine that same molecular change occurring within your own body, every day, every time you dwell on emotions such as anger and on feelings of worthlessness and hopelessness. Now imagine those powerful energy vibrations impacting your partner as well.

Life isn't chaos that is completely out of your control. Your relationship isn't hopeless. Your sex life doesn't have to be passionless. You can decide what type of life you want to live and how you want your relationship to be. You are authoring your own reality. You can create the life you want. Once you realize that your reality can be changed by your energy, you will begin to recognize that your limiting beliefs and painful memories are more than just unpleasant. They are actually preventing you from living the life you desire.

These three quantum principles—that we are all energy, we are all connected, and we create our reality—form the basis of Quantum Love. They show us that anything is possible and that we have the power to shape and reshape our lives and our relationships through the power of our personal energy fields and the strength of our energetic connection with our partner.

In order to begin harnessing this power, we must first understand the limitations that have kept us from this realization for so long.

The Truth about Our Five Senses

By now, you might be thinking: How can these all be possible? Cats are both alive and dead, water responds to music, and people can stop crime with their thoughts? How can any of this be real?

It's okay if this all sounds a little crazy. After all, it flies in the face of much of what we were taught growing up. Like any new thought paradigm, it is challenging to accept, especially when the thought itself is telling us, "There is no paradigm."

Adding to the chaos is the fact that we are not able to see and experience most of the universe around us. As John Maunsell, a neuroscientist at Harvard, says, "People imagine they are seeing what's really there but they're not." He's right. All of the information that comes to us through our eyes, ears, nose, tongue, and skin—and scientists estimate that *billions* of bits of information come to us each day—has to be filtered through our brains in order for us to consciously perceive them. In order to manage the volume of stimuli it has to process, the brain develops patterns, biases, and generalizations that lump the information together in a way that is manageable. Sometimes it will distort the information to make it fit and other times it will delete the information entirely. Your brain *selects* where your attention will go based on what it believes is important. In that way, you are seeing what you choose to see, what you are capable of seeing, and what you are manifesting before you. Your senses mold and shape your reality and then tell you that it's the only reality out there.

But your reality isn't the only reality available to you. In fact, there are infinite realities available to you. Even if you have only 400 billion bits of information available to you (and in reality, that number is probably much higher) you can only be aware of roughly .00001 percent of that information. Otherwise your brain would be overloaded. Let's think about that for a second: your entire reality is shaped by less than one-ten-thousandth of the information available to you! We see and experience just a tiny, tiny fragment of the world and the universe, because our senses limit us to seeing just what is before us.

While our five senses can sometimes be very limiting, they shine the light that allows us to experience the world, but they come with boundaries that can limit our perception as much as they enable it. Our senses trick us into believing that we are viewing and experiencing the entirety of existence, when we are really just viewing a drop in the entire ocean. And they do so because our brains require it.

Why Our Brains Resist Too Much Information

Have you ever seen a movie or television show where a character is given the opportunity to read other people's minds or hear the thoughts and prayers of the world? Invariably, they think it is a cool trick to begin with, but after a while, the countless buzzing of thoughts, pain, prayers, and never-ending information drives them crazy. This is essentially what would happen to us if we were suddenly able to take in the billions of bits of information out there in the world, except it would be on a much, much larger scale.

Famous Georgetown University professor and scientist Karl Pribram found that the brain contains a certain "envelope" mechanism, which works to ensure that we are accessing only the information we need to live on a daily basis. We could not possibly take in the infinite information in the universe without going insane, so our brains take in only the amount of information that we can use and understand.[7]

Our brains continually sift through the myriad possibilities available to us and select which bits of information to "see" and believe. We see, feel, taste, touch, and smell a drastically condensed version of the world, a version that our brains literally concoct, instead of experiencing the world as it truly exists. After all, our brain is performing a huge number of tasks during every second of our existence! Not only is it in charge of our physical properties, but it is also processing 400 billion bits of information a second! We can consciously process only about 2,000 bits—no wonder so many things fly under our radar!

What does all this mean for you? Well, I hope it is beginning to give you some insight into quantum physics and energy as a whole. I also hope it is beginning to teach you that you are so much more than flesh and bone. You are radiating energy that can be felt all around you, especially by those closest to you. If you can get in touch with that energy and harness its amazing potential, you can rebuild your life from the inside out. One of the most powerful ways in which we can do that is through the power of intention.

Intention, Attraction, and Creation

Our thoughts, intentions, and feelings are energy that is as powerful as the energy in our physical selves, and this energy impacts the world around us in material ways. This is because our thoughts and feelings are vibrational energy waves—the same energy waves that exist in everything around us. Every thought you have ever had and will ever have creates a vibration that goes out into the quantum field, extending forever. These vibrations meet other vibrations, crisscrossing in an incredible maze of energy. Get enough energy together and it clumps into mass, becoming a form that is tangible and visible to us. In other words, the energy we send out as thoughts or intentions might just come back to us in a physical form. In this way, the energy of our emotions may be *manifesting* the events and relationships that occur in our lives on an entirely unspoken, unconscious, and quantum level. This is the defining idea behind the Law of Attraction.

Feelings, thoughts, and the intentions that go with them (consciously or unconsciously) have energy and power strong enough to impact the world around us and the people within it. We are all creating our own universe each and every day. Our expectations and our beliefs can literally change how we grow and develop and alter the people we become, not just psychologically but energetically as well.

Intention has led you to where you are today, whether it is conscious or unconscious. And when you don't channel your intention and guide it in the direction you want to go, you are likely going to wind up somewhere you never intended to be.

Focused intention is the key to the Law of Attraction. If you wake up every morning and hold the intention, "I refuse to have anything other than a good day today," you are going to succeed every single time. This doesn't necessarily mean that you won't get a flat tire, forget your wallet, or displease your spouse or vice versa. It simply means that when those things happen, you will remember your intention and you will line up your thoughts and hence your actions with the goal of having a good day.

And here's the thing: if you truly set this as your intention and keep it foremost in your mind, both consciously and subconsciously, I guarantee you that good things are going to happen to you. The more positive energy you exude, the more positive events will come your way. The Law of Attraction is summed up rather simply in a quote often attributed to Albert Einstein: "Everything is energy and that's all there is to it. Match the frequency of the reality you want and you cannot help but get that reality. It can be no other way. This is not philosophy. This is physics."

Einstein is not the only great thinker who knew the importance of one's thoughts and intentions. Buddha said, "All that we are is the result of what we have thought." Zen master Thich Nhat Hanh wrote, "In our consciousness, there are many negative seeds and also many positive seeds. The practice is to avoid watering the negative seeds, and to identify and water the positive seeds every day."

You can't think, "I am a loser" or "I am ugly" or "I will never succeed" and escape the impact of those thoughts on you and your reality. I don't just mean that they will have an impact on your mood or your self-esteem. I mean that these thoughts will literally change your life, and certainly not for the better.

The same is true with your relationship. If you regularly think, "My partner always lets me down" or "I am just not a sexy person," I bet that your relationship and your sex life have suffered greatly and needlessly as a result. I bet that you are afraid to initiate sex, afraid to dress or act seductively, afraid to ask for the love you want and the love you deserve. And, most likely, you unconsciously set an intention every day to be unhappy, to be disappointed, and to be ashamed of your body and your sexuality. Look at where that intention has led you.

The Art of Manifesting: What Is Happening on the Quantum Level?

In Chapter 6 ("Commitment #2—I Will Get Clear on What I Want out of Love"), we will be discussing the art of manifesting in great detail, particularly how to use it to create the kind of relationship you most desire. For now, I want to introduce the steps to manifesting the reality you want and explain how the process works on a quantum level.

As we've seen, quantum physics teaches us that our inside world—our energy, thoughts, and emotions—dictates our outside world, not the other way around. In other words, your internal energy creates the material world outside of you. *All of it.* Everything in your world, your reality, was created by you.

To understand how this big idea works, we're going to have to head back down into Quantum Town.

All physical matter in the universe is manifested in the quantum field. This unformed field of energy waits in a state of infinite possibility for you to create your material world from it, which you do, either deliberately or accidentally every second of every day you are alive. The material world does not preexist, awaiting your observation; you create the material world through your observations on a moment-by-moment basis.

The scientific explanation for this is that subatomic particles exist in a state of mere potential until they are observed. Before you observe them, these subatomic particles merely have the *potential* to become something material and concrete. The double-slit experiment shows us it is *your* expectation that commands subatomic particles to manifest into concrete objects. In this way, quantum physics shows us that intention and expectation cut to the very core of all our physical experiences. You are never a separate, neutral observer of your life.

Quantum physics has forced us to rethink everything we thought we knew about logical outcomes. No longer should we think of formative events (or things that cause outcomes) as sequences that bring a predictable result for us. That is the paradigm of classical physics. According to non-linearity, another component of quantum physics, we need to think of formative events as simply leading to potential outcomes or results.

Nothing in the material universe is a preexisting entity. No material object exists independent of you, awaiting your discovery. The material world is a commingling of your nonphysical energy with the energy of the quantum field, which is energy with the possibility to become anything.

Each observer, quantum physicists explain, sees his or her own individual universe. And this is to be taken literally, *not* metaphorically. You see, physicists call a material object in the universe a *space-time event.* A space-time event is a group of subatomic particles, a part of the quantum field, that have abandoned their status as mere potential because they have been observed and thus commanded to assume a definitive, concrete form. Your body, your hair, your home, your neighbor, your car, and every other material object are all examples of subatomic particles that have been commanded, through your observation and expectations, to form into a space-time event. Material reality is simply the subatomic particles' temporary deviation from their unformed state.

So if we create our reality through our energy state and observation, why shouldn't we create a reality we want? This is where the art of manifestation comes in, and it's possible because of the unity of all things, the shared truth that we are all energy and we are all one.

The universe wants to give you exactly the life and relationship you want. It's a friendly place and wants you to succeed at having all your heart desires. Once you want that for yourself as well (and actually believe that you are worthy of all the blessings of the universe) and you direct your body's energy toward Quantum Love, amazing things are going to come your way. I can't promise that bad things won't happen, but I can tell you that you aren't going to be as affected by those bad things. You won't take the flat tire personally, and you won't let an argument with your spouse make you feel unworthy and unlovable. Instead, you will be able to look at these occurrences with loving detachment and figure out your problems with a clear, concise plan of action. You might even be able to reach a state of mind in which you view your problems with gratitude, as though they are emissaries sent from beyond to help you learn valuable lessons and reach a deeper state of love. And for problems that have no solution, you will be able to sit quietly with them and simply allow them to exist until such time as an answer arrives.

As Einstein would say: It's not philosophy. It's physics.

CHAPTER 3

Discover Your Energy Profile

We are all Vibrational Beings. You're like a receiving mechanism. When you set your tuner to the station, you're going to hear what's playing.

— Abraham*

Life is energy. Emotions are energy. You are energy. Your partner is energy. At our core, that is all each of us really is: energy. This truth is simple, universal, and powerful. Whether it is sadness, joy, fear, or rage, emotions are nothing more than energy moving through our body. In fact, the Latin word for emotion (*motus animi*) means "movement of feelings." And when we express an emotion, that is exactly what we are doing. We are taking that emotional energy and giving it motion, whether it's by yelling at our partner, laughing with our friends, or crying at a sad movie. You are energy in motion, even when you aren't

* Who is Abraham? Well, it's not so much a question of "who" but of "what." Abraham is the collective name of what's believed to be a collection of spiritual guides channeled by a woman named Esther Hicks. Regardless of how weird this may seem and how questionable it may be given our experience of reality and what's possible, the wisdom Abraham shares is beautifully fashioned and makes perfect sense to me. I encourage people to read some of Abraham's work as an aid to getting out of your brain and into your mind (something we'll cover in a later chapter), regardless of its source. Check out this website: http://www.abraham-hicks.com/lawofattractionsource/about_abraham.php.

moving those emotions through you—for example, when you are holding back tears during a horrible job interview or trying not to giggle during a church service. Nor does your energy occur within a vacuum. Energy in motion doesn't just stay within us; it can have a tremendous impact on those around us. Your personal energy can, and will, impact the energy of your partner and your relationship.

Each of us has an energy profile. In this chapter I am going to help you identify what your energy profile is and how it is affecting your relationship, for better or worse. I will teach you about the way the frequency of the energy of your body is creating the realities of your relationship without your even knowing it, and I'll explain how to consciously harness that energy to meet your relationship goals.

Tuning In

It was my children who first showed me that the energy of my emotions had a powerful impact on our relationships—something I had to be conscious of and responsible for.

It started with my own cancer diagnosis, less than a year after my mother's death from cancer. I felt pulled in two directions, first by the desire to take care of my physical needs and second by the desire to manage my own fears. *Holy crap, I have cancer! What will this chemo do to my body? What will my recovery be like? How am I going to pay all these bills?* But on top of that there was the emotional shrapnel flying around me as each member of my family struggled with my diagnosis. My oldest, Ethan, a cancer survivor himself, was in the throes of his own anxiety. My middle son, Sammy, was having nightmares. My youngest, Jackson, was having full-on panic attacks during the day and refusing to go to school.

I was trying to find ways to help them cope while still managing my own feelings and fears. My husband was a phenomenal support, but he couldn't compensate for the family-wide unease my diagnosis created. I realized pretty quickly that this was more than I could take on, so I began searching for a support solution. Therapy and even medication, the usual tracks, just weren't working for my kids. Our situation was too big. I felt like I was grasping at straws, looking for *something* that could help me help my children. That's how I found myself in the office of Dr. Therese Rowley, an intuitive healer and medium.

I was not the sort of person who went to intuitives on a regular basis. But when you go through enough AFGEs and nothing else is working, you start to look in some more esoteric places. And in this case, it changed everything.

During our initial session, I decided to focus on Ethan. As a childhood leukemia survivor, he had always dealt with his own unique challenges. Now he was struggling continuously with attention, focus, regulating his emotions, and anxiety. The stresses of his own life dramas along with my illness were tipping the scales too far and he was acting out, struggling in school, and severely depressed.

With all of these things on my mind, I carefully wended my way along the busy Chicago sidewalks to Therese's office. I was excited about our meeting, but there was a little voice inside me saying, "This is silly" and "What would my colleagues say if they saw me visiting an intuitive?" I ignored the voice. What did I have to lose?

When Therese opened the door with a warm smile, I was taken aback to see that she looked more like a banker than alternative practitioner. She was polished and wearing a suit. I learned later she actually has a Ph.D. and comes from a background in corporate consulting. I followed Therese to her office upstairs in her Lincoln Park condo. The space was warm and inviting, with sunlight filtering in through the two windows behind her. The energy of the room felt peaceful, and it started to put me a little more at ease.

"Please, sit," she said, taking a chair across from mine. "Are there any particular places in your life that you want to focus on?"

Not sure what to expect, I began to open up about Ethan and his emotional struggle.

Therese closed her eyes and breathed in deeply. She explained that, like many energy healers, she does not need to be in the same room as the person she is connecting to. I now know that this is because energy is not contained within the boundaries of time and space, but at the time I thought it was a little wacky. I had to smile, picturing my son across town in school with no idea that a middle-aged former consulting expert was tuning in to his energy.

As I entertained myself with these images, Therese suddenly began to describe how she connects to energy. Her image was so compelling, I was immediately enthralled. She said that we are *so* much more infinite than our human bodies. Picture a huge, beautiful white light, with billions of strands coming down. Your human body is just a single strand of that infinite light. But the rest of your essential self is made up of all those infinite strands together, which are intertwined and connected to everything else. Your physical body is just one small part of your essential self. We are all connected to the greater source and to each other through the shared energy of a great light. It was that light to which Therese was connecting.

As Therese continued to take deep breaths, she softly said, "I'm going to ask Ethan's higher self for permission to tune in to him." Only a few moments passed before her eyes snapped open. "Oh! He's clairsentient!"

"What is *that?*" I asked, marveling at how she seemed to understand a problem I had been grappling with for years.

"He feels the things other people feel, even the things they are in denial about. I think where he is struggling is that he can't discern those feelings from his own."

"So he's feeling other people's emotions as if they are his own?" I asked. I had never heard of clairsentience before.

"Exactly. He can't ground himself because he doesn't understand that these feelings aren't coming from *him*. He's like an ungrounded electrical cord, whipping around with all these energy currents flowing through him and no way to make sense of them all."

It was the perfect description of how Ethan was. He would be so anxious and so upset but often would seem to have no idea why he felt that way. He seemed to be finding things to get upset or angry about even when there were none. Without understanding what was causing his moods, it was difficult (or impossible) to calm him down.

Therese taught me a few grounding exercises to practice with Ethan, very similar to the one I will share with you later in this chapter. "The key," she said, "is to ground yourself first. As you ground yourself, you will ground him." She explained that I had to be very conscious of my own energy when I was in his presence because it could literally dictate his reality. "Once you're grounded," Therese continued, "hug him and send love into him. Picture your love flowing out of your heart directly into his."

I thanked her for her help. Then I walked out of her office, thinking to myself, *There's no way Ethan's going to go for this.*

Ethan is a science brain, and he operates on a very logic-driven plane. I was worried that the idea of clairsentience would be too "out there" for him. I also figured I was already at a credibility deficit by virtue of the fact that Ethan was an adolescent and I was *Mom.* When I went home and told him what Therese had said, I expected him to roll his eyes. Instead, he replied, "I don't know why I'm saying this, but I feel like what you're telling me is true." I then offered to give him a grounding hug and he hesitantly stepped into my arms with a sardonic grin on his face. Within ten seconds, my 16-year-old boy melted into me, the most relaxed I had seen him in weeks.

I took Ethan in for his own session with Therese, and he asked me to stay in the room with them. I sat quietly as she explained everything to him and answered all of his questions. At one point she asked him, "What are you picking up in the room right now?"

He looked right at me and said, "Are you feeling frustrated?"

"No!" I said, startled. "I'm just sitting here listening." But then I thought about it and realized I had just been thinking, *Is this going okay? This is all taking too long and they keep getting off track! When are they going to get to the mood swings?* I *was* feeling frustrated! I wasn't conscious of my mood, but my son could feel it.

It was then that I fully realized how my own thoughts, emotions, and expectations had been working against us. I was always walking into Ethan's room anticipating a fight, and in doing so, I was likely helping to create the same emotional state in him.

From that point forward, I focused on putting myself into a calm, loving state, *coherence,* before I entered into Ethan's presence. And it made a huge difference almost immediately. Our whole dynamic shifted once I took responsibility for the energy I brought into the room with me. With the realization that my sweet son was being tossed around by the energy of others—energy that he mistook for his own feelings—I knew that I had to be accountable for the effect my thoughts, moods, and intentions could have on those around me.

I set my intention on my family feeling whole, happy, and safe, and I consciously kept my focus there. I worked on staying in a loving, openhearted place as I thought about them and envisioned scenarios that were peaceful, playful, and loving. I started executing the Law of Attraction in my relationship with my kids. It was a shift that I created in myself first and then through focused, conscious intention brought into my reality. Then I started to apply it to my relationship with my husband. That was when the real fun started. But more on that later.

It's important to be conscious of our energy because it doesn't exist in a vacuum. It doesn't even stay within our bodies! We are tuning forks. When struck, a tuning fork starts vibrating, sending its vibrations out into the world. We can hear those vibrations in the tone they create. Our personal energy works in very much the same way by sending our vibrations out into the quantum field. Others will *entrain* to our frequency, just as another tuning fork will start vibrating when it picks up the vibrations of the one that was struck. Those vibration waves move, and they have the power to influence, impact, and set physical objects into motion. This is the most basic principle of the art of manifesting. *This is how we create Quantum Love.*

Vibrations, Waves—What Are You Talking About?

As we discussed in Chapter 2, what we think of as empty space isn't really empty at all. That so-called emptiness is the quantum field: filled with energy, buzzing along across an infinite field of interconnectedness. Conversely, things we think of as solid (matter) are made of buzzing energy too, but it's just energy that is vibrating slowly enough for our senses to pick up on it. In order to discover and understand our personal energy profile, we're going to have to take a quick dive into some deep science to learn about energy density.

In *You Are the Placebo,* neuroscientist Joe Dispenza teaches us that atoms give off different electromagnetic frequencies. These energy fields can be invisible, like gamma rays, UV rays, or X-rays, or they can be visible, like rays of light. And he explains that just as invisible radio waves carry a frequency encoded with information, each different frequency in us carries its own vibration as well. The different frequencies carry different information and, depending on how fast they're vibrating, create stronger or weaker fields.

I like to picture these frequencies as blades on a fan that is constantly spinning. The faster the blades spin, the stronger the breeze they create. If the blades spin slowly, then the force they create isn't as strong. Similarly, the faster the blades spin, the harder they are to see; they just look like a blur. As Dispenza writes, "The faster an atom vibrates and the more energy it generates, the less time it spends in physical reality." In other words, like the fan blades that spin so fast we can't see them, once an atom starts vibrating fast enough, we will no longer be able to see it. Our five senses can't keep up.

Penney Peirce, an intuitive and author of the book *Frequency,* is a woman who truly understands the quantum principles I'm teaching in this book. She writes about the idea that all of life is built on energy and its movement (sine waves, octaves, and spectrums). Everything in us has an energetic frequency—our body, our thoughts, our emotions—and each of us is emitting our own frequency that changes throughout our day (or even in seconds) as our vibrational waves contract, expand, speed up, and slow down. Our frequency can be high-intensity or low-intensity, and the intensity levels of our emotions can hold some big implications for our relationships.

I look at frequency like a radio: You've got a knob that controls the different stations, and a knob that controls the volume. (People still know what radios are, right? Bear with me, millennials!) You can scan from one end of the radio dial to the other until you find a station you like, and then you can turn the volume high or low to blast out a song or turn down a commercial. Now imagine that the different stations aren't country music or pop or jazz, but different emotions. In this case the "radio station" is your emotional energy and the "volume" is the intensity. Picture yourself scanning from Anger to Trust to Forgiveness to Understanding. Then imagine yourself cranking up the volume on Understanding!

Our personal frequency is basically the intensity and speed at which our body's energy is vibrating. The higher the frequency of thoughts and emotions, the better the reality we are creating for ourselves, but more on that in a moment. It's an amazing thing to think about our emotions having a measurable existence, but that is exactly what is going on. The field of kinesiology, the study of the body's movement and our muscles' reaction to different stimuli, has opened up a whole new way of approaching our personal states of consciousness, energy levels, and vibrational frequencies. It turns out that our emotions have quantifiable energy, and our emotional *states* affect our body's energy frequency.

The Map of Consciousness

In his book *Power vs. Force,* Dr. David Hawkins explains that different emotions have different frequencies. These feelings exist on a continuum, and the higher the frequency, the better the feeling. He calls this the Map of Consciousness. Hawkins has actually devised a system of measurement that charts the vibrational frequency of our different energy states. He has captured the actual energetic motion of our emotions!

Hawkins was able to calibrate the energetic force of our emotions through a process called kinesiology. This study of movement (*kinesis* being the Greek word for "movement") has been around since the 1960s, when George Goodheart found that certain indicator muscles in our bodies would strengthen or weaken in response to positive or negative stimuli. Positive or benign things would strengthen the indicator muscles, and negative stimuli would have the opposite effect. In other words, your muscles get stronger or weaker depending on your mental state. The strength of the muscle is an indication of how much energy is present. With kinesiology, muscle strength is tested against pressure exerted by the kinesiologist on the muscles of the person being tested. If the muscle stands up to pressure, it's deemed "strong" or "locked." The muscles that give way to pressure are considered "weak" or "unlocked." This muscle response is independent of actual physical strength: a petite woman testing a giant football player will get the same response as the reverse. Goodheart called this applied kinesiology.[1]

Dr. John Diamond took Goodheart's work a step further, refining the idea of behavioral kinesiology. He turned his attention to the stimuli to see if different kinds of stimuli produced a different effect. And, in fact, it did. He found that certain music, pictures, literature, even single words could induce a stronger response in the body's movement than others. In other words, he found that an inspiring speech, a beautiful landscape, or uplifting music could actually make a person stronger. He also found that the truth could produce a strengthening response and that telling a lie would weaken the body of the person who told it.[2]

Then came David Hawkins.

For more than 20 years and with thousands of patients, Hawkins correlated the kinesiologic findings with a logarithmic scale to calibrate the relative power of the energy of different attitudes, thoughts, feelings, situations, and relationships. What he created was a consistent scale that correlated with what psychologists, sociologists, and medical doctors could all tell you anecdotally.

Hawkins's scale calibrates from 1 to 1,000, forming a continuum that encompasses the entire range of human consciousness. What Hawkins calls "energy levels" calibrating at 200 or below weaken the body, while energy levels at 200 or above strengthen it. According to Hawkins, these calibrations do not present an arithmetic progression of energy levels, but a logarithmic one: for instance, 300 is not twice the amplitude of 150, it is 300 to the tenth power (300^{10}). So an increase of even a few points on the Map of Consciousness represents a major advance in power, and the rate of increase as you move up the scale is enormous.

Let's take a quick look at the emotions at the low end of the scale, below 200. There is Shame, then Guilt, Apathy, Grief, Fear and Anxiety, Craving, and Anger and Hate. No fun. These low-calibrating energy levels are what Hawkins refers to as Force. They weaken you and make you feel pretty lousy.

Now let's move up the scale. At the 250 mark (Neutrality and Trust), we see a turn for the better. Then we continue on to Willingness, Optimism, Acceptance and Forgiveness, and Reason and Understanding. These are all much better. They are strengthening you. Let's keep going: Love and Reverence, Joy and Serenity, Gratitude and Praise, and then Peace and Bliss. These energy levels are what Hawkins refers to as Power.[3] They strengthen your body and make you feel pretty good. These higher energy levels are where we want to be, as I will explain shortly. At the top of the scale you have Enlightenment and Ineffability, but most of us won't reach this energy level. A few may have—Buddha, Jesus, and Krishna, to name a few. But don't stress out if you never find yourself calibrating at 700 to 1,000!

The 200 point is the balance point between negative and positive, Force and Power, weakness and strength. All attitudes, thoughts, feelings, and associations below 200 *will* weaken your energy, and that can have a huge impact on your reality and your relationship. Below 200 is the zone of anger, shame, and blaming others or ourselves. It is the zone of our ego self, vibrating at ego frequency. As we tip past 200 and move into courage, the shift is palpable. What lies beyond is the zone of our essential self, humming in home frequency. And that's where we start moving into Quantum Love. I'll tell you more about ego frequency and home frequency in a moment.

Frequency and the Law of Attraction

Frequency plays a *huge* role in how we create, or re-create, our reality. Whether we are conscious of it or not, we are always sending our frequency out into the quantum field. It is interacting with the energy of the field to shape and create our world and experience. If you are in a low-frequency state, such as anger or blame, your frequency is attracting things with like energy into your field. As we discussed earlier, the Law of Attraction is "like attracts like." Your energetic state is going to attract the things that are vibrating at a like frequency; the things in your world are going to be on that station.

Think about the commonly quoted line from the New Testament, Gospel of Matthew 7:7: "Ask, and it will be given to you; seek, and you will find; knock, and it will be opened to you. For everyone who asks receives, and he who seeks finds, and to him who knocks it will be opened."

I have probably heard this passage referenced hundreds of times over the course of my life, but I have only recently started to really understand it from a self-empowering standpoint. "Ask and it will be given to you" had always sounded to me like a passive move: ask for what you want, and then hopefully it might come your way. That didn't fit at all with the "Assert yourself and don't be a doormat" story I had grown up with. I was raised to believe that with lots of hard work (and type A behavior) you could achieve what you wanted. It wasn't enough just to *ask*. But examining the passage from a quantum perspective made me realize that it could indeed be referring to what we now understand as the Law of Attraction. When you use the power of the quantum field, honing your emotions and intention to create the frequency or vibration of that desire, you will draw the things you want to you. "He who seeks finds"—because his resonant frequency has drawn it into his reality!

What I also love about this passage is that it speaks from a place of fullness. There are no conditions or caveats; no hoops to jump through before you can get what you want (or before you are even worthy of asking). It certainly doesn't say, "To him who knocks it will be opened, provided that he loses ten pounds first." This passage says that we are enough simply by virtue of the fact that we are *here*. We deserve to ask and receive, seek and find, knock and be answered, because we are each perfect and whole as we are.

Most of us are unaware of how our body's energy is being affected by the world around us. We are like ping-pong balls being ricocheted all over the table, seemingly helpless over where we end up. Our moods, our thoughts, and our feelings are out of control as we bounce from one situation to the next. Our partner doesn't give us a good-bye kiss? Our mood plummets. Our boss gives us a raise? Our mood soars. Our kids are rude to us? Our mood sinks. Our body's energetic frequencies are typically all over the place and are driving our experiences instead of the reverse.

Quantum Love comes when we raise and stabilize our body's energetic frequency and stay, as much as possible, in a state of coherence. As we learn how to hone our perception and alter our repetitive thinking patterns—especially the patterns that are based on our early experiences and the beliefs we formed as children—we can start to create new beliefs and new ways of reacting to the world. We can begin to live in our home frequency, rather than in our ego frequency.

Home Frequency

Dr. Jill Bolte Taylor is a neuroanatomist who went through a tremendous AFGE of her own. In 1996 she suffered a major stroke that essentially wiped out the functions of her brain's left hemisphere, the place that processes language, numbers, and our sense of identity and of past and future. She could no longer feel the boundaries between her body and the rest of her environment.

In her book, *My Stroke of Insight: A Brain Scientist's Personal Journey,* she writes that at the time of her stroke, the constant chatter of her left hemisphere suddenly went silent, "just like someone took a remote control and pushed a mute button." She was completely disconnected from the side of her brain that held her sense of self, the ego side of her brain. Time and space didn't exist. Her body didn't exist. She just saw magnificent, powerful energy. She felt at one with the beautiful energy of everything around her; she knew she was full, worthy, and whole exactly as she was. Of course, none of us would ever wish to go through the serious physical trauma that Taylor experienced to gain her "stroke of insight," but her experience offers the powerful knowledge that this state exists in every one of our brains and, as she says, it is something we can tune in to.

That is home frequency. That is a state of coherence. That is when you are vibrating at your highest frequency and are able to attract all manner of wonderful things into your life, whether material or spiritual. Don't worry. If it seems unrealistic or unattainable, it's not. I can help you find your home frequency and return there whenever you wish. This perspective of fullness, worthiness, and wholeness is the perspective of home frequency. Our home frequency is the state in which we can truly draw the things we desire to ourselves.

Our home frequency is one of pure, perfect love and faith. This is the state each of us was born in and in which each of us truly belongs. I also think of our home frequency as being equivalent to a state of coherence. Coherence, as we discussed in Chapter 2, is when you drop into that feeling of unconditional love and connection with all living things. It's when you let love surge through you and out of you. When you are in this state, you feel wonderful and at peace. You send out a high-vibration energy that allows you to attract nothing but positivity. Your personal tuning fork is drawing good things to you; high frequency attracts high frequency. Your interactions with the world are coming from a state of authenticity and power. Your relationship with your partner is blessed with a feeling of limitless love and trust.

The good news is that you can always switch your frequency, and as you begin your journey, you might find that you have to switch your frequency constantly throughout the day as you keep slipping into a state of ego frequency. That's okay. It will become like changing channels; it's just a matter of continually shifting back to home frequency. More on that in a moment.

Being in a state of home frequency is quite different from being in a state of ego frequency. Home frequency requires nothing except faith and surrender. I don't mean faith in God or a higher power per se (although that could be part of your home frequency), but rather faith in your own self and your own inherent goodness as well as in the inherent goodness of the world.

Ego Frequency

So what is ego frequency and how can you tell if you are in it? The answer isn't just "If you are unhappy, you are in ego frequency," because you can actually be quite happy in ego frequency, or at least content there! You can feel accomplished, secure, envied, and important. You can even feel loved and respected.

But there is one way to know *for sure* if you are in ego frequency: if you are *struggling*. Ego frequency can be rewarding and even enjoyable at times, but it never comes easy. You have to work your fingers to the bone for every single crumb of satisfaction and approval. You always have to be "on your game." You're anxious and worried and stressed most of the time in order to get everything working the way you want or keep it going in the right direction. From being the perfect partner to the perfect parent to the perfect employee to the perfect child, you have to constantly push yourself. Why? Because doing so is how you feel worthy of love.

This typically isn't something we think of consciously. Most of us don't think, "I have to do *x, y, z* in order to earn love," but that is how we behave. Ego frequency is not just about earning love from other people; it's about the love we give ourselves as well. Those of us who live mostly in ego frequency can't be loving and forgiving with ourselves unless we feel that we've earned it, whether it's by staying up all night to bake cookies for our kids' bake sale, working at a job we hate in order to provide plenty of material goods for our family, or giving up on our own needs and desires in order to serve everyone else. This mentality is pure ego frequency. It comes from the belief that we aren't enough and that the world isn't a place of unconditional, bountiful love. Love comes with expectations, with conditions, with costs, with requirements. Not only do we believe that love must be earned and that the amount of love available is limited, but many of us truly fear that living without love is a very real possibility. No wonder we work so hard to try to earn it! We are in a constant anxious state trying to ward off living in a cold, dark, loveless "reality."

Ego frequency typically stems from a deep belief in our own unworthiness, in life's unfairness, and in the hopelessness of our station. We are "stuck" trying to earn love and approval, whether it's by losing weight, earning more money, or even chasing after seemingly spiritual goals such as being a better Christian or living with a Buddha heart.

When we are in ego frequency, we are vibrating from a place of scarcity. And when we "ask," we aren't at a frequency that allows us to create the reality we desire. We are in fix-manage-control (FMC) mode. We are working hard for answers. We are looking everywhere for clues. We are knocking, and knocking, and knocking . . . and the door just never seems to open. Sometimes it swings open for just a moment and we get a glimpse of what's on the other side, but then suddenly it slams shut again. Maybe you had this experience when you held your child for the first time, or when you had a religious epiphany, or when you first got sober, or when you finally let go of a toxic relationship. For a moment you felt as though you understood everything, and you were awash in love and purpose and hope . . . and then SLAM! You lost it. The world came crashing in, and all the stressors of your daily life dropped you right back to ego frequency.

To Me, By Me, Through Me

The authors of *The 15 Commitments of Conscious Leadership*, life coaches Diana Chapman, Jim Dethmer, and Kaley Warner Klemp, talk about three key states of consciousness that turn out to be a great model for understanding and increasing your frequency. They talk about it in terms of being above or below a certain "line." Above the line is a state of openness and curiosity and commitment to growth and learning. Below the line is closed-mindedness, defensiveness, and commitment to being right. Below the line is on the left side of the Quantum Lovemap, which I will explain later in this chapter, and above the line is to the right, where we want to be in Quantum Love.

TO ME State of Consciousness

The To Me state of consciousness is below the line and in ego frequency. Most people spend most of their time there. All of us spend some time there. When you are in To Me consciousness, you see yourself at the effect of other people, circumstances, events, and so on. Things are happening, or being done, *to you*. This is victim consciousness. Those in To Me consciousness assign blame to others (or themselves) for the current condition of their relationship. Their conversations and thoughts are dominated by the question "Why me?" Most of us were raised there and stay there. This state essentially says, "I am the effect of the world around me." Or "If only this were different, then that would be better."

BY ME State of Consciousness

This is above the line. You move from living in victim consciousness to living as a co-creator of your reality. The By Me person chooses to see that everything in the world is unfolding perfectly for their benefit and development. As my friend, intuitive strategist, and leadership coach Susan Hyman likes to say, "That which is right is unfolding." The person in this state chooses curiosity over defensiveness and the need to be right. Instead of asking, "Why me?" individuals in the By Me zone are thinking about what they can learn and taking 100 percent ownership of their circumstances.

When you are in the By Me state of consciousness, you are in home frequency. You can see the gifts in this world and how they might serve you. Life is in your service, and you are clear that what is happening is *for* you and will make sense, even if you can't see it yet. In the By Me zone we can hold a state of wonder in our lives. We have less need to be right in our relationships and in life in general. We are in the Quantum Love zone.

THROUGH ME State of Consciousness

In this state, you are *really* in the Quantum Love zone. Curiosity begins to guide you to the big questions and to the knowledge that you are truly creating all of your reality. You recognize your power. You know there is a greater universal power beyond yourself. You are in the space of enthusiasm, faith, and curiosity around what you are creating, the great stuff and the harder things as well. When faced with a challenge or an undesirable situation, you ask yourself, "How is this serving me? What wants to manifest through me in life and in this relationship?" In this space you are in full-on surrender to what is being created and in home frequency. You give up the need to fix, manage, and control, and you focus on staying in that energetic state, making decisions and connections from that place.

The fact is, you are *powerful* in each of these states because your energy will impact those around you. If the By Me state is moving into Quantum Love, then when you are in a Through Me state you have fully arrived there. When you are in a higher state of consciousness, either a By Me or a Through Me state, you will be able to positively impact others whose own energy will entrain to yours.

THE QUANTUM LOVEMAP

The Quantum Lovemap (Figure 1) is a model that provides a visual reference point for where you are in your relationship and where you want to be. I created it by synthesizing the work of David Hawkins; Abraham; Chapman, Dethmer, and Klemp; and a variety of other coaches and personal empowerment writers whose work I believe in and respect.

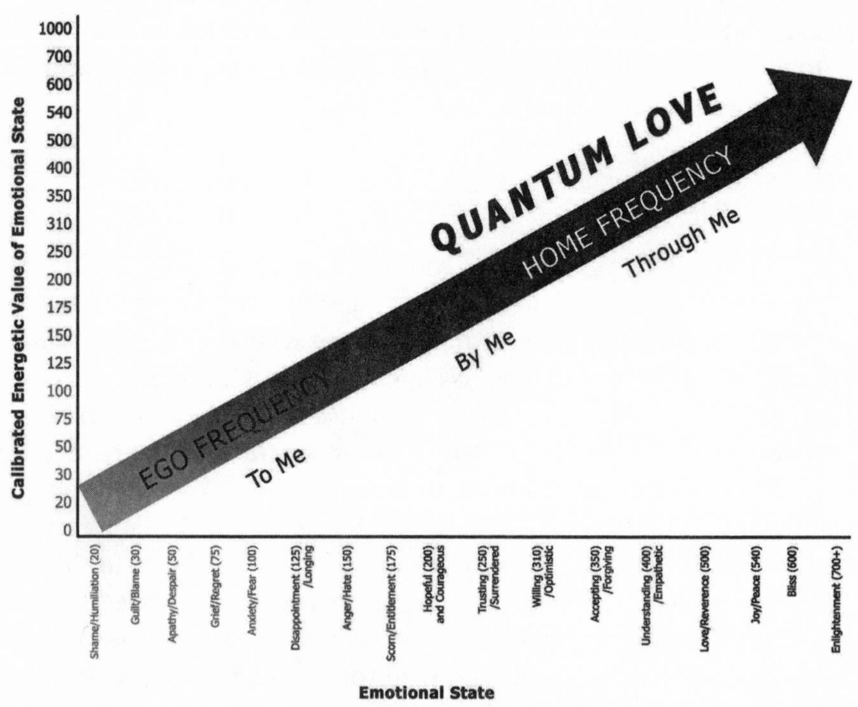

Figure 1: The Quantum Lovemap

On the X axis is a series of emotional states, and on the Y axis is the calibration of your body's energy when in those emotional states. Both the emotional states and the calibrations are from Hawkins's Map of Consciousness. When your body is calibrating below 200, you are in the To Me state, in ego frequency. As you move up the scale, between 200 and 400 you are in the By Me state, in home frequency, and in the beginning of the Quantum Love zone. Above 400 you are really humming in home frequency and living in the Through Me state, fully experiencing Quantum Love. As you can see, while most of us rarely get to a calibration above 700 (much less stay there), the possibilities for Quantum Love are simply infinite and the scale never ends. The Quantum Lovemap can be your template for getting a clear perspective on where you are with any struggle you have in your life, but especially your relationship. It works whether you are looking at a particular issue (your sex life or co-parenting synergy, for instance) or looking globally at your relationship.

What you also need to know is that home frequency has an amazing capacity for counterbalancing those who are calibrating at a lower frequency on a personal level as well as a global one. When you move yourself into home frequency, you are not only drastically improving your relationship dynamics, but actually changing the world for the better! According to Hawkins's calculations of the different calibrations and their impact: one individual calibrating at 500 (love and reverence) counterbalances 750,000 individuals below 200 (in ego frequency); one individual at 600 (in bliss) counterbalances ten million individuals below 200; and just one individual at 700 counterbalances 70 million individuals below 200. Okay, most of us aren't going to spend much time in enlightenment, but it's a worthy goal, and I bless and thank the monks and sages in the world who can hold that place for us!

If this works exponentially on a global level, imagine what happens in your relationship. When we are in home frequency, our high-vibrating energy can help balance or even raise the frequency of those around us as they entrain to us. This is especially helpful for our purposes in love relationships. One of the key principles of Quantum Love is that you must create in yourself first. When you are in home frequency, a place of fullness, wholeness, and love, you will move your relationship and your partner up the Quantum Lovemap with you.

To see where you fall on the Quantum Lovemap right now, go to the Appendix to take the Quantum Love Quiz or go to www.drlauraberman.com/quantumlove for an online version. You'll notice that the quiz is broken up into separate domains that will yield a set of scores rather than a single relationship score. This is because, for better or worse (I say for better), relationships are not that simple. You may find that in the domain of your sex life you are in home frequency, but when it comes to self-expression, you are more likely to be in ego frequency.

Whatever the case, this exercise is intended to give you important information about where you are and help you set goals for where you want to be in Quantum Love. There are no wrong or right answers. By the time you finish this book, you will be primed to be a master of home frequency and Quantum Love.

You can plot where you are on the Quantum Lovemap on the pages in the Appendix, copy the Quantum Lovemap on another paper, or go to www.drlauraberman.com/quantumlove to use the online version. But before you do, please read the section below.

The Keys to Coherence

Before you take the Quantum Love Quiz, I want to teach you two of the most fundamental components of dropping into home frequency, because it is from there that you can most openly and honestly answer the questions. There are two key steps to bringing yourself into coherence: grounding and opening your heart. The applications of this state to your love life cannot be overstated.

First comes grounding. I first learned how important grounding is from an amazingly gifted and loving energy healer, Linda Hall, who worked with my mother during her illness. Her presence during that terrible time was a gift, and the lessons she taught have stuck with me to this day.

So what is grounding? It is putting ourselves back into our body through our consciousness. We spend most of every day completely outside of our body and the present moment. We're thinking about what has already happened, or what is going to happen in the future; we're thinking about our mate, our kids, our jobs, and the logistics of our life. We even put our attention on perfect strangers like the jerk who won't let us move into the next lane on the highway. But rarely do we turn our attention solely to our body to check in with it and to move ourselves back into it instead of dragging it along with us. This is what grounding is all about.

When we are grounded, we feel a greater sense of presence, security, and belonging. It's almost like a settling-in. It takes only a few moments to do and creates a wonderful feeling of safety and connection to the earth and our place on it. Grounding can also be really energizing because we are tapping into the most primal and vital energy out there (as we will learn in Chapter 7). From the place of safety and presence that we move into by grounding, we are able to move more effectively into our coherent state. Without it, we are more like an ungrounded electrical cord!

The Guide to Grounding

Get into a comfortable, seated position, close your eyes, and take some deep breaths. As you breathe in, imagine a beautiful light, whatever color you want, coming in through the top of your head. As you exhale, imagine the light moving straight down the center of your body and coming out through your tailbone, going straight down deep into the earth and branching out like the root system of a tree.

With each in-breath the light comes in and with each outbreath it roots deep into the ground. Let the roots expand, spreading out in all directions. Linda Hall taught me that just as the roots of a tree in nature are double the width of its widest branches, your grounding roots into the earth should be imagined as two times as wide and deep as you are extending yourself in that moment. For example, when I'm about to go on television to be seen by millions of people, I imagine my roots spreading out in all directions across the United States. If I'm staying in home frequency with my family and need to ground, I imagine my roots fanning out to double the size of our home.

Envision your body being anchored to the earth by the strength and reach of your roots. This is how it feels to be grounded.

To hear a guided meditation for grounding yourself, go to www.drlauraberman.com/quantumlove.

Heart-Opening Meditation

Once you have grounded yourself, I suggest moving directly into opening your heart. By performing this exercise, you are moving into home frequency. You are opening yourself to giving and receiving love. It is this final step that will move you into coherence, which is a state of pure, unconditional love.

Just as we move through life outside of our bodies, we all too often move through life outside of our home frequency. We close or constrict our energy channels, partly out of self-defense from this noisy world, and close our heart to others. When we are in that state, we are in ego frequency, and as I've mentioned, it is not possible to even catch a glimpse of Quantum Love from that place. Opening your heart is how you find home frequency.

Close your eyes and continue to breathe deeply. First, think back to a time when you felt pure, unconditional love, when all was right with the world. It could be when you held your child in your arms for the first time, or perhaps when someone who loved you unconditionally held you. It could involve being in a place you loved on a beautiful, sunny day—use any memory you have of a time when you felt like you and everything around you were in perfect harmony.

Now, as you continue breathing in your grounded state, focus on the scenario you are choosing, as if you were there *right now.* Be there as if you are experiencing it in the first person. You aren't watching yourself in that situation; you are *there,* employing all your senses. If your visual is holding your baby for the first time, you can look down and see the baby in your arms, feel what it's like to hold him or her, imagine smelling that sweet baby smell . . . What do you see? How do you feel? Be in the emotions of that state as if it is happening in this moment. Feel your heart opening up to receive the unconditional love that you are experiencing in this moment. You will likely feel a shift in your body—a lightness spreading in your chest—or a smile may come to your face. You are now in coherence.

To hear a guided meditation for opening your heart, go to www.drlauraberman.com/quantumlove.

Grounding and opening your heart is a great way to center and move into home frequency at any time. I've even done this in the car on my way to an appointment (keeping my eyes open, of course). I find it especially helpful to move myself into coherence in this way before I have to express myself honestly and authentically. For this reason, I highly recommend that, before assessing yourself with the Quantum Love Quiz, you put yourself in a grounded, openhearted state.

The Wisdom of Ego Frequency

Now that you have learned all about how amazing home frequency is and the wonderful way the universe (and a partner) will respond to a person who is vibrating at this state, you might be disappointed and regretful that you have spent so much of your life in ego frequency. You might worry that you will still slip into ego frequency frequently and that you won't be able to do coherence in the "right way."

Here's the good news: There is no right way! It's okay to slip into ego frequency and even stay there for a while. In fact, when you slip into ego frequency, it's usually because your body or your spirit is calling out for something. Something isn't serving you. So rather than fearing ego frequency and feeling disappointed when you notice you are in it, choose instead to really drop into that state and get up close and personal with what is going on inside of you. There is wisdom to be gained there.

Once you realize that ego frequency and your ego self may actually have important lessons to teach you—lessons that can help deepen and encourage your home frequency—you will easily be able to get back into coherence. The key is embracing the contraction that comes with ego frequency. Like the physical contractions of labor, this sort of energetic contraction can sometimes be painful in an emotional way, but when you surrender to the pain, you can create and release life-affirming energy. Contractions are a rhythmic cycle of tightening and opening. Anyone who's experienced labor knows that when you relax into the contractions and don't fight them, breathing into them, they are less painful and pass more quickly. The same is true for ego frequency. In fact, I encourage you to see your time spent in ego frequency as a mini-labor that gives birth to a new facet of yourself.

Ebb and flow is such a key rhythm in our natural world. It's present in almost everything, be it as big as the ocean or as small as our cells. Energy is always moving, contracting, and expanding. This is why, if we are going to figure out where we are on the Quantum Lovemap, it isn't as simple as plotting a point on a graph. In order to fully understand where we are on the map, we also have to understand how our unique energy profile works within it. You may tend to land at one spot on the Quantum Lovemap and rest there for the most part, but in my experience, each of us tends to vacillate a bit around that point, moving into and out of higher and lower frequencies. So the next step in using the Quantum Lovemap is learning what I call your Ego/Home Frequency Index, or EHFI. Your EHFI is basically a way of mapping out *your* typical pattern of contractions into ego frequency and expansions out to home frequency. When you are clear about your EHFI pattern and how you move around the Quantum Lovemap, you can use that awareness to more quickly shift up out of lower frequencies and into higher ones.

For each one of us, the contractions and expansions are happening in a constant flow that looks like this:

Figure 2: The Shape of Your EHFI

It is not a coincidence to me that this image is shaped like an infinity symbol, because the contraction and expansion that is always happening in our natural world happens endlessly in our emotional world too. Your EHFI fits onto the Quantum Lovemap and can show you how you tend to vacillate between home and ego frequency.

The left side of the EHFI tends to be your typical lower-frequency state of being, and the right side represents your higher-frequency state. The midpoint tends to mark the emotional state (and calibration) that is your usual point of transition from lower to higher—and hopefully from ego to home frequency. When you understand your point of transition, it becomes a beacon that alerts you to the fact that you are experiencing a shift in your energy so that you can direct the shift up the Quantum Lovemap.

Consider Figure 3 as an example. I call someone with this EHFI the Quantum Love Beginner. At this person's most pessimistic, he or she feels apathy, and at the most optimistic, acceptance. In the example, it would be important for the Quantum Love Beginner to know that anger and scorn are a powerful point of transition for them when they are moving back toward joy. For more examples of typical EHFIs I see in my practice, go to www.drlauraberman.com/quantumlove.

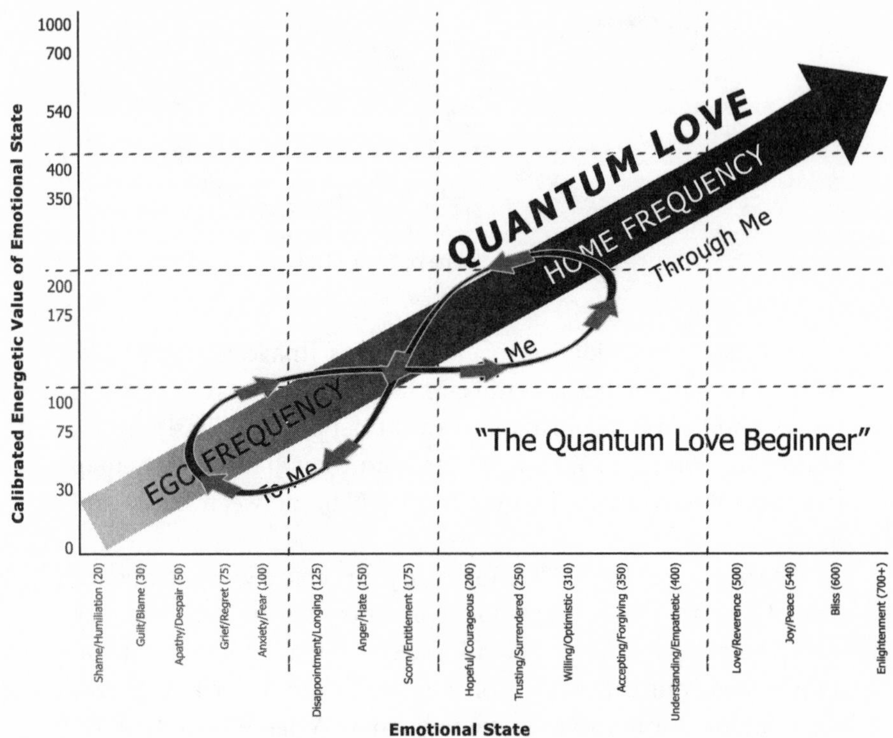

Figure 3: EHFI Example—The Quantum Love Beginner

What's Your EHFI?

The EHFI Quiz will help you identify your energetic ebb and flow and determine your own point of transition between expansion and contraction. Each set of questions will ask you to characterize the way you feel at your most optimistic and your most pessimistic when you think about different facets of your relationship. Like the Quantum Love Quiz, there will be some elements of your relationship in which you vibrate at a higher frequency energetically than in other parts of your relationship, and that is perfectly normal. In the chapters ahead, you will learn all about how to move up the Quantum Lovemap in *all* areas of your relationship.

If you don't presently have a partner, it doesn't matter. All you have to do is think about how you typically feel in relationships or use your last significant relationship as a guide. It can also be really helpful, not to mention illuminating, to have your partner take the quiz as well and compare notes. Knowing each other's EHFI can give you a lot of great insight into not only your partner's emotional patterns but also their perspective on your relationship. You may find that the two of you experience your relationship in very different ways.

Now go to the Appendix to take the quiz, then come back to these pages to learn more.

Interpreting the Results and Plotting Your EHFI

As with the Quantum Love Quiz, you'll notice that the questions are organized into different relationship domains. You may find that the EHFI for your ability to work with your partner in tackling the logistics of your life is in a place very different from that of your sexual connection. Or you may see that your EHFI sits at a high energetic frequency when it comes to communicating with your partner, which means it's probably pretty easy for you to do. But your spiritual connection may be at a lower frequency, meaning that you find it difficult to "read" him or her at an intuitive level.

Also as with the Quantum Lovemap, you will use the results of the EHFI Quiz as you move into the next chapters and learn practical strategies to get to Quantum Love.

Each of the two mind-sets, which for simplicity's sake I refer to as "optimistic" and "pessimistic," will represent a different point in your EHFI. Your most optimistic is how you feel when you are the most hopeful and enthusiastic about that element of your relationship. Conversely, your most pessimistic is how you feel when you are at your lowest low regarding that aspect of your relationship. Your most optimistic mind-set will be the highest-frequency end point of your EHFI; your most pessimistic mind-set will represent the lowest-frequency end point of your EHFI. Plot each point on the Quantum Lovemap. Now determine the middle point between your two ends, and plot *it* on the Quantum Lovemap as well. This is your shift point.

Next draw a sideways infinity symbol (like the example in Figure 3) connecting your three points, with the middle point as your cross mark. As with the Quantum Love Quiz, you can draw on these pages, copy the Quantum Lovemap on another paper, or go to www.drlauraberman.com/quantumlove to use the online version.

This sideways figure eight is your EHFI energy loop, uniquely personal to you. Some people's loops will be elongated, and some short. Some will be more in home frequency, some more in ego.

The idea of the EHFI Quiz is to recognize your typical energetic pattern so you can notice sooner rather than later when you are moving into contraction (from home frequency) and then use shift moves and other tools I will explain in the next chapter in order to shorten the transition back to expansion. This awareness is part of figuring out how to harness your energy and build your EHFI out to be as much in home frequency as possible. Remember: no one is in home frequency *all* the time.

I want to bring special attention to your point of transition, the middle of your EHFI. This is where you move from contraction to expansion (and vice versa), so it is especially important to be aware of this emotional state, what it looks like, how it feels to you, and what usually sends you there. That way, if you find yourself in that state, you will be able to tell yourself, "Oh, I might be heading for a contraction" or "I'm getting closer to expansion." If you do notice that you are moving toward the low-frequency end of your EHFI, don't judge yourself for it. If you can shift your energy up in the moment (using techniques that I will teach you in the coming pages), then that's great, but sometimes it's best to just surrender to the ebb. Let it carry you down, allow yourself to feel the emotion that you need to feel, and then do what you can to move yourself into a more coherent state.

Remember: these are just patterns and not set in stone. Awareness is the first key, and in the following chapters I will show you everything you need to know about how to shift your energy pattern to a higher frequency and greater Quantum Love.

Whence Your EHFI Comes

Why don't we just naturally stay in home frequency? If home frequency is our perfect state—the one we were born into, where our energy is highest and most loving—then why isn't it our default mode all the time? Why is it possible for us to be knocked out of it?

The short answer is *you*. Or, rather, the *you* your ego loves chattering about: your sense of individual self, the boundaries between you and the rest of the world, your past and future, and your years' worth of emotional baggage. Basically all the elements from which Jill Bolte Taylor's stroke broke her free. All that noise in your brain (the to-do list, the anxiety, the fears for the future) is not coming from your essential self, it's coming from your ego self, which Michael Singer refers to in *The Untethered Soul* as "a crazy roommate."

This loud, inconsiderate, sometimes rude *you* is your ego frequency, which I believe is a mirror (a reverse image) of your soul's purpose for being here. As I mentioned above, your crazy roommate loves to chatter on about scarcity and unworthiness, with extra emphasis on the struggle. *Loudly.* And when you give yourself over to the beliefs your ego self is spewing, you throw yourself into a state of resistance, shame, and fear. You tune in to and attach yourself to the stories that come from your external world. You are thinking of what could go (or is going) wrong and looking for ways to protect yourself. It's a pretty easy thing to do, especially because all too often we don't even know that we're doing it.

The truth is that each of us was born with pure, perfect energy within us, a full physical expression of our home frequency. We radiated light, love, hope, ease, and truthfulness. We were born without shame, fear, doubt, anger, or self-blame. You only have to look at a newborn baby to see that this is true. No matter what family or situation they are born into (be it a mansion in Hollywood or a hut in a war-torn third-world country), babies come into this world with nothing but pure love and trust. They trust their parents wholeheartedly, without reservation. They trust the world to be warm, kind, and receptive. They believe. They hope. And they do so with absolutely no effort and no walls of self-protection. This pure, perfect energy is your essential self. It is unchanging, immovable. Its perfect light is inside you right now, no matter what is going on in your world, and it's not going anywhere. Your crazy roommate ego self can't touch it.

Like all humans, though, on a practical level babies are very adept at adapting to their situations. Darwin and most psychotherapists would agree that babies are programmed to learn to adapt to their caregivers' reality as a key to their survival. We learn early to emulate the tone of our home, to fit into the boundaries, and to mirror those who are essential to our survival. We learn how to express emotion based on how our family expresses emotion (and, as we know, emotion is just energy). So essentially we learn how to control our energetic state based on how our family does it. Even though most of us eventually question those norms and assumptions at some point, our sensibilities, how we handle conflict, how loud or quiet we are, how joyful or scared we are, are built during those earliest formative years. These are the facets of our personality that we tend not to question; instead, we just think, "This is how I am." Our family's energetic style becomes our heritage and the beginnings of our ego frequency. At our core, each living creature on earth has one goal: to survive. And a baby's survival hinges on its ability to adapt to its family unit. Sadly, adapting often means developing skills of anger, mistrust, doubt, and putting up walls. That is why children grow from uninhibited, loving beings into hesitant, fearful adults who are afraid of being hurt and afraid of being made fools of, or making fools of themselves.

Michael Singer explains that each of us is walking around with numerous sensitive "thorns" within us.[4] They represent points of major trauma and pain in our past, negative messages, fears, and humiliations. These thorns come in all shapes and sizes; some are very obvious, like an AFGE or trauma, while others are much smaller or so deeply imbedded that you might not even know they are there until something touches them and triggers you. Imagine accidentally brushing your hand over a cactus plant. You get most of the thorns out, but there are still those tiny, almost invisible ones in your skin. They don't hurt until something touches them. Then watch out!

When it comes to our emotional thorns, the same is true. We get triggered when something inevitably happens to touch one of them. We find we are unreasonably angry when someone cut us off in traffic or completely devastated when we get on the scale to learn we've gained five pounds. Our reaction doesn't fit the "crime." Why? Is it the traffic incident or the weight gain alone? No, we react out of proportion because that incident brushed against one of our thorns and hit a nerve. Whenever this happens, we immediately switch into ego frequency.

One couple, Jackie and Jake, came to see me after a medical diagnosis flipped their life upside down. They also had some serious thorns. Jackie's mother had been very critical of her as she was growing up. She was never really allowed to speak her mind, and if she did have an opinion it was usually slapped out of her for being "disrespectful." Jake was very kind and accommodating, and Jackie felt she had full permission to express herself in the relationship. Recently Jake had been diagnosed with a brain tumor. The tumor had been found in the pituitary area of his prefrontal cortex, the part of the brain that regulates impulse control. His new impulsivity led him to say things that were perhaps a little *too* authentic. He was reactive and prone to big outbursts of anger. It was triggering Jackie like crazy.

Intellectually, Jackie knew what was going on and that Jake didn't have control over his outbursts. She fully understood that he was not trying to hurt her. Jackie knew she liked to be in control, but she had never realized to what degree she needed to feel that she had a voice. When Jake started to behave in ways that made her feel as if her voice was undervalued or disregarded because he wasn't filtering his thoughts and reactions, she became extremely resentful and started to shut down.

Through our work together, Jackie was able to recognize her thorns and understand that the emotions kicking up inside of her were not really about Jake. Her thorns had colored the lens through which she viewed the relationship (and Jake). Once she realized that, everything started to change.

When Jackie was able to recognize these thorns, she was more capable of recognizing when they were being touched. Then, with that clarity, she could start to consciously decide how she wanted to feel when Jake behaved in a way that seemed dismissive, angry, or controlling. Instead of just dropping down into ego frequency and creating more bad feelings, she was able to release them and move more into home frequency.

On her EHFI, Jackie realized that she vacillated between guilt (75) and acceptance and forgiveness (175). The guilt was from the story that because Jake was sick, she should be giving him a longer leash, not taking his comments personally. Scorn and entitlement came from the feeling that she was sacrificing so much to be a caretaker. Instead of being in home frequency even part of the time, Jackie realized her EHFI was solidly in ego frequency.

She began to honor how scared she was and used the techniques I will show you in the following chapters to begin to move into willing/optimistic and even accepting/forgiving. She was forgiving not just Jake but also herself *and her mother.* She began to feel compassion toward all of them, the compassion she wasn't given as a child. Then she started spending more time in the By Me state, and everything in her relationship started to change.

Jake even had an unanticipated recovery of all brain function after they were able to operate on the tumor. "Do you think it's because I manifested it?" Jackie asked me. I smiled at her, shrugged, and said, "Who knows?"

Most of us aren't even aware that we have emotional thorns that hurt to be touched. We just recognize the emotions of hurt when we feel them. But just like you can get a magnifying glass and a pair of tweezers and remove the thorns the cactus left behind, we can address our emotional thorns as well.

Each of us has built walls around our heart and our mind, consciously and subconsciously, in order to block out what we imagine is the danger in the world. It's easier to stay closed off and defensive, to stay in ego frequency. But I can promise that Quantum Love is there for you, and in the following chapters you will learn to challenge your assumptions and beliefs and discover strategies for changing your frequency and moving your EHFI up the Quantum Lovemap.

This brings to mind the wonderful quote from the Sufi mystic and poet Rumi, who said, "Your task is not to seek for love, but merely to seek and find all the barriers within yourself that you have built against it." So, too, your task is not to force yourself into a state of coherence or muscle your way into your home frequency, but merely to bring consciousness to your journey and find out where your resistance is coming from. What makes you close up with rage and hurt when your partner is late for dinner? What makes you turn away from your partner in the bedroom when you desperately want to cling to him or her? What energy comes to the surface when you think of your relationship with your spouse?

In examining these questions, you will likely find some surprising answers and hidden truths about yourself. Especially when you drop into home frequency. From that quiet place of the essential self, you may find that it isn't anger holding you back from your spouse, but fear and sadness. Maybe you will find that you are capable of deep levels of forgiveness and unconditional love that you didn't even know you had. Maybe you will be able to look at your spouse when he or she is angry and feel not irritation but love. Maybe you'll see a big teddy bear inside the anger, or a raging lion cub or a grumpy manatee. Whatever image works for you! In doing so, you will be able to reframe your perspective. You will see your partner as the person who loves you and just wants to be heard, valued, and respected.

In the next chapter, I will be giving you lots of tools for getting out of ego and into home frequency. From the coherent state of your home frequency, you will be able to explore these questions and reach the wonderful clarity that comes when we connect to our essential self and quiet the voice of our ego.

The good news is that even though every last one of us has been influenced by our upbringing and experience, *our essential selves haven't.* If each of us is born with perfect loving energy within us, and energy can never be created or destroyed, that means that this energy is still there. It hasn't tarnished, aged, or decreased over the years. It has merely been hidden. That love has been there all along, waiting for the time when we will discover it, waiting for us to become conscious and receptive once again.

Jill Bolte Taylor used the words "I'm in here. Come find me," to describe how she felt while in the throes of early recovery from her stroke. I believe that our essential selves AND the essential selves of our partners are saying the same thing: *I'm in here. Come find me.*

This is the path of Quantum Love.

CHAPTER 4

Commitment #1

I Will Take Responsibility for the Energy I Bring into My Relationship

You don't attract what you want.
You attract what you are.

— Dr. Wayne Dyer

Now you understand your energy profile—where you fit on the Quantum Lovemap, and your body's energetic style in your relationship, either in one parameter or in general. You also understand how that style developed and how the frequency of your energy is determined by your most common emotional states. You've gotten clear that the higher the frequency or calibration, the more positive experiences you will notice and create in your relationship and in those around you.

Commit yourself to noticing when you are moving from home frequency into ego frequency, and take steps to put yourself back into coherence. After all, your energy and consciousness are creating your reality, *including* your relationship reality. Commit to doing what it takes to keep both on the path of Quantum Love.

Remember, when you are calibrating above 200 and moving in the By Me and Through Me states, you are really in Quantum Love. You are going to vacillate—contract and expand—toward higher and lower vibrations. But now you know what your style is, and how to identify that transition point toward expansion or contraction, between higher and lower calibrations. In this chapter I am going to show you some ways to shift more quickly out of lower energetic calibrations, regardless of how stuck you feel, and stay longer in higher calibrations, putting yourself in home frequency as much as possible.

As you've learned, there is nothing wrong with ego frequency. It serves you well, and you are constantly moving in and out of it as part of your energy's natural ebb and flow. The goal here isn't to lock your energy in the By Me or Through Me state. That would be impossible. The goal is to move your EHFI up the Quantum Lovemap. When you take responsibility for your frequency, it puts you in the driver's seat. Remember, when you are in home frequency, your partner is entrained to you and you are creating the reality you most desire.

Below are the five key principles that I have found are amazingly effective at allowing you to shift out of ego frequency and into home frequency, no matter what the circumstances are. Most of these we will dive into more deeply in the chapters ahead. These five keys are: opening your heart, tapping into the energetic field around you, gratitude, surrender, and mindfulness.

Home Frequency Key 1: An Open Heart Is the Fast Track to Home Frequency

Opening your heart—which also means opening yourself to giving and receiving love—is a wonderful way to move into home frequency from those lower-frequency calibrations, especially when you are feeling anxious or angry. It will immediately shift you into home frequency, and you will feel it in your body. Several years ago I had the opportunity to interview Harvard psychiatrist Srinivasan Pillay, author of *Life Unlocked*, on my radio show, talking about strategies for managing fear and anxiety. He was the one who introduced me to the concept of visualization as a way to activate the prefrontal cortex of the brain and shift neurologically out of fear. It has since become a strategy I use with many of my patients. When we are in fear, the prefrontal cortex—the part of the brain that creates organized thoughts, sees solutions, and understands the larger picture—shuts down and the amygdala, the reptilian part of the brain, takes over. We will discuss this process in depth in Chapter 9, but for now it is important that you know that when your brain shuts down in this way, you are in fear. And it is nearly impossible to move into Quantum Love from a place of fear.

When you do the heart-opening meditation I shared with you in the last chapter, there is a sensation of widening, spreading, even a bubbling in the area of your heart. It's as if your heart is lightening and expanding. This is actually putting yourself into coherence, which is the state in which the energies of your body, mind, and spirit are in harmony.

Recent research performed by the Institute of HeartMath discovered that the heart is an energetic powerhouse for shifting and affecting energy around you, a subject we will be examining in Chapter 7. You can do the heart-opening meditation on its own as a regular practice, when you are feeling stuck in negative thoughts, or when you simply want to increase your own vibration with the intention of holding that state so your partner can entrain to you. However, a great additional practice is to use it as a kind of *energetic biofeedback*. Then you can learn to move into this powerful openhearted energetic state in a split second.

First, practice the heart-opening meditation several times and get familiar with it when you *aren't* particularly stressed. You will notice changes in the physical sensations in your body, improved mood, and more positive outlook, and likely the same shifts in those around you. Over time you will be able to move into openheartedness without having to think about or put yourself in a beautiful place of unconditional love in your mind. You will be able to move into home frequency without thought, knowing what it feels like in your body.

Heart-Opening Energetic Feedback Exercise

1. Ground yourself and get into the openhearted state as I described to you in the last chapter.
2. Now, move into constriction: Think about something that really triggers your thorns, really makes you feel scared or angry. Stay there for a few moments and notice how you feel. You will likely notice tightness in your chest, back, and jaw. You won't be feeling bubbly and light anymore.
3. Now, move back into openheartedness.
4. Repeat steps 1 and 2 several times, and you will notice that it becomes easier and easier to move into openheartedness from a place of constriction. Your body and your essential self are most aligned when you are in home frequency. You will get familiar with the sensations and build a mind-body connection that will allow you to shift into home frequency in a snap, whenever you desire and without thought.

Home Frequency Key 2: Tap Into the Energy All Around You . . . on Your Terms

As we have learned, we are all energy, affecting and being affected by the energy around us. This means that if we are not conscious of our own energetic state, we may find that it is being moved by something else in our field. This is something that every one of us has experienced in our relationships. Do you ever feel that your mood changes based on your partner's mood? If you are feeling happy, light, and carefree and she walks in the door with a sour look on her face, you can almost feel a mood of dread and misgiving building in your stomach. "What's wrong?" you ask immediately as your mind races over the possibilities. *Did her boss yell at her? Did her hours get cut? Did the kids act up in the car?* In the blink of an eye, your positive mood has been shattered into a million little pieces . . . and you don't even know what your partner is upset about yet, or if she is really upset at all. Maybe she just has a stomachache!

Why do we do this? The answer, as I alluded to in the previous chapter, is survival. Most of us had childhoods in homes with lots of "upper limits," the voices that kick in to tell us when we've been "too happy" or "too comfortable" and prime us to wait for the other shoe to drop. (We will be discussing upper limits further in Chapter 9.) Or we may have had an alcoholic or addicted parent, or lived in a family where love felt conditional. But the ability to read and sense energy is something we all have within us, even if it's been squelched or we've been distracted from it. To live more in home frequency, the goal is to use this ability to connect to the energy in and around you on *your* terms, not the other way around.

I have found that those who had really difficult childhoods often have super-sensitive intuition and an uncanny ability to read the energy in the room. It isn't necessarily that they have greater intuitive power than the rest of us. They just have easier access. The truth is, they often developed and exercised the intuitive connection out of the need to survive. Some children can tell from the very moment they walk in the door if Dad is drunk or Mom is angry, simply by feeling the energy radiating through the house. Robert Ohotto, a well-known intuitive life strategist, once shared with me that he believes his awareness of intuitive gifts began as he grew up in an alcoholic, often unsafe, and tempestuous household. He got to the point where he would walk into the house and know immediately if it was safe to stay, or if he should hop back on his bike and pedal away to the park as quickly as he could until the coast was energetically clear. Today, he is able to use these skills to help him in his career and to help those around him reach a level of wholeheartedness.

Unfortunately, Ohotto's case is somewhat rare. Rather than using their sensitivity to their benefit, many people find that their highly attuned intuition can work against them. Instead of elevating people around them to their energy, they tend to sink to other people's low energy levels, just as I described my son Ethan's old behavior in the previous chapter. They may even slip into codependency. I have come to believe that the only difference between these people and people like Robert Ohotto is awareness, and the ability to harness that awareness and move freely back to home frequency.

Assessing and Accessing Your Intuition

Intuition is a priceless and beautiful gift that each of us already has inside us, whether we realize it or not. In *Frequency,* Penney Peirce offers a "vibrational sensitivity survey" for taking the measure of your own sensitivity, and I've adapted this tool to give you the Intuition Quiz that follows. It is designed to help you determine your feeling habits and how they might be affecting your ability to access the intuitive voice of your essential self. Those places where we are not allowing ourselves to feel are probably also areas where we are carrying the energy of things we need to address. If the quiz indicates any areas where you might be closing off your energy, I encourage you to get curious about them so you can determine the source of your negative feeling and then move into it and release it.

For the following questions, rate your response on a scale of 1 to 5 (1 being "Never" and 5 being "Always").

Intuition Quiz

My Intuition About . . .	Never	Rarely	Sometimes	Often	Always
Others:					
My mood is easily impacted by the mood of others.	1	2	3	4	5
I can usually tell whether I can trust someone very soon after we meet.	1	2	3	4	5

I can sense when I am being lied to.	1	2	3	4	5
I can feel other people's moods, even if they do not verbalize them.	1	2	3	4	5
I can tell what other people are thinking before they say a word.	1	2	3	4	5
Myself:					
I trust my gut instinct.	1	2	3	4	5
I trust my internal compass and ability to make decisions.	1	2	3	4	5
My emotions tell me a lot about how I really feel about something.	1	2	3	4	5
I can sense what my body and mind need, and I give it to them.	1	2	3	4	5
I trust how I feel about something when I am making decisions.	1	2	3	4	5
The World Around Me:					
I can walk into a place and immediately know if it's a place I want to be—or if it's not!	1	2	3	4	5
I can feel when something big is going to happen in world news, weather events, etc.	1	2	3	4	5
I can sense the things that exist outside of our physical world.	1	2	3	4	5
I can see auras or energy fields, feel nonphysical entities or spirits, or perceive the souls of others.	1	2	3	4	5
I am very sensitive to the noisy or tumultuous vibrations of the world around me.	1	2	3	4	5

Now add up your score. A score of 15 to 35 indicates that you have some work to do connecting with your intuition and are likely closing, constricting, or blocking your energy channels with low-frequency To Me beliefs. If you scored between 36 and 55, you have some access to intuition but it's inconsistent, and if your score was between 56 and 75 you have a solid connection to your intuition and likely use it as a guide on a regular basis. Remember, there is no right or wrong level of sensitivity, so do not judge yourself if your numbers are low. Use this assessment as a jumping-off point.

So what can you do if you want to let your intuition speak more clearly to you? One key is to quiet the chatter in your mind. Meditation, even something as simple as the grounding and heart-opening exercises we have discussed, can go a long way toward putting you back into a quiet, coherent space so your intuition can speak up and be heard.

To learn more ways to tap into your own intuition, go to www.drlauraberman.com/quantumlove.

Home Frequency Key 3: Gratitude

Have you ever had a day when, right off the bat, you know you're in for a rough ride? Maybe you wake up cranky, hit every red light between home and your office, and then get called away from your desk for an unannounced staff-wide meeting, only to find afterward that your inbox is flooded with frantic "Where are you?" e-mails from a distressed client. Perhaps you drive home in heavy traffic, wanting nothing more than to sit quietly on your couch and read, watch TV, or vent about your terrible day to your partner. You walk into the house and, before you've even set your keys down, your partner says, "It looks like you forgot to pay the cable bill." This feels like the last thing you need. And you respond angrily. Or you don't respond at all. All the little things have piled up in your day, tanked your mood, and are about to bring your partner's mood down with yours. Why does it feel like the world is out to get you today?

Or maybe instead of a series of small obstacles and annoyances, one big, bad thing happens: an AFGE. Your world feels turned upside down.

No matter how big or small they are, or how frustrating or painful, hard experiences don't pop up just to torture us and make us miserable. Out of our greatest pain come our greatest gifts. It's a truth that can be very difficult to see when you're in the middle of that pain. But though we might not know the reason for the pain right now—in fact, we probably won't for a while—that doesn't mean that no reason exists. When I was diagnosed with breast cancer, my first thoughts were "I can't have cancer. I have a family, a career—I don't have time for *cancer*." As the emotional gravitas set in for me, my thoughts turned to whether I could handle what was now ahead of me, both physically ("How will the chemo make me feel? What will be the long-term impact on my body?") and emotionally ("I just lost my mom to cancer. I don't think I can take more hurt right now"). If there was a lesson to be learned from the AFGE bomb that had just dropped into my life, I didn't see it then. It never even occurred to me to look for it.

If you had asked me what I needed in the weeks that followed, I would have given you any number of answers: An hour of peace and quiet. A hug from one of my sons. A warm blanket and a cold compress. A shoulder to cry on. My mom. But if you had asked me how my cancer was serving me, I might have stood up and walked out of the room.

Not long after I finished my cancer treatment, my son Jackson, then eight years old, asked me, "Mommy, was cancer fun?" Almost immediately I replied, "No! Of course not!" But then I stopped and thought about it. In some ways, looking back from the other side of cancer, there were many parts of it that *were* fun. As tough as it was, cancer was the permission slip I needed to slow down, connect with what was important, and accept the love and help others had to give me. It forced me to take stock of my life and make changes that have led to a fuller, much more fun-filled life. I mean no disrespect to the pain and struggle that comes with cancer. I know it intimately. But I have to say that, yes, in a weird way, cancer can be fun. And, even more strangely,

I am hugely grateful for cancer and the wisdom and clarity that I gained on the journey through it.

The root of the ability to move to gratitude is the ability to surrender to the unknown (and possibly the unknowable) and find things to be thankful for, even when it seems like there is nothing to be found. Just as there is always a lesson in your pain, there is always something calling out for gratitude in your life. I don't just mean that there is food on your table or that your home is warm and safe, which puts you ahead of millions of people in the world as it is. I mean feeling gratitude that you are here, alive, mentally clear and emotionally strong, and grateful for the gifts that are found in the worst of circumstances. You are grateful for breath and awareness. You are grateful for the ability to challenge and consider your thoughts in a new light. You are grateful to have a journey to take and lessons to learn. When you are in a state of gratitude, you almost immediately switch into home frequency. Ego evaporates and you move closer to your essential self.

Before my big AFGEs, gratitude was not where I would go automatically. It sounded hard, like something more for monks than for a mommy with a full-time job and too much stress on her hands. There were so many things that needed to be fixed, managed, and controlled, after all! But my world changed, and yours will too, when you stop asking the usual question, "Why is this happening to me?" and ask instead, "How is this *for* me? What can I gain from this experience? What lessons am I being invited to learn?"

A "gratitude reboot" is an easy way to move into home frequency. It works whether you're in the midst of an AFGE, in a relationship crisis, or in a slump, or even if you just had a lousy day. It's a shift in perspective that creates an actual shift in your energy and consciousness. The idea behind a gratitude reboot is shockingly simple (though it might sometimes take a little creativity): stop trying to fix-manage-control (FMC), surrender to what is happening (even for just a little bit), and commit to looking for something to feel grateful for in every situation.

Gratitude Reboot

Make a commitment that, at least for a while, you will find gifts in anything that bothers, stresses, or annoys you. Even if it's a stretch, like feeling grateful for the symptoms of PMS ("This breakout is a reminder that my reproductive health is sound!"), you are going to recognize some small positive element of your experience. Maybe your computer isn't booting up because you are really supposed to go outside and get a few breaths of fresh air. Maybe you haven't heard back about that job you want because another, more amazing job is about to be offered to you. If you just can't see the bright side of something, perhaps you can commit to being open to discovering how this experience or event is "for you." Maybe your kids are fighting because they are supposed to highlight for you the ways in which you have been unconsciously fighting with your partner. Try it for a day, a week, even two weeks. Once you get to the two-week mark, you will be shocked and amazed at the level of home frequency you are able to maintain and the positive impact it is having on those around you and the reality you are creating.

1. Use this mantra: *I surrender to this moment/this day/ this week. Not only will I surrender, I'll find something to be grateful for in every situation.*
2. If you are someone who doesn't tend to look on the bright side, especially in your relationship, keep a gratitude journal, either written (maybe in your Quantum Love Journal) or in your smartphone. Keep a list of small and larger things you are grateful for about your partner. Maybe he looked really attractive in the outfit he was wearing. Perhaps he took out the garbage—even though he does it every night, you can be grateful that you don't have to. Maybe she just put her technology down for ten minutes while you were hanging out together. Maybe she paid you a compliment. Look for things that you can be grateful for, and keep a running list.

> Go to the list whenever you find yourself struggling with staying in home frequency in general but especially around your partner.

In Chapter 6 ("Commitment #2—I Will Get Clear on What I Want out of Love"), I will be teaching you more about how to apply the art of gratitude to your relationship and how powerful it can be in creating a new relationship reality, moving yourself and your partner into Quantum Love.

Home Frequency Key 4: The Art of Surrender

Surrender happens when you stop looking outside yourself for assurance, acceptance, and peace. You stop *trying* to be worthy. You stop *trying* to earn love. And you accept, maybe for the first time ever in your entire life, not only that you are worthy of love but that you are made for that purpose. You are an instrument that is here only to give and receive love. You have a soul that was built in love's image and a heart that can emit and experience love even across the chasms of time and space.

And you don't have to do anything to earn that love. You don't have to lose ten pounds or earn $100,000 a year or be the perfect parent or the perfect spouse. That love is already yours. You're asking for a candle but you're not in the dark. You're seeking forgiveness but you've never fallen from grace. You are grace. You are forgiveness. You are the candle.

The art of gratitude, as discussed above, is ultimately a lesson in faith and surrender. You have faith that you have something to learn from your pain, and you surrender to the discomfort that the lesson requires. Don't try to fix, manage, or control your way to a state of coherence! When you try to FMC anything in your life, you are in a state of constriction and ego frequency. Your heart is like a clenched fist. Nothing can get in and nothing can get out. Constriction is not going to feel comfortable on a physical or emotional level, and it's not going to help you on an energetic one.

Sometimes we get caught up in our negative stories and feel powerless: "There's nothing I can do to make this better." "My life is a mess right now." We are basically telling our mind, body, and spirit to batten down the hatches. We are caught up in our fear, anger, or sadness and constricting ourselves energetically into ego frequency, closing ourselves up in an attempt to stay safer. We have a really hard time being open and generous and in the moment. And so we create a reality that reflects what's going on inside us. We don't allow ourselves to be in the higher-frequency state that is going to create the outcome that we want. In those circumstances, surrender might seem impossible. And it often feels very difficult and scary. I know it does for me. And that's okay. Sometimes our situations feel too big to willingly give ourselves over to them.

When the going gets tough and we feel overwhelmed by everything around us, clinging to control can feel like the safer, more stable choice, even if what we're clinging to is a negative story we consciously (or unconsciously) have playing on a loop. The more we fight the pain, the more it grows and festers, and the more powerless and hopeless we feel. It isn't until we begin to *surrender* to the pain and allow ourselves to be with it that we begin to see light at the end of the tunnel. The more you surrender, the more open you become.

Maybe you don't think you can surrender to whatever is going on in your world. But do you think you can surrender simply to what *is* in this very moment? Can you surrender just to *right now*? Quantum Love is found when you really surrender to the moment *and only the moment*—it doesn't mean that you're making a larger statement about your partner or your relationship or whatever story you might have. If you can surrender to the moment with your mate in love and alignment, it keeps you in home frequency. You're surrendering your ego to your essential self.

It isn't easy. And it isn't our go-to state. If you are at all like me, you don't want to surrender to the bad things in your life because that feels like giving up. But one thing that I have learned in my life and my work is this: You cannot be at peace if you are in a state of resistance. When you are struggling or in a bad place in your relationship, you aren't going to be able to change anything until you surrender to what is, in this moment. Einstein famously said, "No problem can be solved from the same level of consciousness that created it." In other words, you can't solve a problem from the same state of consciousness that drew it into your field.

Surrendering to what is, just being with reality and getting curious about what might come next and what lessons may be in it for you, is the shift in consciousness that changes everything. That doesn't mean you can't work to change aspects of your life, whether it is your weight, your job, or your relationship with your spouse. But you can really create lasting, powerful change only if you accept that your current state is perfect and has purpose.

The Buddhists talk about the concept of "loving detachment," a state in which you are able to observe thoughts, beliefs, emotions, behaviors, and actions in yourself and others without attaching to them as part of who you *are*. The wonderful Buddhist monk and writer Thich Nhat Hanh refers to the image of a mountain and says that what we are, in our essence, is the *inside* of the mountain. Anything can happen around the mountain and on its surface—storms, high winds, mudslides—but the inside of the mountain is unaffected. Some people may come to see the mountain and exclaim over its majesty, while others will be less impressed, saying they have seen bigger, better mountains elsewhere. But regardless of the judgments made on its external self, the *inside* of the mountain doesn't change. Your essential self, the inside of your mountain, is perfect, strong, and brilliantly radiating light in your optimal frequency. No AFGE, relationship crisis, or any other external force can touch it.

Loving detachment plays fundamentally into surrender and our ability to let go of our long-held stories, beliefs, and thought patterns. Most of us have unwittingly woven these stories into the fabric of who we think we are. Loving detachment allows us to stop identifying with our stories. It's also key when we are talking about the art of manifesting because when we really want something, the natural inclination is to cling to it. When we do this, we move into a place of scarcity from which we cannot access Quantum Love. By viewing our well-worn stories or the things we really *want* through the lens of loving detachment, we can surrender and move back into the By Me and Through Me state from which we can actually create a positive reality.

Here are a couple of exercises that can help you move out of FMC and into surrender.

Say Hello to Your Essential Self

Your essential self is an immutable, powerful force that is unmoved by anything you've got going on in your life, no matter how big or bad. It is ready to offer you insight and clarity when you ask for it. It can be hard to hear this amidst the noise of the ego self. This is where saying hello to your essential self comes in.

In *The Untethered Soul*, Michael Singer teaches us that while it's easy to think that our beliefs, emotions, or state of being are "who we are" and encompass our whole self, our essential self is always an observer instead of a participant. When you say hello to yourself, there is a part of you that says it, and a part of you that hears it. The you that *hears* the hello is your essential self.

The point of this exercise is to ground yourself, open your heart, and quite literally say "Hello!" inside your head. Try it now. As you say the word in your mind, the part of your mind that is listening to the hello is your essential self.

Ask for Loving Detachment

When you are stuck in FMC mode and finding it difficult to move into surrender, try to access your lens of loving detachment. Begin by moving into a grounded, openhearted state and then ask your essential self, the lovingly detached version of yourself: "What would the lovingly detached thing to do be?"

You will find, as I and so many of my patients have, that the answer will come to you fairly quickly.

Home Frequency Key 5: Mindfulness

Most of us have heard the term *mindfulness* thrown around in one self-help capacity or another. But what is it really, and how does it apply to home frequency? Mindfulness is when you bring attention and awareness to your body and mind by experiencing complete sensory connection to this present moment, this moment alone, and not any other. You are not thinking about what happened two weeks or two years ago, what you're cooking for dinner, or when the mortgage payment is due. You are just right here, right now, nothing more.

In Chinese characters, the symbol for mindfulness is two characters put together: the top one means "presence" and the bottom one means "heart" (see Figure 4). So mindfulness is, simply, presence of heart. It comes when you stop living in your head and in your to-do list and start living in your heart. I will be sharing more about mindfulness, including some mindfulness meditations, in Chapter 10 (Commitment #4).

Figure 4: Chinese Symbol for Mindfulness

When you are fully mindful, you are aware of all five of your senses. You are fully tuned in to the here and now, utilizing all your senses to experience what *is* in this present moment. Whether it's while having a meal, making love, or walking to work, so many of us are only partially in our bodies. In today's world we are masters of multitasking, almost always doing more than one thing at once, waiting for the bus while typing on our smartphones, making dinner while helping a kid with homework, surfing the Internet while hanging out with our friends. It's not all bad. After all, multitasking allows us to get a lot of things done at once. But multitasking is in the world of the ego self, not the essential self. Even though you might be in flow, and perhaps vibrating at a higher emotional frequency while multitasking, you aren't fully present in your body. I believe that this is one of the reasons it is so easy for us to be unconscious of our body's energetic states, whether we are in home or ego frequency. Dropping into mindfulness allows you to tune in to how you are really feeling and make necessary adjustments to your energetic frequency.

Here are a couple of mindfulness exercises that can help you move into the practice. To learn more mindfulness practices, go to www.drlauraberman.com/quantumlove.

Mindfulness in the Moment

The next time you are in the park pushing your child in a swing, walking down the street with your partner holding hands, or even just eating an apple, put your awareness on all your senses: seeing, hearing, smelling, tasting, and touching. If you are pushing your child on a swing, hear the sounds of the park around you and the laughter of your little one as the swing goes higher and higher. Watch the look on your child's face and notice the leaves on the trees and the beautiful colors around you. Feel the wind on your face as the breeze blows across the playground, and notice how it feels to have your hair ruffled by it, how it feels on your skin. Smell the hair on your child's head as you catch the swing for a moment and plant a kiss on her head, and notice how her hair feels against your lips. If you are holding your partner's hand, put all your attention into the hand that is being held and use all your senses to experience it fully. This is mindfulness in the moment. And, quite frankly, when you put all your attention on the moment, it's next to impossible not to find something for which you can be grateful.

MINDful Love Intentions

Every day when you wake up, set a mindful love intention for the day. In the following chapters you will have a chance to clarify some Quantum Love Goals, and your love intention may be characterized by those goals. For instance, if your goal is to feel more romantic, perhaps your mindful love intention for the day will be to take in the energy of a romantic connection. Ground yourself and open your heart, then take some deep breaths and imagine in your mind and body what a romantic connection would feel like.

If you need to, you can imagine a specific scenario, as if you are there in first person (not unlike the heart-opening exercise). Or you may be able to get there just by asking the question "What would it feel like in my five senses if I had all the romance I ever wanted in my life?" Allow yourself to be in that space for a few minutes, enlisting all your senses in the process. Maybe you are seeing and smelling beautiful flowers, or tasting champagne or your partner's surprise kisses. Maybe you are having a massage, or just feeling a tingling, warm, loving, accepted feeling running through your body. As you finish your imaginings, open your eyes and try to hold that energetic state for as long as you can. Now you are creating a mindful intention to build the kind of love connection you most desire.

Honoring your responsibility for your own energy state is one of the most positive and impactful things you can do for yourself, your partner, your relationship, and your life. Whether you are aware of it or not, your energy and consciousness are shaping all of these things every second of every day. You are indeed creating your reality through the resonant frequency you are putting out into the field. As you will learn in the next chapter, the ability to move your relationship into Quantum Love is yours for the taking . . . and it begins with you. This is why it is so important to commit yourself to taking responsibility for the energy you bring *into* your relationship. Understand what you will create from a place of coherent home frequency versus what will manifest when you are vibrating in ego frequency. Use these techniques to train your awareness, to notice how it feels when you are in home frequency and what it feels like when you are moving into a contraction and looping toward the low end point of your EHFI. Know what you're transition point is, and use these techniques to steer your energy back onto the path of Quantum Love.

All of these things are within your power. Quantum Love begins with you.

CHAPTER 5

Falling in Love versus Quantum Love

Love does not consist of gazing at each other, but in looking outward together in the same direction.

— Antoine de Saint-Exupéry

By now, you probably have a good grasp on how your thoughts, perceptions, and emotions impact your body's energy. You understand the fundamental role your frequency, ego or home, plays in the reality you are creating around you, in all things, but especially in your relationship.

This book isn't about getting you back to that time when you had just fallen in love. I know we are talking about quantum physics, but this isn't the DeLorean time machine! Instead, this book is meant to help you learn how to fall inward and upward into Quantum Love. I speak about love and sex all around the country, and people always want to know how they can spice up their love lives. They want to make their relationship "like it was in the beginning." I could give you a book with 365 different things to try, one for every day of the year, but it would never be enough. The real intensity comes when you take full responsibility for your thoughts and feelings and learn to use home frequency as a way to create exactly the relationship experience you desire.

Let's face it. Falling in love is an amazing feeling. The biological, psychological, emotional, and spiritual powers of love make you feel like you're getting caught in the pull of an exhilarating wave. You can think of nothing but being with your beloved, of intertwining in body and soul again and again and again. *What could possibly be better?* you think as you fold into your beloved's arms. In that moment, you're not likely to be aware that this high is fleeting. The intensity of your feelings is going to wane, and this will be a good thing.

The truth is that every relationship invariably reaches a point of predictability. You feel numb from day-to-day life and the natural conflicts and resentments that can build up over time. You're desperate for a little variety. But the biggest mistake is resigning yourself to the idea that this burnout is love's inevitable conclusion when, in reality, there is a relationship waiting for you that far exceeds the excitement and novelty of the honeymoon phase. The energy in the human body, in its purest potential, has been calculated by physicists to be ten times greater than the energy in a typical hydrogen bomb. This was calculated with Einstein's famous equation $E=mc^2$, using the mass of an average human body (155 pounds or 70 kilograms). If you're willing to claim and use your energy and apply it to this world that is nothing but pure potential, Quantum Love is yours for the taking.

Remember, in Quantum Love, everything starts with *you*. Quantum Love is a state you must move into within yourself first, and once you do, you don't need your partner to do anything, change anything, or show up in a different way. He or she doesn't even need to know you are reading this book or buy into its concepts. Because when *you* change, *your partner* changes. When you harness the power of your body's energy and consciously use it to create Quantum Love, you get everything you are looking for in your relationship.

By understanding and harnessing the power of your own energy, you can unlock and encounter a more evolved version of yourself. It's a self who can handle every obstacle with strength and grace, who lives authentically and freely, and who loves and is loved unconditionally and passionately. But first, I have to take you back to the beginning and show you your love story from a different perspective. Once you understand the science of attraction, infatuation, and attachment, you'll have a clearer understanding of how it all leads to Quantum Love.

Attraction

The day I met my husband, I felt a huge, intense, energetic connection.

Sam and I had known each other when we were kids. Our families were friends and we even vacationed on the same street. There was no energy exchange between us then, however. Sam was a full four years older than me, and he never noticed me at all, nor I him, for that matter.

That all changed a couple of decades later in Chicago.

I was in town from Los Angeles with my sister, her then-husband, and a friend. We had traveled to the Windy City for my first-ever *Oprah* appearance promoting a book my sister and I had written together.

As we were heading to lunch, my sister casually said, "By the way, I invited Sam Chapman to join us. Do you remember him?"

I did, though we had not seen each other since my family moved away when I was ten. He had really been my sister's friend, as they were the same age. Neither of us had seen him in about 25 years. However, he had recently reached out after seeing us on television, remembering our families' good times together. He told us to call him if we ever came to Chicago, so my sister had followed through (and for that I will always be grateful).

When Sam joined us at our table, I certainly wasn't disappointed with what I saw. He was handsome, confident, and extremely smart. But there was something else too.

As the group was talking, I caught myself staring at him. I felt this unequivocal pull toward him. I couldn't look away from him. At least not until he looked at me. When he suddenly glanced my way and caught me staring, he held my gaze for just a moment before I panicked and looked away.

Months later, Sam would tell me that was a pivotal moment for him. He couldn't stop thinking about how it felt when I was looking at him, and he couldn't keep from trying to think of ways to get me to look at him again.

Several months after our lunch, a friend of his suggested, "Hey, remember that woman you felt that intense connection with? Why don't you just go out and see her?" The pull that Sam felt toward me was strong enough that he fabricated a reason to visit Los Angeles without giving it a second thought.

Of course, he didn't tell me that he was flying out to see me. He simply e-mailed my sister saying he was coming to town. He just wanted to check out the situation, determine if I was available, and see whether that charge he felt was still there.

We were all supposed to go out to dinner together: my sister, her husband, Sam, my parents, and me. However, it turned out I already had another engagement for the same night, a date with a man I had met online a few months prior. I was new to Internet dating, and I was not completely sure I wanted to move from e-mail to an actual meeting. After repeatedly breaking our dates, I had promised to keep this one and felt compelled to follow through on it. So after drinks, when my date suggested grabbing dinner, I thought on my feet and proposed we meet my parents and "an old family friend" who were dining down the street. I felt bad about dragging my date along with me, but I didn't want to miss out on seeing Sam. My plan was to join in the dinner but not to linger; we'd stay just long enough to satisfy my curiosity. Then, I reasoned, I could focus on my date without any distractions.

That plan fell apart as soon as Sam and I caught each other's gaze again. When our eyes met across the table, I felt the same pull that I had felt months earlier, except this time I didn't look away. Looking away felt impossible. As the dinner conversation continued around us (no one else noticed that he and I were in our own world), it was like the entire table faded away. I was overwhelmed—in a very, *very* good way.

Three Minutes

To me, "love at first sight" was little more than romantic fantasy. This was entirely different. The intense energy of the connection between Sam and me felt stronger and more immediate than I could logically explain, almost as if I recognized him on a cellular level.

While you too may be tempted to write off love at first sight as wholly unrealistic, don't be too hasty. Your brain is hardwired to say *yea* or *nay* at high speed, making cuts faster than the rose ceremony on *The Bachelor.* In fact, your brain sizes up a potential mate within the first three minutes of meeting. That's right. *Three minutes.* It's an intuitive skill developed millions of years ago to distinguish friend from foe, mate from mistake. So let's break down the chemistry of those all-important first three minutes.

At any given moment, your brain is taking in 400 billion bits of information. However, of those 400 billion bits, you are consciously processing only 2,000 bits. So no matter how many mindfulness meditations or therapy sessions you might have attended this week, you will not be conscious of most of the information you are taking into your brain. It's a good thing, too, for the sheer volume of information would completely overload you. But just because you are not aware of them doesn't mean that those unconscious pieces of information don't have an impact. They are being processed and synthesized to create your preferences, and your romantic and sexual preferences are no exception. Your brain has constructed a template of everything it desires most out of your relationships.

A well-known researcher named John Money dubbed this template the "love map" (not to be confused with the Quantum Lovemap). It is a totally subconscious breakdown of everything that turns us on neurologically and emotionally.[1] Love maps vary in nature: one person's love map might determine that only waifish, short-haired brunettes do the trick, while another's might prefer buxom redheads. Your love map locks in your physical and even emotional type as well as your more atypical sexual needs, behaviors, and fetishes—and all by the age of seven. That's right: by first grade, your brain had already cemented the bulk of your sexual preferences. My husband maintains that this is why I look like his first crush—his kindergarten teacher!

Your brain has essentially already written up a casting call for your ideal lover, and it turns out the first audition is less than one second long. The seemingly intangible sexual chemistry between two people actually has a biological source called pheromones. In 2008, researchers discovered an almost imperceptibly tiny olfactory nerve called "nerve 0" that they believe is the route through which pheromones are processed. The fibers of this nerve start in the nose but completely bypass the olfactory cortex, the part of the brain that processes smell, and go straight to the sexual centers of the brain. So even though you are not conscious of a smell, your partner's scent is a huge factor in your attraction. You have an unconscious sniffer you are not even aware of that helps you choose your mate.[2]

Typically, we are attracted to a particular kind of smell too: the smell of a person who has a different MHC from ours. MHC, or major histocompatibility complex, is a set of genes that play a fundamental role in your immune system. Family members share similar genes and therefore often share similar immune systems. So the idea that we are unconsciously seeking out a mate with a different MHC suggests that, in part, scent cues evolved to protect close family members from procreating with each other. (I know, I know—we're really setting the mood here.) Research has demonstrated, too, that pregnant women are actually drawn to the scent of people with a similar chemical makeup during this crucial time, which indicates that their brains are prioritizing the safety of a familial tribe over sexual needs.[3]

Of course, poets and painters haven't been praising merely a dry biological or chemical response for thousands of years. Truly, there's a sacredness and intangible beauty about the way two people are drawn to each other. You've felt it: a shiver of energy, an immediate recognition, a magnetic pull, and the electric excitement of the novelty and discovery of this other being. It's a completely spiritual—a *quantum*—experience.

Let's take a look at what is happening on the quantum level.

A New Energy Field

As we discussed in Chapter 1, we are all made of pure energy, and that energy is constantly interacting with the energy of everything (and everyone) else in the world around us. It's one big field, in which the energies of everything wiggle and dance, create and interact. But just because we are all connected, that does not mean our energy is not individual to us. As we learned in Chapter 3, "Discover Your Energy Profile," we are each humming at our own frequency. Our frequency is how our energy interacts with all the other energies out in the field.

The people who populate your world are likely a "frequency match" to you, meaning that they have a personal vibration that is in tune with your own. Your shared vibrations recognize each other and draw you into each other's field. It's a crazy thing to think about, but this means that every person with whom you have ever crossed paths was drawn to you by a shared vibration, and you were drawn to them! As Penney Peirce puts it in *Frequency*, "If they occur in your world, you occur in theirs. You mutually create each other for a shared purpose."

Of course that shared purpose is not always love and sex; it can be anything. There are times when I'll be standing in line at the store checkout and happen to notice the outfit on the woman in front of me and feel the urge to compliment her. I might say, "Your dress is very pretty," to which she replies, "Thank you"; then we go back to staring straight ahead. After we finish buying groceries, we are likely to part ways and never see each other again; clearly our shared purpose is something much smaller, something neither one of us is likely to be aware of. Maybe I have a need to be kind; maybe she has a need for kindness. It could be anything. Our interaction, brief though it is, serves a purpose, even if we don't know what it is.

Now here's where quantum physics comes in. The really amazing thing about our interactions with people with whom we share a vibrational frequency is that when our energies come together, they actually combine to create their own energy field, or relationship field. This new relationship field comes with its shared purpose (no matter how big or small) and its own voice. And when we start talking about the relationship field and the combining energies that occur in the early moments of attraction, that's when things start to get really interesting.

Neale Donald Walsch describes this moment perfectly in his wonderful book *Conversations with God.* He sets the scene: Two people, Tom and Mary, are on opposite sides of a room. They each radiate their personal energy. Their energies meet midway between them and unite to create a new energy unit Walsch calls TomMary. As they both feed energy to TomMary, energy is sent back to each of them through the quantum field. And the closer they draw to each other, the shorter and more intense the cord of energy between them becomes. With each step in the other's direction, that intensity vibrates and burns wider, brighter, and deeper. The intensity of their shared energy field, their relationship field, will continue to be amplified by their individual vibrations, which are a clear frequency match.

But what made Tom and Mary see each other across the room in the first place? Let's look a little more closely at the energetic source of relationships.

Resonance

Have you ever heard someone say, "That really resonates with me"? What they are trying to express is that a story or concept really hit home for them; they feel connected to it on an emotional and spiritual level. Resonance in quantum physics works in a very similar way. Best-selling author, scientist, and speaker Gregg Braden puts it very simply when he says, "Resonance is an exchange of energy between two things. It's a two-way experience allowing 'something' to come into balance with another."[4] Another way to think of that "balance" is to say that two things sync up with or tune in to each other. Every object has a frequency at which it naturally vibrates, and if another object (or person) shares the same energetic frequency, if they are a frequency *match*, they can sync up and even influence each other. One can even set the other into motion!

Resonance speaks in *YES* and *NO,* and it works quickly. Think of how quickly the brain assesses a potential mate against its love map: *NO, NO, NO, YES!* When I was out with my online dating match, I knew *NO* pretty quickly. My energy tuned in to his and said, "Next!" Our frequency match brought us together, but our shared purpose was definitely not to date.

To get a picture of *YES* resonance in action, we need to look no further than my first lunch with Sam. Remember, the very fact that Sam *occurred* in my life is because we share a vibrational frequency. As he was talking to my sister, he was not conscious that I was staring at him. But my energy was resonating with his, and it was saying, *Look at me*—even though that was a message I would have been too chicken to ever consciously send! His essential and physical self responded *YES,* and his eyes met mine.

In other words, my individual energy frequency sent his into motion without my ever having to say a word or even seductively bat an eyelash. Yet at that lunch, there was something more than pure physical attraction at play. When his eyes quickly moved across the table and caught mine, in that instant, we were both conscious of the energy between us.

Knowing what I know now, I can't help but wonder if, in that moment when our eyes met across the dinner table and we became conscious of the intense energy between us, our energies entrained or even entangled with each other. Remember from Chapter 2, entanglement is when two energies behave as if they are exactly the same. Even if they are separated by time and space—by miles and years—if one unit sets into motion, the other one does too. The connection is instantaneous, as if they truly were *one* thing.

A few days after Sam left L.A., I couldn't stop thinking about him. I finally worked up the courage to type him a quick e-mail, something easy, breezy, and not at all indicative of the fact that I was smitten. I can't tell you how long I spent writing this "easy, breezy" e-mail, and how many different drafts I deleted in frustration. *War and Peace* felt easier and breezier by the time I was done! Finally, though, I had it perfect, and I sent it off with excitement. It read: *It was great to see you. If you find yourself back in L.A. and would like to have dinner without the peanut gallery, give me a call.* The second I hit "Send," I heard my own e-mail account ping with the arrival of a new message. It was from Sam: *I can't stop thinking about you. When can we see each other again?* Despite the thousand miles and two time zones between us, we had behaved identically and instantaneously. I smile now to think that our timing was no accident and wonder whether our energies were already entangled. It was another quantum moment between us, the first of many, many more to come.

Resonance is what moves people into your life in the first place, and it doesn't fade as the relationship progresses past the attraction phase. It is an incredible tool that, once understood and harnessed, can be used to influence the flow of your relationship. Resonance is a form of coherence, and as more and more things resonate *YES* between you and another person, the more you can fall into coherence with each other. As your energetic coherence intensifies, your attraction deepens. Your relationship field gets bigger and begins to draw other things in. Your individual frequencies vibrate in a way that supercharges your shared frequency, drawing you closer and closer.

Let's revisit Neale Donald Walsch's scene with Tom and Mary. He describes how, as Tom and Mary come together, the intensity of TomMary gets brighter and wider. As they interact, their *YES* resonances are firing like crazy and create a noticeable response in their physical selves: goose bumps, flushed cheeks, a sense of anticipation and tingling excitement. As they touch, "the sensation is almost unbearable . . . exquisite. They feel all the energy of TomMary . . . all the compact, intensely unified substance of their combined being."

As they embrace, Tom, Mary, and TomMary all fill the same space. They are desperate to literally meld and feel this union in physical form. And as they enter and receive each other, they become one in the flesh. They heave, move, explode, and convulse. "And in the explosion of their oneness they have known the god and goddess . . . the alpha and the omega, the all and the nothing, the essence of life."

This is the very first soul connection that can take the energy of physical passion between two kindred spirits to the Quantum Love level. And it is this soul connection, not the novelty of first encounters, that can be grown into a deeper, more fulfilling, and more mind-blowing relationship.

But first comes the all-consuming, rosy-hued infatuation stage.

Infatuation

Infatuation. The honeymoon phase. You can't eat, can't sleep, can't *think* of anything else but this person who has invaded and conquered your head, heart, and body. Typically it can last anywhere from three months to three years, depending on how much time you spend together and how quickly the relationship becomes a committed one.

Sam and I were obnoxiously infatuated with each other for that full three-year span, much to the chagrin of everyone around us. I remember snuggling with him, full of bliss, and begging him to promise that we would always keep this head-over-heels honeymoon phase going. It was so yummy, I didn't want it to ever end. Plus, I knew how awful it could be when it went away.

The infatuation stage is when the energy of sex comes in to increase the intensity of your energy and conscious feelings tenfold. It combines an intense physical interaction with the energetic interaction that was jump-started during the attraction stage. A shared psychological intensity comes into play too as you both show off your best selves.

In fact, you're not only putting your best self forward, you're also seeing the best in each other. Things that might typically annoy you seem like endearing and charming traits. Your partner is smart and funny, enchanting and interesting, and he or she thinks that you are all those things too. This is one of the reasons why the infatuation stage feels so good: you are seeing the most fabulous version of yourself reflected in your partner's eyes.

Beneath those psychological processes, there is a lot happening in quantum terms. Your energy frequencies are entrained to each other on a fundamental and intense level. If we think about it in terms of a radio, you and your partner are on the same station with the volume cranked up! Both you and your partner are humming along at this intense level, opening yourselves to each other emotionally and physically and operating in a big YES state.

Infatuation Is Full-Body YES

In the infatuation state, you get to experience a condition that was first introduced to me by life coach Diana Chapman: the Full-Body YES. I believe this is how our essential self communicates with us as it responds to the resonant energy of our environment, other people, and even the energy of our own thoughts and ideas.

Whether you knew it or not, you've experienced a Full-Body YES before. It's that feeling of lightness that comes with a thought or a suggestion, a buzzing, excited feeling that blazes through your body and mind. It's when you think, "Wow, that would be *amazing*!" or when you experience a sensation of just *knowing* something. It's a powerful barometer that you have at your fingertips, and you'll learn more about how to use it as this book goes on.

In infatuation, as your partner reveals a new piece of information about himself or herself or does something incredibly sweet, your mind is probably in a state of YES. As your physical interactions become more affectionate, something as simple as holding hands can put you theretoo. And as you each start to figure out what the other really likes in the bedroom, your sex life can certainly throw you into a state of Full-Body YES.

So what is going on at the quantum level of Full-Body YES? Coherence, baby! Your energy is in coherence with your partner's, of course, but it is also buzzing and humming inside of *you*. Amazingly, even though they are all part of you, your body, mind, and heart can have different energy frequencies that are communicating with one another and, hopefully, working together to create your positive state.

Personal coherence is essentially when all of the little subatomic energy particles that make up each of us can cooperate with one another. We already know that they are highly interlinked (after all, that's why we are solid instead of liquid, gaseous, or formless) and that they're held together by their electromagnetic fields and vibrating together. These vibrations come together to create a wave pattern, and as they do, they begin to act as one wave that behaves as a single entity. That wave is then able to communicate and come into sync with the other waves inside you through coherence. The stronger the coherence, the more refined the wave patterns are. When all of those subatomic particles are in a perfect state of coherence, we have what we refer to as "health."

Have I made you go cross-eyed yet? Let's make it more concrete. Think of your body. Your body has *lots* of systems contained within it: respiratory, circulatory, and neurological, just to name a few. When all of your systems are working well, you get the "good health" stamp from your physician and feel great. Well, on a quantum level, that means that all of the waves within each system are in coherence. But sometimes one or two of those systems can go out of whack, and when they do, you tend to know it right away. It can be as simple as the flu, in which the interloping energy of an invading virus (yes, they have their own energy too) interferes with the energy of your body's systems, or it can be far more serious. It's possible for individual systems within the body to be out of coherence without taking the other systems out too (you don't lose muscle control just because you have the flu). The different systems within your body are highly intertwined but still distinct. It is the same with the interaction between your overall body system and the other systems within you, your mind and heart systems.

When your systems are all in coherence within themselves *and with each other,* you are at your very, very best. You feel amazing, assured, and perfectly happy in your given moment. This perfect state of alignment—when you're solidly in home frequency—is where you want to be. Full-Body YES is this personal coherence in action.

The gift of the infatuation stage is that there is effortless coherence between you and your beloved. There's nothing knocking you off center in this relationship, so you get to experience this YES feeling toward your partner again and again. It's no wonder you want it to last forever.

This Is Your Brain on the Drug of Love

So many of us fear or lament a decline (or just a leveling out) in the intensity of our feelings in the infatuation stage. We think it's the same as a declining interest. So we actively try to avoid it or head it off at the pass by pushing the relationship forward ("I think we should move in together!") instead of letting things progress organically. But in doing so we create a self-fulfilling prophecy of defeat, because we're asking our brain to do the impossible.

You see, by pressuring your relationship to stay in the infatuation stage forever, what you're really asking your brain to do is maintain a permanent high. And no, that's not a metaphor. During infatuation your brain is literally, biologically, high on love. In one study, 37 people who were madly in love, both happily coupled and recently dumped, were put in a functional MRI brain scanner to see what romantic love does to the brain. Researchers found high levels of activity near the VTA (ventral tegmental area) of the brain in A10 cells, the cells that make dopamine and send it to other brain regions.[5] This is part of the brain's reward system, operating below emotions and reason in that reptilian core associated with wanting, craving, focus, motivation, and addiction—the same part of the brain that lights up when on cocaine.[6] And when you're denied what you want, when someone you love breaks up with you, you're actually experiencing withdrawal. All of those serial monogamists you know, jumping from relationship to relationship, are very often infatuation junkies craving a new high. Once they come down, they have to find another fix of the dopamine high of new love. But your brain isn't designed to sustain that high forever.

Attachment: A Sweet Comedown

On a psychological level, it is impossible to present only your very best high-energy self forever. There's another drive that is supposed to kick in and supplant infatuation: attachment. It allows us to stay connected but still be functioning, contributing members of society. Think about it: if everyone were in the infatuation stage all the time, nothing would ever get done. We'd all blow off work and our other commitments to be with our beloved. Millions of people would take insane, desperate risks to secure affection. We'd be an entire society of love junkies, and civilization would collapse!

That's why most long-term relationships eventually move into the attachment stage, which is typically characterized as a softer, sweeter, more sustainable kind of love. But for many, moving into attachment can feel like a loss of intensity, joy, and connection or even like a rocky road to nowhere. Our instant-gratification culture doesn't promote this next phase of love—but attachment is where the really good stuff in a long-term relationship is. This is where Quantum Love can be found.

When we are moving from deep infatuation to the attachment stage, we usually begin dropping into ego frequency. During the infatuation stage, you were seeing your best self reflected back to you through your partner, and that made it easy to be in home frequency. But over time you find it harder to maintain that perfect self and begin to expose your more authentic self. That's when ego can start to take over with the low-frequency emotions of jealousy, fear, and negativity. We wonder, *What is wrong with me? What's wrong with him/her?* We get so caught up in our own negative state that we don't even recognize the fact that this transition is a good thing. Our egos are dying for a fix and telling us that the mutual connection we have enjoyed on a psychological and energetic level is going away.

Science tells us a different story. MRI scans of couples claiming they were still madly in love after 20-plus years together confirmed they were telling the truth. Researchers found that those dopamine centers associated with romantic love and sex drive were still lighting up, but there were two big differences between the brains of the long-term couples and those who were newly in love: the long-termers' had a drop in the obsession region and a huge boost in the opiate system. This is the reward system of the brain. It acts as mediator between wanting something and actually enjoying it. And on top of that, there was a crucial added bonus: researchers found activity near the base of the brain associated with calm and pain suppression and almost no activity in the region linked with anxiety.[7]

On a quantum level, the attachment phase is all about entrainment. This is where you see couples' heartbeats coming in sync with each other; their moods and energetic states can directly impact their partner's. The thing to remember is that just because they are entrained, it does not mean they are in coherence with each other. And if a couple goes too long without being in coherence, one or both of them might start feeling as if "something" is missing. This is often what makes the transition from infatuation to attachment feel a little rough.

Yes, leaving the infatuation phase means you lose some of the obsession and intensity. It might feel a little less thrilling. But by practicing Quantum Love, you take love to a whole new level. You gain more intense pleasure, a true sense of peace, and the ability to enjoy the beautiful partnership you've created on a deep, connected emotional level. That means more intense sex, a more intimate relationship, and a strong sense of security. Biology is urging you to move past the craving to real satisfaction. You were made for Quantum Love. All you have to do is claim it.

The Quantum Love Difference

Quantum Love isn't just about your relationship. It's a spiritual path to your truest self. It doesn't start with your partner, the story of your relationship, or even your mutual connection. Quantum Love starts within *you alone*.

The key difference between love (in its attraction, infatuation, and attachment stages) and Quantum Love is that in the latter you consciously use the energy of your body, heart, and mind to create exactly the kind of love you seek. Your partner doesn't have to do anything differently, but just naturally entrains to your energy, and you mutually create a relationship field that feels joyful, passionate, and fulfilling. In Quantum Love, you are already connected to your essential self and the conscious choice to be with your partner. You accept your partner not only in spite of her or his so-called flaws, but *because* of them. In infatuation you only see your partner's best self. In Quantum Love you see your partner's whole, authentic self and you love him or her *for it*. Seem like a tall order? I promise it won't feel that way by the time you finish this book.

The most important thing to remember for now is that your partner exists in your life because you are already vibrating at a similar frequency. You are already in harmony, even if temporarily out of tune. When you get back to or remain in the By Me or Through Me state, in your home frequency, you move your EHFI up the Quantum Lovemap. Your partner, who is already in harmony with you, will entrain with you. You don't need to do anything but focus on what's going on energetically inside you, and your whole relationship will change.

In Quantum Love, *You* Are Complete

When you are in Quantum Love, you don't *need* your partner or your relationship to feel complete. Now, of course, that isn't to say that you wouldn't be devastated if it were to suddenly end; but once you picked yourself up off the floor, you would still go on. I've always rolled my eyes at that line from *Jerry Maguire* when Jerry says to Dorothy Boyd, "You complete me." *Nobody* completes you, and you can't have Quantum Love until you are complete on your own. In Quantum Love, you don't *need* to be in a relationship, you are *choosing* to be in your relationship. And because it is your choice, you exist in your relationship in your home frequency with a fully open heart.

Before you can move into Quantum Love with your partner, you have to get into Quantum Love with *yourself.* This is a truly transformative and positive process that will move your EHFI right up the Quantum Lovemap. While I will be sharing numerous tools in the following chapters that you can use to build Quantum Love with and in your partner, I will also be helping you fall in Quantum Love with yourself.

Fully accepting and even adoring yourself really is the solution to resolving any conflict or longing. If you are constantly seeking affirmation and approval *outside* yourself, you're coming into your relationship from a place of lacking. Conversely, when you are able to find affirmation and approval within yourself, by and for yourself, you are entering into your relationship in a state of fullness, a state that you can feel in your mind and your body. And when you come into a relationship in a state of fullness, you're less likely to try to fix, manage, or control. You're less likely to slip into ego frequency. You are already complete and in your home frequency.[8]

In Quantum Love, Your Partner Is One of Your Greatest Teachers

Holistic health expert Deepak Chopra uses the term *communion* in his writings to refer to the recognition in a relationship that each of you has strengths that the other one lacks. You learn to share in each other's strengths, to complete *yourself,* and to honor the parts of your partner that touch your "thorns." This means reimagining the idea of two becoming one. It is not simply that your strengths and weaknesses balance each other out. *Communion* means that you consciously model traits from your partner and learn to incorporate them into your being.[9] Let's say your partner is really great at standing up for himself and expressing anger in a healthy way, while you tend to let people violate boundaries and retaliate passive-aggressively. As the two of you come into communion with each other, you learn to stand up for yourself, and maybe your mate learns how to listen empathically. Consciously, you borrow each other's strength to become even more whole.

But it can work the other way too. One of the most fascinating things about the work I do is seeing how perfectly my patients are matched through their greatest point of conflict. After almost 30 years working with couples, I have come to truly believe that we are drawn to someone who will force us to face our most complicated issues and deepest fears. In the hit Broadway show *Rent*, Mimi hits the nail on the head when she sings, "I'm looking for baggage that goes with mine." Your unconscious has selected your soul mate for this very reason. If you are willing to surrender to the process of Quantum Love, to harness your energy and take responsibility for what you bring to the relationship, your partner can serve as your greatest teacher, helping to usher in a version of you that is healed, loved, and whole.

This idea was perfectly demonstrated by a couple I treated recently in an intensive retreat, Sarah and Pete. They had been married for 25 years and had never had sex sober. No matter what they tried, Sarah was incapable and unwilling to have sex unless she was drunk. As we unraveled things, it became clear that this was tied to her history of abandonment and abuse.

After the death of her father when she was 12, Sarah's mother emotionally—and eventually literally—abandoned her. Starved for care and supervision as a teenager, Sarah started acting out and drinking. At 16 she secured a summer job and was raped repeatedly by three of her adult co-workers.

Meanwhile, Pete came from a background of abandonment through a work-obsessed father and an emotionally mercurial mother. Also around the age of 12, a financial crisis propelled him to become the family hero, going to work to help earn extra money, becoming the go-between for his parents and the emotional soother of his mother. This laid the groundwork for a lifetime of codependent behaviors. As an adult, Pete's self-worth was still wrapped up in being the hero. He had to be exactly what others needed in order to emotionally care for them. He was incredibly successful socially. But he was also severely stressed and suffered from chronic back pain and immobility.

The word that kept coming up for both Sarah and Pete was *responsibility*. Both of them came from families with impossibly high standards, where an A-minus still wasn't an A. Sarah felt responsible for letting her parents down, even though her mom left *her*, and like many victims, she ultimately felt responsible for her rapes, as if she had brought them on herself. And her shame and guilt had prevented her from taking responsibility for her own sexuality. She felt 100 percent responsible for her husband's satisfaction and not at all connected to her own. Meanwhile, Pete felt completely responsible for *her* satisfaction and took no responsibility for *his* own. He didn't even masturbate outside of the three or four times a year they had sex! After a lifetime of codependence, his entire focus was on making Sarah happy. The problem was that this task was impossible until she was ready to take responsibility for her own happiness.

Pete *chose* a woman whom his superstar emotional and social skills could not reach, a woman who couldn't stand the emotional spotlight and even resented it. Unconsciously, the highest, most loving part of him selected someone who would challenge his codependency. That was his work: to learn to hold others accountable for their own happiness instead of assuming responsibility for it himself.

And Sarah *chose* someone who was going to require that she be present with him and open her heart. On an unconscious level, she knew that Pete was going to call on her to move through her issues, confront her demons, and take responsibility for her happiness in the relationship.

As soon as she made that connection, we started working on Sarah's ability to take ownership of her sexual response. She was eventually able to have great, sober sex, with orgasms. Ultimately, what created a shift toward Quantum Love for Sarah and Pete was not just the acceptance of their roles and responsibility, but the recognition that the source of their conflict was the point of their greatest personal growth. Sarah and Pete chose each other because in bringing out each other's demons, they were truly able to save each other—and themselves. Once they both recognized this, their relationship was transformed.

When you accept that your partner is your greatest teacher, you will love his or her whole, authentic self. You will recognize that your souls have a contract to grow, evolve, and expand your essential selves together. You were unconsciously attracted to your partner not in spite of his or her flaws or shortcomings, but *because* of them. Your partner's traits were all selected by your essential self to help you grow, face your fears, and become the most complete version of yourself. Yes, even the traits that drive you absolutely crazy. This means that you never have to love your partner "in spite of" certain traits or habits; you can love your partner specifically *for* them because your essential self sought them out!

Quantum Love comes when you seek to discover what lessons your partner can (and is here to) teach you. Next time you catch yourself wanting to roll your eyes over something your partner says or does, stop for a moment and ask, "Why is this resonating with me in this way? What is my reaction telling me about *me*?" Even better, look at that characteristic that bothers you and ask yourself, "How does this serve me?" Chances are, when you drop into home frequency and consider the question, the answer will be clear. If it isn't, then you have found a powerful path that is worthy of exploration.

Quantum Love Is Not a Battlefield

Legendary marriage researcher Dr. John Gottman studied newly married couples for six years. He observed the couples in their home environments, and he also brought them into his lab and asked them to talk to each other about conflicts they were having as well as positive memories they shared. While doing so, he used electrodes to measure their blood flow, heart rate, and even the amount of sweat they produced. And he was able to predict with 94 percent accuracy whether a couple he studied would last or call it quits.[10]

With the data he collected, Dr. Gottman was able to separate the couples into two groups: the Masters and the Disasters. The Masters continued to be happily married years later, while the Disasters were divorced or miserable in their relationship.

So what was the difference between the Masters and the Disasters? As Dr. Gottman evaluated couples in his office and observed them in their home environments, he found that the Disasters projected a calm, relaxed facade during their arguments with their spouses, but underneath, their blood pressure and heart rate told a different story. Their pulses were racing and they were sweating. Even during seemingly easygoing conversations with their mates, the Disasters' bodies were responding as if they were facing off with a saber-toothed tiger.

Why is this? As we will learn in greater depth in Chapter 7 ("Your Body Is an Energy Powerhouse"), arguments (especially heated ones) can initiate your body's stress response, putting you into fight-or-flight mode, squarely in ego frequency. Your brain will often exacerbate your stressed-out state by reverting back to negative beliefs and well-worn emotional patterns, which in turn creates an even worse physical state. Compounding matters even further, your body has only *one* stress response. So whether you're in a conflict with your partner or staring down a hungry bear, your body's reaction is the same.

This stressful, low-frequency state can steer you away from productive communication and toward escalation, withdrawal, negative interpretations, or put-downs.[11] You don't have to be a relationship expert or a quantum physicist to know that behaviors like stonewalling or flinging insults out of your own hurt feelings are neither good for resolving conflict nor good for the relationship at large. Nor are they good for your energy state.

So were the Disasters simply doomed because they had a more sensitive fight-or-flight response? Why are some couples and not others able to have conflict without feeling defensive and enraged? I believe that the Disasters had accidentally "taught" their minds and bodies to energetically respond to conflict in that manner. They had no idea how to unlearn this lesson, or even that unlearning it was an option. They might have learned their behavior around conflict as young children watching their parents interact. They also might have developed particular behaviors as coping mechanisms to manage the scary and even dangerous situations in their own home. Perhaps later in life their hearts were broken and they've been in fear and reactivity ever since.

That's why the Disaster couples immediately switched into fight-or-flight mode and why they were unable to move out of ego frequency, staying in that fight-flight zone even when later discussing a pleasant event. It was almost as though their brains were clinging to the feeling of being threatened, thinking, unconsciously, "I might still need this adrenaline," "I might still be attacked," or "I'd better stay on guard." Essentially, what separated the Disasters from the Masters was that the Disasters never felt safe.

It is impossible to open your heart and move into home frequency if you are on high alert and don't feel safe, literally or emotionally. In this state you can't experience a partner's love and forgiveness, nor offer love and forgiveness in return. Pat Benatar told us in her hit song that "Love Is a Battlefield," and for these Disaster couples, that was true on many levels. They were never willing to lay their weapons down, and so they never were able to create a relationship of trust, safety, surrender, and unconditional love.

In Quantum Love, You Speak Your Partner's Language of Love

Gary Chapman popularized the concept of love languages in his mega-selling book *The 5 Love Languages*. In the book, he defined our five love languages as gifts, quality time, words of affirmation, acts of service, and physical touch. These are the ways in which we communicate or demonstrate our love for our partner and the ways in which we best understand or receive love—how we love and how we want to be loved. When partners don't speak the same love languages, signals can get crossed and messages can get lost.

Let's consider my friends Adam and Ronnie. Adam had been putting in a lot of time at the office lately to wrap up a big presentation, leaving his husband on his own until late evening and then often collapsing right into bed upon getting home. Adam felt bad that he'd been so absent and wanted to do something loving for Ronnie. Though he didn't know it yet, Adam's love language was gifts, so on his way home one evening he dropped by Best Buy and picked up a gadget he knew Ronnie had had his eye on for some time. When Adam delivered the gift, however, Ronnie, whose love language was quality time, was confused more than delighted. *Why did he buy this?* Adam's expression of love and appreciation for his husband didn't fully *resonate* because Ronnie would have been happier if Adam had just taken a long lunch break one day to come see him at his office. If you know your partner's love language, you can make sure that you are loving him or her in a way that lands.

As important as this is, I think our language of love is more than just the five means of expression Chapman introduced. In my mind, learning your partner's love language is also about identifying and understanding your partner's thorns (as well as your own), which is a big part of Quantum Love.

Shira and Andy had been married for three years when they came to see me. They were a loving, successful, and driven couple. Andy owned an IT company and Shira was a talented actress. Although they deeply loved each other, they had been fighting frequently for months. Their sex life was all but nonexistent, and there were resentments brewing just under the surface. I could feel the tension and irritation the second they walked in the room.

Andy fidgeted while Shira smoothed a strand of dark hair over her shoulder. "I just can't take it anymore," she sighed. "All we do is fight. We used to be so happy!"

Andy reddened a little but nodded in agreement.

Shira rolled her eyes. "Of course he says nothing! This is how he always is at home! I'm upset, and he sits there without saying a word. I can't get any reaction out of him."

"You have more than enough reactions for both of us," said Andy. Then, looking at me, he added, "She cries nonstop. She throws things when she's angry. She threatens divorce."

"And the madder she gets, the quieter you get?" I asked.

"Exactly," said Andy.

As I started to see their dynamic fall into place, I asked them about their childhoods. Andy told me he'd been raised by a single mother who had to work two jobs to support him, and Shira revealed that she'd grown up in an abusive home with a violent and unpredictable mother. "One second she was crying, the next she was yelling," said Shira. "The next she was saying how much she loved you."

Andy squirmed in his seat a little.

"What?" Shira asked with annoyance in her voice.

"I was just thinking . . . that sounds a little like you."

Shira's eyes flashed. Andy quickly continued, "Not that you are ever violent! But you threaten divorce even though you know it breaks my heart. Then the next morning you want to hug and kiss me and apologize."

"And you punish me with the silent treatment," accused Shira. Then she turned to me. "He can't take a freaking apology."

"I can't move from zero to sixty like that!" Andy said. "I forgive you, but I am still hurt and confused. And I guess a little scared."

"Scared of what?" I asked.

"Losing you," Andy said to Shira, his voice breaking. "If I lost you, I would never recover from it."

Tears streamed down Andy's face while Shira watched in shock. "He never cries," said Shira, handing Andy a tissue.

"Is that true?" I asked Andy.

"Yeah," he said, taking a shaky, deep breath.

"I cry all the time," laughed Shira. "Everyone in my family cries constantly. You should see us at weddings."

"What about your family, Andy?" I asked.

"We don't cry in my family. No matter what. My mom lost my dad and my sister in a car accident when I was just two years old. But I don't remember ever seeing her cry."

"What about you?"

"What do you mean, what about me?"

"Did you cry?"

Andy seemed confused by the idea. "No. What would be the point?"

I began to clearly see the thorns around Andy's and Shira's hearts, and how deeply rooted and ancient these thorns were. Shira, reeling from a violent home, had no clue how to regulate her emotions or express her needs in a way that wasn't antagonistic. "Acting out" wasn't just a career for her; it was her way of getting attention and love. I explained this to both of them as best I could.

"Andy, when you see Shira starting to get loud or throw her cell phone across the room," I said, "I want you to picture her as a little girl, maybe four or five years old. She wants something: a drink of water before bed, a teddy bear, a hug, or a story. But in her home, love and attention weren't easy to come by. Imagine how scary and lonely that must have felt, and the lessons she learned by watching her mother's anger. She learned that the louder you are, the more powerful you are. So when you see Shira start to get loud, I want you to see where that anger is really coming from: from a deep fear of not being heard and not being protected.

"But, Shira," I said, "that doesn't mean that you're off the hook. Andy can love your thorns and understand them, but you still need to learn how to manage your anger and control your words."

"What about Andy?" Shira asked. "Does he have deep thorns?"

"Him? I think his thorns are very deep indeed." Turning to Andy, I said, "I think you are afraid that if you let yourself cry, you might never stop. That if you give in to the feelings of pain and loss, those feelings could consume you. So instead, when things get hard, you shut down. Which triggers Shira to up the ante and act even bigger and louder for your attention."

"So what should I do instead?" asked Shira.

"Love him *and* his thorns. Understand that he isn't being distant because he is punishing you or holding a grudge. It's because he is scared to talk about things that hurt. Ultimately, both of you are just trying to protect yourselves and keep your tender spots safe. But my recommendation is that you have to bare those tender parts to each other. You have to have a home where it is okay to be angry and it is okay to cry, and it is equally okay to need space and time to process things. Neither one of you is 'right' or 'wrong.' You are both just dealing with your emotions the way you were taught as kids. Now, as grown-ups, you can offer each other grace and understanding for those thorns, and you can make positive steps to remove some of the more prickly and painful ones."

Almost one year later, Shira wrote me a long, effusive e-mail, as was her style. She was happy and had wonderful news to share: They were expecting a baby! She also had other news. She had taken an anger management class and now was taking a Buddhist approach toward dealing with stress. And Andy? That was the biggest surprise of all. Andy took an acting class on a whim with Shira, and something amazing happened. "He's no Robert DeNiro," Shira wrote, "but taking the class taught him how to get in touch with his emotions in a very real way. I am still the crier in the family, but my tears don't make him shut down anymore. It's awesome!"

Quantum Love allows you to show powerful compassion and embrace change in a loving and inspired way. If you can use the spiritual component in conjunction with the powerful physical energy of your body, heart, and mind, you'll experience a deeper, richer, wider, more energized, more inspired and inspiring spiritual kind of love.

Now let's get to some specifics about how you can design and create the kind of Quantum Love relationship you want.

CHAPTER 6

Commitment #2

I Will Get Clear on What I Want out of Love

When we love, we always strive to become better than we are. When we strive to become better than we are, everything around us becomes better too.

Paulo Coelho, *The Alchemist*

Each of us has the power to shape and reshape our life and our relationship into whatever we desire. The principles of quantum physics not only prove this, they also show us how. Remember what quantum physics has taught us: we are all energy; we are all connected; we all create our own reality (meaning anything is possible).

It can be difficult to wrap our heads around the concept that anything is possible—that we live in an entire universe of pure potential—because it contradicts the limiting stories we have been telling ourselves for years, and also because it carries a lot of responsibility. The principles of quantum physics tell us that there is no passing the buck. Our reality, and our relationship, can be whatever we want it to be, provided that we own our responsibility for making it so.

Knowing what you know about the impact your personal energy has on your relationship, you've made the commitment to take responsibility for your energy. Now, understanding the difference between the common conception of love and the vast possibilities of Quantum Love, you're faced with a classic red pill/ blue pill decision: Do you choose to do nothing and keep moving along down the comfortable path you're on? Or do you choose to take conscious action to move into Quantum Love?

You can trust me on this or not, but I can tell you one thing I know for sure: all that is working and not working for you in your love life is 1) being created by you and 2) of the greatest service to you. The good news is that you can create the love you want through the power of your own energy, and you can deliberately shift your energy and your relationship into Quantum Love. To do this, you need to get clear on exactly what you want. In this chapter, I'm going to show you how to determine what you really want to *feel* in your relationship and how to set your Quantum Love Goals.

Then I'm going to lead you through a process of determining how close or far away you are from those goals, help you uncover areas that you might not even have realized were off the mark, and show you how to start closing the gap between what you currently have and what you want in love. You are going to learn how to use the art of manifesting to create a new relationship reality, one that is aligned with your core desired relationship feelings. I will teach you about the powerful role your intention and awareness play in creating what you want, and I will explain why getting clear works.

Finally, I'm going to help you overcome some of the relationship challenges that so often stand in the way on the path to Quantum Love. I will teach you ways to deepen your connection to your partner, break down any barriers that stand between you, and connect in ways that you never have before. Then I'll show you why it is so important to *surrender*—to move out of fix-manage-control mode and scarcity thinking—and I will reveal the gifts that come with living in a state of wholeness and faith.

Getting Clear on What You Want out of Love

The Quantum Love you want starts with determining how you want to *feel* in your relationship and understanding what that means in an emotional sense. Think of this as determining your *core desired feelings*. It's a concept laid out by poet Danielle LaPorte in her book *The Fire Starter Sessions,* a series of sermons written to expand personal consciousness. In her sessions, LaPorte teaches that our goals should be about how we want to *feel,* not what we want to *do.*

She came to this idea in the time leading up to New Year's Eve one year. She was starting to do what so many of us do in preparation for a new year and all the promise it holds: making resolutions. This time was different, however. She wasn't excited about it at all. She was so sick of setting goals she never followed through on that she decided to try something different. Instead of setting resolutions for things she wanted to change or achieve, she set her sights on how she wanted to *feel.* "Does it contribute to or detract from the feeling I want to create in my life?" became the litmus test for all her actions. And everything flowed from there.

The concept of core desired feelings is essential to manifesting what you want through the Law of Attraction. As we have learned in the previous chapters, everything, including our thoughts, beliefs, expectations, and feelings, is pure energy. And, as we know, like attracts like through resonance. So whatever the frequency of your thoughts, feelings, beliefs, and body, your tuning fork will be drawing experiences into your field that will reinforce, perpetuate, or exacerbate that energy state. At a very simplistic level, I view this as the reason why I always seem to stub my toe when I am in a bad mood. At a much more complex and impactful level, it's why I believe Sam walked into my life at a time when I was ready for him.

The sheer power you have to create what you want is the core reason why getting *clear* on what you want out of your relationship is such a crucial step in getting to Quantum Love. After all, how can you manifest Quantum Love if you don't know what you want it to look like?

So with this in mind, I want you to ask yourself: *What are the top five things I want to* ***feel*** *in my relationship?* These are your *core desired relationship feelings,* which will shape and ultimately help you realize your Quantum Love Goals.

What Are Your Quantum Love Goals?

I love the idea of extrapolating the concept of core desired feelings out to our relationships to make them our core desired relationship feelings. How you feel is fundamental to what you create, and your core desired relationship feelings are what you want to manifest. Now, remember, these are the big-ticket-item feelings you want to feel in your relationship. They are not the things you want to do, like your bucket list of travel destinations. Nor are they an "improvements" list the way most sets of New Year's resolutions can be. They are the emotions you want to *feel* in your relationship. These emotions will set the frequency that attracts the reactions and experiences you want to bring into your reality.

So now I'm going to ask you to choose the top five feelings that will make up your Quantum Love Goals. Your goals may change, and that is great, but this is a good place to start. Before beginning this exercise, I recommend taking a few minutes to get yourself into coherence by grounding yourself and opening your heart, using the exercises I outlined in Chapter 3.

As a starting point, take a look at the list of feeling words on the next page. You may find that some of these words stir an emotional or even a physical movement within you. In other words, they resonate with you. Do not ignore them! Remember, resonance comes from vibrational frequency, and words can resonate as much as people can. So if a word resonates with you, it is a good indication that the emotion behind it will be very impactful in your relationship. If any feeling words make you feel a Full-Body YES, then move them to the top of your list.

The list here just gives you some examples of feeling states. (For an expanded list, go to the Appendix.) Feel free to come up with and write down any other feelings that come to mind. You can use your Quantum Love Journal. Anything goes! But notice that core desired relationship feelings are all positive and high frequency. You should focus on how you *want* to feel, not on how you *don't* want to feel: instead of "less anxious," try "calm." Also, if you find it hard to choose only five core desired feelings, don't be afraid to take your time. Set your list down for a little while and then return to it. Or shake up your energy by going for a walk or doing something else that's active. Then come back, ground yourself, open your heart, and see if your essential self has any answers for you.

In my love relationship, I want to feel . . .

Connected	Turned On	In Alignment	Supported
Joyful	Playful	Comforted	Encouraged
Cherished	Appreciated	Free	Calm
Trusted	Delighted	Seen and Heard	Passionate
Accepted	Honest	Excited	Spontaneous

If you take a quick glance at the Quantum Lovemap, you'll see that these are all high-calibrating feelings. This is the good stuff! When you are feeling your core desired relationship feelings, you will likely be in home frequency and moving toward Quantum Love.

So how close are you to meeting your Quantum Love Goals? It's time to hold up the yardstick of your core desired relationship feelings against how you really feel right now.

Your Quantum Love Goals and Your EHFI

Once you get clear on your Quantum Love Goals, I want you to plot your EHFI on the Quantum Lovemap for each of your core desired relationship feelings, even if it's a feeling state you long to hold more regularly. For example, if you selected "Supported" as a Quantum Love Goal, look at the Quantum Lovemap again and choose a feeling state to describe how you *feel* when you think about the level of support you currently experience in your relationship at your most optimistic as well as your most pessimistic. Maybe at best you feel *bliss*-fully supported and at worst you feel *anger* that you're not supported more. Even though the Quantum Lovemap consists of feeling states, you have feelings about your ability to achieve those core desired feelings in your relationship. Not long ago I worked with a woman who wanted to feel more trust in her partner and their connection. When consulting the Quantum Lovemap and thinking about the level of trust between them, she found that at her most optimistic she felt understanding and empathetic and at her most pessimistic she experienced anger and hate. Ironically, *trust* and *surrender* were her point of transition! To plot your Quantum Love Goals, you can use the worksheet provided in the Appendix or go to www.drlauraberman.com/quantumlove for an online version.

1. *At my most positive and optimistic, I feel ___________ about how much [core desired relationship feeling] I feel in my relationship.* Plot this point on the Quantum Lovemap. This will be your high end point.
2. *At my most negative or pessimistic, I feel ___________ about how much [core desired relationship feeling] I feel in my relationship.* Plot this point on the Quantum Lovemap. This will be your low end point.
3. Draw a figure eight connecting the two points. The center of the figure eight is the point where you transition between expansion and contraction, as discussed in Chapter 3, and as such it's a guidepost telling you when you are approaching an energetic shift.

Here is an example:

Mary and Ellen have been together for six years. They have three kids. However, Mary feels resentful that Ellen doesn't support her enough when it comes to the children. "I am always the bad guy," she complains. "No wonder my kids hate me."

When Mary got clear on her Quantum Love Goals, she determined that first and foremost, she really wanted to feel "In Alignment" with her mate. She plotted her high end point at Hopeful/Courageous and her low end point at Disappointment. She could see that she was sitting just at the brink of the By Me state and home frequency. Once she was able to move her energy up using the feeling state techniques I will teach later on in this chapter, she was all set to manifest the relationship experience she wanted.

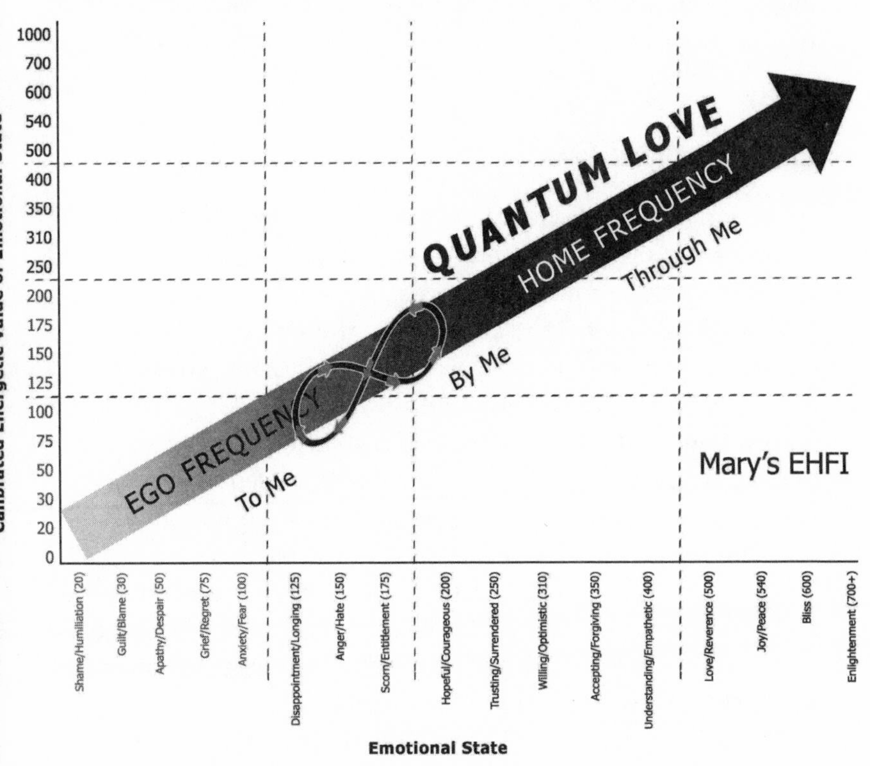

Figure 5: Mary's EHFI

By plotting your points on the graph, you will be able to notice any areas where, like Mary, you might be falling short of your Quantum Love Goals and are more in the To Me state than you would prefer. That's okay! This is just your starting point.

If you want to—though you certainly don't have to—you can engage your partner in this process and do this exercise together. Take one of the goals you've set, plot out your own graph, and ask your partner to do the same. You and your partner may have different goals, but there is likely some overlap as well, and it's illuminating to see how you each feel about a range of qualities in your relationship. You can also invite your partner to set his or her own Quantum Love Goals and then do the exercise using those. Discussing the results, especially if you keep it positive, will help you get on the same page about how you want to build better love together and more successfully meet each other's needs.

Closing the Gap

Having set your Quantum Love Goals and looked at how your current feelings in your relationship measure up, how do you start working toward those goals? There are a couple of ways you can go about it. You can focus on the area where there's the biggest gap between how you want to feel and how you currently feel, or you can charge ahead with the feeling that gave you the biggest Full-Body YES. Choose to put your focus on one per day, one per week, whatever feels natural to you. Keep all your Quantum Love Goals in your mind and put your attention on working on them in the ways I will show you in the pages to come.

First, ask yourself this question: what can *you* take responsibility for in your Quantum Love Goals? Look at each of your goals. Are you creating that feeling in yourself, in your life? Chances are the answer is no. Are you instead looking to your partner to create those feelings for you? If you're totally honest, my guess is the answer is yes. Remember, though, that as we learned in Chapter 4, your relationship with your partner is really just a relationship with yourself. Your own feelings, beliefs, and stories color the lens through which you view your partner, and your own actions and behavior determine the experience you're having in your relationship right now. In Mary's case, if she is not feeling in full alignment with Ellen because she thinks Ellen is contentious and stubborn, it is probably because *Mary* has (also) been contentious, stubborn, and stuck in ego frequency. Start by owning up to your 100 percent responsibility (a concept I will be teaching you more about in Chapter 10) for how you are feeling in your relationship. Then turn your focus toward what you can do to create your core desired relationship feelings for yourself.

You may not know right away how to close the gap between what you currently feel and how you want to feel. That's okay. Right now, I just want you to commit to seeing your partner and your relationship through a new and more generous lens. Generosity is one of the cornerstones of Quantum Love. Choose to be generous in how you see your mate, and you will start to notice that this generosity comes back to you. Now, through your generous lens, get ready to start looking for the evidence that the new reality you want to create is already in your life and building to your new Quantum Love reality.

Change the Lens and Change Your Reality

The fastest way to increase your frequency toward your Quantum Love Goals is to look for pleasing attributes your partner has—even if they don't match any particular one of your goals. Maybe your partner doesn't show passion but does demonstrate attraction. Or consideration. Or anything you can see through your new, more generous lens. Put your awareness on those things. Appreciate them. Feel gratitude for them. And don't keep your appreciation to yourself.

Look for pleasing examples of your partner's care, consideration, focus, attention, romance, sexual function, sexual energy, and so on. And give him the feedback of appreciation. Let him know that you've noticed what he is doing, that he is making you feel cared for or understood or desirable, and that you appreciate it and him. Then stay with that feeling, and with your appreciation of it, for as long as you can.

Look for evidence that you are moving closer and closer to your Quantum Love Goals everywhere. You can even keep a collection of these moments. If you are the journaling type, you can write them down in your Quantum Love Journal, or go to www.drlauraberman.com/quantumlove to download an electronic version.

The most important part of this exercise is to keep your lens open wide to Quantum Love. Maybe you don't trust your partner much when it comes to the discipline side of co-parenting, but you can appreciate how willing he is to play with the kids and give them his time and attention. Tell him how much it means to you that he is such an active presence in their lives. Or maybe your partner has an "alpha woman" persona (as I call it, being a recovering alpha woman myself) that just really irks you. Take a generous perspective on her behavior and express out loud your appreciation for the way you can trust her to attend to all the details as she manages everything in your lives. Whatever reality you want, notice evidence of it wherever you can and turn away from other, less generous realities on which you've been putting attention.

It is important to note that resisting the instinct to focus on what is *not* working will *not* come naturally. If there has been ongoing disconnection or conflict in your relationship, you might worry that you are somehow putting your head in the sand, or that if you don't focus on what's wrong and work on it, things won't get better. That is FMC thinking, not Quantum Love thinking. So maybe you start by using a more generous lens and focusing on the positive in your partner for just an hour, or just a day, or just a week. I promise that once you do, you will be amazed at the positive changes in your relationship. When you turn your attention to finding evidence of what *does* feel good, you get more of it, and the positive energy between you and your partner grows. And as you remain for longer periods of time in home frequency, you are in the perfect position to fully manifest your Quantum Love Goals and the relationship reality you desire.

Remember, the three important steps here are:

1. Notice a quality to appreciate in your partner.
2. Express your appreciation of what you are noticing in your partner's words and actions in the moment.
3. Feel the appreciation for as long as you can.

When you express appreciation, it not only impacts the quantum field, it also energetically changes the reality you are creating. There are tangible effects as well in what I refer to as the *logistical field*. If the quantum field is the field of energy that you and your partner are made of and that interconnects the two of you, the logistical field is the concrete and tangible impact of your words, deeds, and actions, the field of cause and effect. Imagine how your partner, who is likely already very aware of his or her shortcomings in your eyes, experiences your appreciation. Not only do we, like all other animals, respond to positive reinforcement, you are also modeling a different way of treating and being treated. Chances are that more and more of what you are appreciating will show up, and very likely you will get appreciation back from your partner as well.

I saw this unfold firsthand with a woman named Geri who came to me about a problem with her stepson. "My marriage is wonderful," she said. "I met the man of my dreams and I feel unconditional love for the first time in my life. There is just one problem: I can't stand his son." She put her hand up before I could speak. "I know that sounds terrible! Who hates a child? But I am telling you, this kid is a menace! He is sixteen years old and he thinks he knows everything. He never listens to a thing I say. I feel like he wishes I would disappear. It's horrible."

I sat there for an hour, barely saying a word, as Geri regaled me with story after story about her stepson. I heard about the time he called her the B-word. I heard about the time he mocked her cooking and the time he didn't get her a Christmas present. I almost felt as though I were a judge listening to a court case. "Be on my side," she seemed to be saying. "Listen to how wrong he is. Listen to how right I am."

"Is there anything you like about your stepson?" I asked when she finally paused for a sip of water.

Geri sighed. "His father is a cool guy," she joked. "That's about it."

"Let me give you a challenge," I said. "I want you to spend the next week appreciating your stepson. I want you to create a notebook where you write down things you like about him every day. When you come back in here, I want to see a few pages filled up."

Her mouth dropped open. "No way," she said. "First of all, I hate homework. I am forty-three years old. I am not doing homework. Second of all, I wouldn't be able to fill a single line, let alone a page."

"What do you have to lose?"

She stared at me.

"What do you have to gain?"

She swallowed. "I'll buy a notebook on the way home."

I sent her on her way with some trepidation. I didn't have high hopes for her assignment. When she came back the next week and sheepishly handed me her notebook, I thought I would find it blank. Instead, in neat, delicate penmanship I saw:

He ate my lasagna without complaint.

He made me laugh with his celebrity impersonation.

He didn't take the last soda.

When he smiles, he looks just like his dad.

He sings (badly) in the shower.

When he fell asleep on the sofa, he looked like a little boy. I covered him with a blanket.

He let me give him a hug.

He asked me to make my lasagna again!

I smiled as I read the list aloud.

"How do you feel about your stepson today?" I asked.

"We still have a lot of work to do," she said, taking back the notebook from me. "But I don't want to think of him as the enemy anymore. I understand why he lashes out sometimes. I can take it. But I am not going to give it back."

"That's wonderful," I said.

"He's being nicer to me too lately," she said. "It's weird. I think maybe an alien invaded his body."

"I think it could be even more miraculous than that," I said.

She looked puzzled for a second, then joked, "Like this is some kind of magic notebook?"

"It felt pretty magical to me," I said.

"Well, I'd better keep writing it in, then," she said. "Besides, I was really starting to have fun!"

I ran into Geri at Whole Foods a few months later. I asked her if she was still keeping her notebook.

"No," she said, shaking her head and depositing tomatoes in a produce bag. But as my face fell, she crowed, "I have a whole binder now." She gave me a triumphant smile. "And guess what? He keeps one for me too!"

"No kidding?"

"Yep. The first two pages are just about my lasagna." She laughed, motioning to her cart. "The secret is in the sauce."

I smiled. "Sounds magical."

The Law of Attraction: Manifesting Your Quantum Love Goals

It's important to remember that, just like everything else in this world, your energy is dynamic and moving, ebbing and flowing, a constant cycle of contraction and expansion. You might have a day in which you notice all kinds of evidence that the relationship experience you want to manifest is becoming part of your reality, followed by a day in which you feel like you've taken ten steps in the wrong direction. That's natural. Later in this chapter I will teach you some techniques to cope with those moments when you feel disconnected from your partner or are finding it difficult to color your perspective with a loving and generous lens. The key with the Law of Attraction is to be patient and to *surrender* your desires to the universe that serves you. (More on that later.) Right now, I'm going to walk you through a simple process for focusing your intention and tapping the power of your essential self to bring your Quantum Love Goals into being.

Step One: Ground Yourself

Time to get the energy of your mind and body ready for a different reality. The key to manifesting is to put your mind and body into a grounded, openhearted space. Do this every time, using the grounding exercise I taught you in Chapter 3.

It is so, so, *so* important to get yourself into a grounded, coherent state. Remember, the fundamental principle of the Law of Attraction is that your energy will resonate with and attract that which is vibrating at a frequency similar to yours. If your energy is down in the To Me ego frequency, you will not be able to manifest the core relationship feeling you want. You certainly won't be able to get into Quantum Love.

Step Two: Enter the Thought State

Choose one core desired relationship feeling to focus on (passion, trust, unconditional acceptance, etc.), then move in your mind to a time when you felt that feeling. Try to remember as many details as you can. "See" the surroundings, the people. Be there, in that moment, in first person, as if it is happening to you *right now.*

If you can think of a time you felt the feeling in relation to your partner, that's wonderful, but it isn't necessary—it can be *any* time you felt it. The delivery system (the specific person) isn't so important here. We are just looking to get you into the thought state of your goal.

Step Three: Get the Imagination Engine Running

Now it's time to really get into your imagination. Go deeper into the thought state of your Quantum Love Goal. What might it actually *look* like if your goal were a reality? Let your imagination run wild. If your relationship goal is more romance, imagine a scene in which your partner is being, saying, or doing exactly what you would dream him or her to be, say, or do in a specific romantic scenario. Once again, be there in first person.

Step Four: Move into the Feeling State

As you play out your fantasy scenario in your mind in first person, as if it's happening right now, *how do you feel?* Allow yourself to imagine that right now there is absolute abundance of the core desired relationship feeling and experience you want. Now you're moving from thought and imagination into the actual *feeling* state of your goal. What are the sensations in your body? How does it feel in your heart to soak up those good, high-frequency vibrations? Breathe into that. Stay there for at least a few moments.

Step Five: Release It

This is the hardest part and the most counterintuitive. This is where the FMC-er in each of us has to let go of our attachment to what we're trying to manifest. The reason is this: When you *need* something, you are aligning your energy with scarcity rather than abundance.

In all things, especially love, when you long for it, miss it, *need* it, feel you're not complete without it, and put your emotional and mental attention on that *need,* you are in ego frequency. The result is going to be the opposite of what you want, because the universe is going to give you exactly what your frequency is attracting: more scarcity.

That all might make sense on a logical plane, but as we have discussed, when it comes time to actually *surrender,* it can be shockingly difficult. Here's what works well for me. When it's time to let go of what I want to manifest, I ask my deepest essential self to help me release it and to remind me that everything I want already exists—it just hasn't come into my field yet. My intention is to place the lens of my core desired relationship feeling over my experience, so that I can see the evidence of this feeling state in my partner's actions and stay openhearted to express the feeling myself, for myself, and toward my partner without expecting anything in return.

I guess this is a kind of prayer, if you want to think of it that way. Some people think of prayer as something you do during desperate times, but I see prayer more as connecting with, communing with, or communicating to a higher power, whatever that higher power is. In my mind, my essential self is part of the infinite energy of a perfect, loving universe, and that's the "higher power" I'm connecting with. If you are someone who prays, then you surely believe in a higher power, and you know (I hope) that whatever is going on in your life is part of a much bigger plan. You understand that you are being held and that ultimately all is well. That understanding makes it much easier to surrender.

Help for Letting Go

Surrender is ultimately about faith: trusting even that which you can't see. It's definitely a hard thing to remember when you're going through an AFGE, or even just hard times in your relationship. If the reality is not yet clear that you already ***have*** what you want, then the key is in recognizing the desire, feeling the reality of ***that*** as if it has already happened, and then letting it go. In Chapter 10, we will be discussing some specific shift moves that will help you do this. Here are some ideas to get you started:

1. Commit to just stop thinking about what you desire for one night, and pretend that what you want is already there. If you can't do a whole night, then try just one hour. Think, "For one hour, I am going to pretend to be a person who doesn't have this problem. If I think about it, that's okay. But for this hour, I am not going to obsess about it." Build your way up slowly until you can do two or three hours, and finally a whole night.

2. Find a way to shift your mind in a new direction. Sitting and stewing isn't going to do it. Go for a run. Take a walk in a nearby park. Volunteer at an animal shelter. Offer to babysit your younger sister's three kids. Take a yoga class. Cook an elaborate dinner. Have sex!

3. Distract yourself with other thoughts about things you *can* appreciate. For every negative, stressed-out thought you have, try to follow it with a positive thought. Think of it like breathing. In with the good, out with the bad. It's okay to have stressed, anxious thoughts. It's part of being human. But it is just *part* of it. Don't make the anxiety the whole story. You have a lot of other things to celebrate and appreciate.

The Importance of the Feeling State

The feeling state is an essential component of the art of manifesting, so it's worth spending a little more time talking about it. When it comes to *why* getting into the feeling state of what you want is so key to bringing it into your reality, there are a couple things at play.

First, as we've seen, in order to have the relationship you desire, you must become a vibrational match for the qualities you seek. This is because what comes to you always matches you. It starts with you! The really crazy thing is that the frequency of the reality you want to manifest is already there in you. Yes, that's right. The exact relationship you want, the person you want to be with, the person *you* want to be in the relationship, the way you want to feel, is all there, vibrating, waiting for your tuning fork to align with it.

Second, if you insist on looking for the positive in others, in time only (or mostly) the positive will be shown to you. You will have incrementally adjusted your vibrational point of attraction to align with your Quantum Love Goals. When you practice the thoughts of the things you desire, they must show up in your experience. That, ultimately, is the Law of Attraction.

Keep going, and be patient. Your vibrational point of attraction will change until there is an obvious tipping point. For a while, the only evidence of progress will be your improved emotional state as you choose to view your partner through a more generous lens. And that will feel great. Then the change at the logistical field level will kick in as you notice more and more evidence that your desired relationship experience already exists in your reality. And then things will really start clicking and humming at the quantum field level as the Law of Attraction does its work.

My friend Patty had what I consider a very quantum experience just recently. Let me start off by saying Patty is a bit of a skeptic. The first time I told her about my research for this book, she made a horrified face and said, "Oh, God, you're not going to turn into one of those people who speak to the spirits of dead dogs or something, are you?" I had to laugh. She's never afraid to speak her opinion. However, after I gave her some of what I had been writing and lent her a few of my favorite books (check the Quantum Love Resources section for a similar reading list), she started to open up. Last January she sent me a very powerful e-mail. She has given me permission to share it here with you.

> *Hi Laura,*
>
> *Had to share something very cool that happened to me on New Year's Eve. Really was amazing. Here goes:*
>
> *It was New Year's Eve afternoon. I was happy to be home with my fiancé and our two daughters, but I was feeling a little less than loved. In fact, I was feeling really stressed. I didn't want to deal with cooking a big special feast for all of us—a feast that would take hours to prepare yet just minutes to gobble. I didn't want to be the one who had to lead all the games and pop the sparkling grape juice and keep the girls from fighting over the Wii. I felt pretty resentful.*
>
> *But then I thought, wait a second. Is this how I want to start the New Year? Pouting because I don't want to make scallops for my kids? I took a few breaths and I got deep inside myself. Okay, Patty, I thought: What do I really want here?*
>
> *As you know, one of my New Year's resolutions is to be 100 percent responsible for creating what I want. I then realized I was being*

called on to work on one of my core desired relationship feelings: playful romance. That's what I wanted: A playful New Year's Eve that was fun, cohesive, easy, connected, not just with my kids but my fiancé too. Time to get manifesting. Okay, Patty, you can do this, I thought. Step 1, ground and open my heart. Check. Step 2, get into the thought state of a time in the past where my core desired relationship feeling of playful romantic time was experienced.

I started thinking about a time we were all playful together and when I felt deeply connected to John at the same time. I remembered a recent ski vacation where we were all riding up the lift together, spread out over a couple of lift chairs, catcalling each other up the mountain and racing each other down. I could imagine looking down and seeing the huge grin on the face of my littlest one and looking up and seeing the similar grin on my fiancé's face as our eyes met and we had a warm kiss on a cold night. I let myself be there in first person as if it were happening now. I felt the bubbling in my chest, the lightness in my shoulders, and the smile on my face. Step 2, in the playful zone, now it's time to let the imagination engine start running.

What might a playful romantic New Year's Eve look like with my family at home? One where I wasn't the only one in charge of making the fun happen, where my fiancé was engaged and attentive to me and the kids were having fun and getting along—just enjoying. I imagined myself giggling and cuddling with John and the kids, eating a great meal, and having a Silly String fight. I was there in my mind, in first person. Step 3, get into the feeling state as if that were happening right now. That was easy because as I was already there in my imagination, I just had to tune in to my five senses and notice a similar lightness and bubbling joy in my body.

Now it was time for step 4, letting go. I knew that no matter what happened, the kind of New Year's Eve I was going to have was completely up to me. So I decided that no matter what happened and who was awake to share it with me, my intention was to have fun; to be playful and to see in John the romance I wanted to see that night. I could do that no matter what happened or who did or didn't step up to participate with me.

Not long after, I was standing by the window watching the snow falling and John came up behind me and put his arm around me. Had I still been in my ego frequency and snarky mode, I would have stood there quietly, likely hoping he noticed my wistfulness and asked me about it so I could complain to him. He would likely then get defensive, feeling like I was setting us up for a lame night, and be insulted that I expected the worst of him. Instead, I decided from my home frequency state to look for evidence of what I wanted to see. When he came up to me, I leaned my head on his shoulder and complimented him: "Thank you for being such a sweet partner. I love the way you are always so warm and romantic with me; the way you cuddle on me." I went into full-blown appreciation mode for the little gesture he had just made. I did it a few times. I was determined to find every piece of evidence I could—no matter how small—and to then show him how much I appreciated it. No surprise, he just kept going.

The next thing I knew, he'd piled the kids in the car. When he came back, they had food from my favorite takeout place and they'd also stopped over at the convenience store. They came back armed with Silly String and noisemakers . . . the very Silly String I had just been thinking about, without me having said anything! We ended up having this crazy night where we dressed up in costumes and went out and Silly Stringed in the alley . . . I will never forget it.

I truly believe I created that within myself. And to think, I could have missed out on it all and pouted instead!

P.S. But no contact from any dead dogs yet. ☺

Xo Xo Patty

The key to moving into Quantum Love is to move *yourself* there before anything else. Your partner will entrain to your powerful high-frequency energy and shift along with you. You have the power to create or reshape your relationship reality in any way you want, and it starts by following the advice famously attributed to Gandhi: "Be the change you want to see in the world."

We are the ones leading the way to Quantum Love; therefore, we must be the change we want to see in the relationship. I encourage you to move into home frequency and then tap into the wisdom and clarity of your essential self, asking: *What is my core desired relationship feeling here? What would the experience of that feeling look like? How does my partner already demonstrate it, and how can I let him/her know how much I like it?* And finally: *Have I been (your core desired feeling)? Why can't I create the experience?*

By creating Quantum Love in yourself first and then being the change you want to see, you will quickly find that your partner moves right along with you in both energy and action. Together you will move in Quantum Love.

Overcoming Challenges

While you have the power to create any reality you want, that doesn't mean your partner is an empty energetic vessel. Your partner has his or her own frequencies, moods, wants, core desired relationship feelings, and thorns. So what can you do when your relationship is being challenged? How do you move into Quantum Love if one of you can't break out of ego frequency? And how do you form a deeper, lasting connection if there are barriers (intellectual, energetic, or otherwise) between you?

You and your partner are multifaceted human beings with very different histories, perspectives, lenses, and beliefs. For that reason, I could never recommend a one-size-fits-all approach. When you face a relationship challenge, the key things to focus on all lie within you. Do what you can to keep your tuning fork attuning to the Quantum Love you desire, in spite of what your partner is doing—and even because of it.

See Truth in Reflection: The Seven Mirrors

Remember that your partner is your greatest gift and one of your greatest teachers. If you are feeling stymied, take this opportunity to ask your essential self, "What does this have to teach me?" After all, if something your partner is doing or saying is resonating with you enough to stir up negative feelings in you, it means you've got a thorn that is being touched.

In his book *Walking Between the Worlds: The Science of Compassion,* Gregg Braden describes the "Seven Mirrors of Relationship," a concept he gleaned from the ancient texts of the Essenes, an ascetic sect that lived between the 2nd century B.C.E. and the 1st century C.E. along the shores of the Dead Sea. While there has been much debate about how (or even if) the Essenes lived, their teachings are an enlightening and inspiring way to consider the relationships that come into our lives.

All of our relationships are integral steps in our spiritual evolution and an opportunity to know ourselves better if we can determine what truths are being mirrored back to us by the people in our lives. "Our world is a mirror of processes within," Braden says, as we draw into our external world the things that are going on in our internal workings. He is essentially describing the Law of Attraction and our energy frequency at work in creating our external world to reflect our place in the To Me, By Me, or Through Me state. His focus, however, is not on the experiences that come into our lives; it is on the *relationships* that do. He believes the people who come into our lives, especially our partners, are our mirrors in seven distinct ways.

The first mirror reflects who we are in the moment. This is the energy that we are vibrating right now.

The second mirror reflects what we judge. This reflection is of an emotional pattern, usually rooted in anger or fear. This mirror can illuminate for us beliefs or feelings we might not otherwise see. Remember, if something triggers a strong feeling in you, it is *about you.*

The third mirror reflects what has been lost or taken from us, or what we have given away. If we feel a magnetic connection to someone, it is possible that we are recognizing in him or her something that our essential self loves and misses.

The fourth mirror reflects our forgotten love. It often highlights an addictive or compulsive behavior that we have rearranged our life to accommodate. The stark light of this reflection may show you areas of scarcity that you are trying to fill with something else.

The fifth mirror reflects our mother and father. This reflection can hold feelings of love and security as well as old thorns and worthiness-killing beliefs. It is the reflection of our relationship with our parents and the spectrum of truths that contains.

The sixth mirror reflects our own quest for darkness, our soul's desire to confront and work through our greatest challenges, biggest fears, and deepest thorns. As we will discuss more in Commitment #4, asking, "What does this have to teach me?" can help you make great strides toward healing.

The seventh mirror reflects the way in which we see ourselves. The big question that comes with this reflection is "Does what I see make me happy or unhappy?" If you feel unhappy, then it is time to figure out 1) why that is, and 2) who you are measuring yourself against that makes you feel as though you are coming up short.

The people in your life don't represent just one mirror each. The mirroring is constantly shifting according to what is going on inside you. At any given moment, a person in your life can be any one of the seven mirrors. And the more time you spend with someone, the more likely it is that you will see all seven reflections of yourself in him or her.

This, I believe, is part of what makes your partner your greatest teacher. Your interactions with your mate, especially the ones that give you a strong positive or negative feeling, are reflecting a truth of your deepest self back to you if you are willing to see it. If your partner is driving you crazy leaving the kitchen cabinets half open and you're ready to launch into full-blown nagging mode, take a moment and ask why this has come into your field. What is your partner reflecting back to you with this small, albeit annoying, habit? It is probably not something your partner is intentionally doing to annoy you; it is simple inattentiveness. So try to determine in what ways inattentiveness has been showing up in *your* thoughts, beliefs, or actions. Have you been inattentive toward your partner lately, distracted by the goings-on in your busy life? Or are you judging the behavior because it connects to other, more painful instances in which you felt neglected? Maybe you have been feeling down on yourself lately for not being on top of your game in the organization department. Whatever the reason might be, this little annoyance that is pulling your attention has a message for you—about you.

The constant external mirroring of our internal energies (and it is *constant*) gives us an opportunity to learn and address whatever is going on inside us to create a more positive reality. This is the foundation of Quantum Love. We have to be the change we want to see in our reality and our relationship and shift our frequency to manifest something better.

Are You in an Emotionally Abusive Relationship?

When you look at the fear you feel in your life, especially when you drop into your essential self by grounding and opening your heart, you might get the message, perhaps (but not likely) for the first time, that your partner is actually abusive. While physical abuse and domestic violence are much easier to recognize and harder to ignore, emotional abuse is very insidious. It's possible to be in an emotionally abusive relationship without understanding it for what it is.

You may be in an emotionally abusive relationship if your partner engages in these behaviors:

- Constantly putting you down or being hypercritical
- Humiliating or meanly making fun of you
- Asserting control or dominion over you
- Ignoring, excluding, or refusing to communicate with you
- Making everything your fault or guilt-tripping you
- Acting provocatively toward others or cheating
- Withdrawing affection
- Being unreasonably jealous or constantly calling to check up on you
- Isolating you from your friends and family

If you feel you may be in an emotionally (or physically) abusive relationship, please refer to the Quantum Love Resources section at the back of the book for resources and information on how to get help.

Break Down Barriers

Sometimes it may feel like there is a wall between you and your partner that you just can't get past. Maybe you are worried that something is wrong or that your partner is mad at you. Or maybe you just feel disconnected, as life and all its crazy logistics have been in the way for too long. Among the things you can do to break down barriers between you, one of my favorites is the Energy Read, in which you try to get close to your partner and see if you can get a sense of how he or she is feeling through the powerful energetic connection you share.

This exercise is very simple. First, ground yourself and open your heart. If you relax into your home frequency and imagine the barrier disintegrating between you and your mate, you will actually be able to feel his feelings. I now do this much more effectively at work and at home. I can tell what someone needs in order to be in flow with me, often without his needing to say a word.

Then, from that place of home frequency, just put your awareness on your partner and let your mind go soft and receptive to him and his energy. If thoughts occur, you can identify with them or let them go, or you can add energy to them and shape them before letting them go. There's no "right" thing to do or "right" thought to have; this is just fun creativity. It is your soul expressing itself. So be in the moment and be soft. Let realities come and go. Your energy and awareness radiate through and beyond your skin to the quantum field in which we all exist. As you play with this process, you will experience yourself in new ways.

When you let go of preconceived ideas and focus your attention and sensitivity on something, really feel into it, especially with a true desire to know and appreciate it, amazing knowledge can be revealed. You can feel into your mate and know if she needs something. Maybe you'll know she needs to get something off her chest so her heart can reopen, because *your* heart feels tight and *you* want to talk.

You can use these energy reads to let go of fear that is in the way of intimacy. I think one of the biggest blocks in our relationships are the negative beliefs and fears, stories we have that take us out of home frequency and into ego frequency. In my own life, I know these beliefs are a part of my own thorns, so when I notice myself attaching to these stories and moving into ego frequency, I try to drop into home frequency and feel into myself and into Sam. Invariably, I don't feel control or stoicism or manipulation when I feel into his energy. I usually feel fear and sadness, and I recognize that whatever he is doing or saying that feels limiting or critical to me is coming from his own fears and sadness, which in turn come from his own beliefs and thorns. When I can stay in my home frequency, I feel deep love and compassion for him at those moments, and it is easy to find a win-win where I feel powerful and he feels cared for in the way he needs.

The Power of Focused Connection

The following two exercises, sitting in silence and the 30-second hug, are wonderful ways for you and your partner to become allies in your relationship and overcome the challenges you face. They focus attention in the same way that you would focus in a meditation. It's sharing an openhearted, high-frequency state that will elevate both of you toward Quantum Love.

Sitting in Silence with Your Partner

How often do you sit there and *listen* to your partner talk for 20 minutes? This is a great exercise for couples who don't really talk to each other much, and it's great for couples in which one partner is a little more of a talker than the other. I tend to be someone who likes to talk . . . constantly. To me talking is bonding, sharing, connecting, but for my husband it's not. For him, the opportunity to be listened to without interruption is a really meaningful thing. Sam *loves* this exercise because I can't say a word.

This exercise allows a release of energy that you may have been carrying inside you, and it's also extremely bonding because you're giving your partner your full attention. You can take turns doing this, or just do it as a gift to your mate. The talker's job is to talk about something specific or just to free-associate and see what comes up in the one-sided conversation.

You don't have to be staring into each other's eyes during this exercise, but don't multitask or do anything else that is going to pull your attention away from your partner. Be really attentive and really curious about what he or she is saying. If your mind wanders to the laundry you wanted to do, that's fine. Just quietly notice, and bring your attention back to your partner. Twenty minutes can feel like a long time if you're not used to it, but it is well worth it. Your partner will feel the energy of your attention and feel seen and heard. Also, there's no pressure to respond in a certain way or say the right thing. In fact, you don't have to respond at all. This exercise is all about listening, focusing, and connecting.

30-Second Hug

This quick exercise is a powerful way to start or end your day (or both). Face each other, then give each other a 30-second heart-to-heart hug. Use this as a time to consciously *choose* to love your partner today and to be in the relationship. Breathe into the embrace and imagine a cord of energy connecting your hearts. Send your love and trust and comfort and optimism, any positive feelings you are having, into your partner's heart, and imagine yourself receiving his or hers in return. It's a long hug, to be sure, but it's a great way to reboot and reconnect with your partner in the midst of all the craziness life throws at you every day.

Nothing Risked, Nothing Gained: Sometimes Love Means a Heart Smashing

I can't tell you how many times I've had patients in my office or callers on my radio show who describe the ways in which fear of getting hurt is holding them back from the love they want to feel: "I was cheated on in the past." "I had my heart broken." "My parents got divorced." "I'm scared to love again."

We spend so much of our energy guarding our hearts. It's as if each of us is walking around subconsciously thinking *Please don't hurt me, please don't hurt me* as we interact with every person in our lives. I've found that this is a reason why so many of us stay stuck in low-frequency emotions. If you've built huge walls around your heart because you want to protect it, then your heart isn't open and you're not in home frequency. You're vigilant, looking for signs that your partner is cheating or that he or she will let you down. When you get into an argument, you get really controlling because you're not going to let anyone control you. Or you threaten to leave so you won't be the one left. You're the energetic equivalent of a closed fist.

The only way to have a healthy, loving, mutual Quantum Love relationship is with the openhearted willingness to have your heart smashed. Often with callers like this on my radio show I say, "Okay, let's say you totally open your heart to this person. You tell them you love them, jump into the relationship with both feet, and decide to let your guard down and trust them. And then let's say they break your heart. What is the worst thing that could happen?"

"Ugh, I wouldn't be able to deal," is all too often the response. "It would be horrible and painful."

"Yes, it would be painful," I reply. "Absolutely. You'd probably curl up in a ball for a while. You'd need to lick your wounds and maybe even hate life for a little while. Then what would happen?"

"Well, I guess I'd be okay."

"Right! You'd pick yourself up, brush yourself off, and get on with your life. And you would have been through an AFGE that would make you not only stronger, but so much clearer about what you want and need out of love. You'd be fine. No matter what."

But if you don't open your heart to the possibility of being smashed, then you can never fully love because you're always holding yourself back. It's impossible to move into Quantum Love from this place. Quantum Love comes from a place of fullness in you, not a place of scarcity. It's great if you and your partner have a wonderful, long-term, committed relationship and walk off into the sunset together, but if you don't, you're going to be okay. With or without *any* partner or *any* relationship, you are enough. When you understand that, then you are in a place of Quantum Love.

CHAPTER 7

Your Body Is an Energy Powerhouse

The body never lies.

— Martha Graham

By now you have discovered the basic principles of harnessing your personal energy and the power you have to change or re-create your reality, shifting everything in your relationship up the scale so you can begin to experience Quantum Love. You know all about your energetic profile, your EHFI, and where you are on the Quantum Lovemap. It's time to start talking specifics, and there's no better place to begin than the body: the vehicle of your soul and the source of the energy you are putting out into the world. In this chapter, you'll discover how you can use your body's energy to create the reality you most want to experience in life and in your relationship. You'll learn to prime your body to be a channel for the high-calibrating frequency of Quantum Love.

You'll also discover how to tap into your body's wisdom, to listen and understand the powerful truths it wants to tell you. Trust me when I tell you that it's better to tune in and take action sooner rather than later, because the body wants to deliver its message, and it isn't afraid to use an AFGE to get your attention.

What Cancer Taught Me

The first thing almost anyone who knew me well said when I told them about by cancer diagnosis was "How could that be?" I prided myself on taking good care of my body. I wasn't a smoker, I ate healthy and drank green juice daily, I exercised regularly, I did yoga, and I rarely drank. And I agreed with them. When I got my cancer diagnosis, I felt like my body had betrayed me. However, in the end, my body turned out to be not my betrayer but one of my biggest teachers. It was my body that called upon me to stop, to shift, to be silent. Had it not been for my cancer diagnosis—my AFGE—I would still be living my life as I had in the past: always on the go, always trying to be perfect, pleasing everyone, and making sure that my husband and my kids acted the way I wanted them to act and felt the way I wanted them to feel.

It was my body that grabbed me and shook me to get my attention. And this is no wonder. It is often our physical selves that ultimately cry out for a change. This is because our bodies are more than just vessels. Our mental, spiritual, and emotional processes impact them in the same way our diet and our exercise habits do. Think of your mind as the wind and your body as the ocean. Just as the wind causes waves of varying speeds and sizes on the water, so too does your mind have a tangible, physical effect on your body. So, as my body was being buffeted by cancer treatments, I had to look inward and ask myself, what does this cancer have to teach me?

The Power of the Mind-Body Connection

Louise Hay's book *Heal Your Body* is an amazing compilation of symptoms and conditions, their probable causes, and most interestingly, I think, the thoughts behind them. Louise explains the thought pattern that underlies each condition, then offers a new pattern to replace your old one. The book had sat on my shelf for years, serving as a trusty reference in my work with clients and even with my family. When my own body was fighting cancer, I was drawn to the book yet again.

I thumbed through the C chapter until I found my C: Cancer. There I read: "With cancer, the cause is almost always deep hurt, long-standing resentments, and deep grief that is eating away at the self." *Deep grief.* The words almost seemed to jump off the page at me. *Could my grief over the loss of my mother have caused my illness?*

The new thought pattern Louise suggested was this: "I lovingly forgive and release the past and choose to fill my world with joy. I love and approve of myself." She wrote about how she believes (as so many others do) that everything that happens in your body is the result of the thoughts you repeat in your mind. Coming from a medical family and being trained in the hard sciences, I had always found this difficult to accept. But now, in the midst of my AFGE, it made a lot of sense. I personally believe that illness stems from a combination of internal *and* environmental factors. But from a quantum perspective, we are creating everything in our world, including illness. Our body is a messenger of what's going on in our deeper selves.

I've become really curious about this connection. As a result of my scientific curiosity and the openness with which I have shared my personal cancer journey, I've had the opportunity to speak with hundreds of women about their experience with cancer. I have found there is one common denominator, particularly with women who have had breast cancer. We haven't been nurturing ourselves enough, and/or we have been overnurturing others, often at our own expense. More often than not, the women I've met with a breast cancer diagnosis are such pleasers and so disconnected from the desires of their essential selves that they've lost themselves somewhere along the way. Their cancer, more often than not, turns out to be a journey back to themselves.

Their stories remind me all too well of when I first received my own diagnosis. One of the first people I called was life coach Diana Chapman, whom I've introduced you to already. She's very direct; it's one of the things I love about her. This call was no exception.

"I have breast cancer," I told her.

To which Diana almost immediately replied, "Well, no wonder. You let the whole world suck off your breasts!"

I had to laugh because in a way she was right. For so many years I had been nurturing, treating, healing, and applying my focus and intention to everyone but myself. None of those things were bad, of course; the problem was that I was doing *nothing* to tune in to what I wanted or what was important to *me*. I wasn't aware of that larger issue at the time because, like most people, I was caught up in the day-to-day. I did know that I was overworked, overstressed, and overtaxed, yet I didn't feel like I could stop doing what I was doing.

Just before my fateful mammogram, I was at a women's retreat where my friend Robert Ohotto, the intuitive life strategist whom I introduced earlier, listened to me as I laid out my laundry list of struggles and stressors. He shook his head. "Honey, you really have to land your plane," he told me. "You've been flying your plane in the air nonstop, and you *have to land it* or you're going to crash." I didn't really understand what he meant by that. I thought, *Okay, I'll do a little more meditation and yoga.* I had been flying for so long that I didn't even know what it meant to land.

My crash landing into cancer came just a couple weeks later.

BC (before cancer), I knew our emotional state of mind affects our physical health, but I didn't understand the extent to which the energy of our unconscious thoughts impacts our bodies. Being a therapist, I always thought of the brain as the main director of the body. And in some ways it is. But body and brain are deeply intertwined. Knowing what I know now, I see illness, aches, pains, and afflictions as the body's way of knocking on the door of our consciousness. And our wise bodies will keep knocking, louder and louder, until we answer the call of our essential selves.

So can our minds really hurt us in a physical sense? A study at Duke University, directed by James Blumenthal, suggests that they can. He identified long-term experiences of fear, frustration, anxiety, and disappointment as examples of the heightened negative emotions that are destructive to the heart and put us at risk.

Fortunately, our emotions can also help us.[1] When we create a positive energetic state in our minds, we also create one in our bodies.

I was able to help my client Debbie use some of this research to address her ulcerative colitis. Like me, Debbie was someone who always lived a healthy lifestyle. She went for daily two-mile walks around her neighborhood, and she always ate nutritious and whole foods. She eschewed harmful chemicals and opted for natural health and beauty products. A self-described "earth mama," she prided herself on her informed choices about what went into her body. However, when she turned 68 years old, she began experiencing debilitating stomachaches and diarrhea. She couldn't leave the house to make her social engagements, and her stomach pain kept her up all night. Not only was she exhausted and grouchy, but she was rapidly losing weight. Soon she was 15 pounds below her normal healthy weight.

The physical problems were leading to problems in her relationship as well. She began to struggle with depression and anger. It was this anger that led her to visit me, as her husband, Tom, had finally become fed up with her constant yelling and criticism. "I feel like I am living on top of a volcano," Tom confessed. "I never know what's going to set her off."

Debbie confessed that she had been angry lately, but she claimed it was just because of the lack of sleep. As for her diagnosed condition, she was full of ideas and plans for how she was going to "fix" her ulcerative colitis. Preferring not to take medication, she was instead going the natural route and changing her diet dramatically. She gave up wheat, dairy, and food from the nightshade family, such as tomatoes, peppers, eggplant, and potatoes. The stomachaches kept coming, though, and as they did, she kept dropping more and more foods from her diet. Finally one day, with frustration and anger in her voice, she said to me: "I give up, Dr. Berman. I can't beat this thing. It has beaten me."

"No, you're a true fighter. You haven't yet given up, but what would happen if you really did?" I asked her. "What if you surrendered to your colitis?"

"What do you mean? Spend my life in the bathroom?" she asked. "I already do that."

"No, I mean what if you just surrendered to whatever lessons your colitis had to teach you?"

She looked at me as if I were insane. "Dr. Berman," she said, "are you seriously telling me that my diarrhea is trying to teach me something?"

I laughed. "Absolutely. What makes more sense? That your body is trying to tell you something with all of this, or that it is all just happening for no reason? Think about it: Why are you, a healthy, wise, active woman, being sidelined by this health condition? In what way is your ulcerative colitis *for* you?"

She looked irritated. "I have no idea."

"Debbie," I said, "I am no psychic, but I bet you won't experience any relief from your symptoms until you figure out what the heck your body is trying to tell you."

I was starting to get her attention. I knew that, as an "earth mama," she was well aware of the mind-body connection. "Okay," she said, "I have nothing to lose, I suppose. What should I do?"

From what I had learned of Debbie up until that point, she was the queen of FMC. She thought there wasn't a problem she couldn't fix. And with that came a great deal of ego and superiority. "If everyone would just listen to me," she would often say, "the world would be a much better place." In other words, I knew Debbie was almost always operating from a place of ego frequency. Anytime someone believes she is always right, or that she is smarter or more capable than the people around her, she is 100 percent in ego frequency. If you are in home frequency, there is no place for superiority. When you are in home frequency, you accept that you don't have all the answers. Not only do you accept that fact, but you also find a way to love that fact—to love the mystery and to love the imperfections of being human. Something told me that Debbie hadn't loved an imperfection (in herself or in other people) in a very long time.

Hence, my prescription to Debbie was simple: learn how to get into home frequency, and then work to stay in that place as much as possible.

It was an uphill battle. It took weeks for Debbie to even acknowledge that her ego was running (and ruining) her life.

Finally, one day after a particularly brutal fight with Tom, she confessed: "Dr. Berman, you're right. I yelled at Tom until he cried last night, all because he didn't put the car in the garage the 'right' way. I spent all night sitting on my living room couch thinking about it. I realized something: I want to be right all the time because I am so scared. I am so scared because I know I can't really control anything. Bad things happen all the time, and I can't protect my family or myself. That thought terrifies me. I guess I figured if I could be Mrs. Right, then I could keep chaos and tragedy at bay. But instead it brought chaos right into my living room."

This was a true breakthrough moment for Debbie. She had experienced great loss in her childhood (both of her parents had died in a car accident), and I believe that this had a big role in shaping her Mrs. Right persona. Bossing people around and declaring her opinions as fact made her feel secure and safe in an uncertain and sometimes terrifying world. But now that persona no longer served her. And I believe that her ulcerative colitis came along to help her realize that.

Once Debbie had her breakthrough, she became dedicated to living her life in home frequency. She had a fail-safe way of helping herself get there. Whenever she felt her body clenching and her mind starting to go into Mrs. Right mode, she would picture the day her grandson was born. The memory of holding him and the pure joy and unconditional love she felt in that moment would quiet her ego almost immediately. After a month or two of living like this, not only did her relationship vastly improve, so did her stomachaches and her sleep. As she puts it: "I still have ulcerative colitis. But I don't suffer from it anymore. I surrender to it."

Happy Mate, Long Life: Mind-Body Connection and Our Relationship

The truth is that the mind-body connection is much greater than most of us realize. It isn't just about powering through a difficult run or forcing yourself to stay awake during a boring meeting. In fact, when our bodies and minds are connected and in harmony, we can be sure that we are in flow, operating in the world from a place of coherence. This is when your mind and body are humming together in your home frequency.

Plenty of exciting research has helped to demonstrate the power of the mind's impact on the body. When we are in a state of distress, it doesn't just make us feel bad emotionally; it can have real, lasting effects on our physical bodies as well, especially our immune systems. Here's a look at how it works.

Immunoglobulins are proteins secreted by our white blood cells (plasma) to fight antigens, such as bacteria, viruses, and toxins. They are a huge part of our immune system, and the body makes different immunoglobulins to combat different antigens (the bad guys). When our stress response kicks in as a reaction to something we are dealing with in our external or internal world, we experience a drop in these important antibodies as part of our fight-or-flight process. What that means is that acute, immediate stress (not just prolonged stress) can have a harmful effect on our immune system.

A while back, there was a study in the *Journal of Advancement in Medicine* that looked at the physiological and psychological effects of compassion and anger. The researchers studied subjects' immune systems over a six-hour period, looking at levels of immunoglobulin A (s-IgA) present in saliva and in mucous membranes in the mouth and upper respiratory system. In the presence of anger, the immune response was repressed up to *five hours* after the incident.[2] As anger was resolved, s-IgA production increased and stayed elevated for five to six hours after the healing incident. Positive emotions also increased s-IgA levels.

It turns out when we are sad, it is not just our brain cells that are experiencing sadness. In fact there are receptors that react to antidepressants in the skin, kidneys, and stomach lining as well. Research has already demonstrated that not just anger but sadness, too, creates a compromised immune system.[3] It has also been established that loneliness puts one at greater risk for heart attack and cancer.[4]

Sickness is the body's wisdom. When you have an illness, even just the common cold, it means your body has a message for you. I've found that I get sick when I need to stop but don't give myself permission to do so. I tell myself, "I can't. I'm too busy to stop," and instead, inevitably, I just "make" myself sick. The cold comes. And then I *have* to cancel plans and stay in bed where no one can bother me!

All illness (especially cancer) has to do with immunity; and immunity has to do with inflammation (or lack thereof); and inflammation has to do (at least in part) with your emotional state of being. On an energetic level, I think every single illness or physical symptom, even chronic pain, has a higher wisdom to share with you, whether it's the cold that's giving you the sign that you need to slow down or the back pain that's telling you that you have some anger stored that needs to be released.

The impact of your emotions on your physical experience is particularly powerful when the emotions are about your relationship with your partner. In fact, a recent study from Ohio State University found that nasty arguments with your spouse can actually have a long-lasting impact on your body, even after the disagreement is over. Researchers took blood samples from couples before and after they had an argument, and they found that those who had the most vicious quarrels (with name-calling, stonewalling, slamming doors, etc.) were the ones who were most likely to have a drop in antibodies in their blood following the fight. Their immunoglobulin levels would return to normal, usually once they resolved the conflict. In other words, couples who fought bitterly actually ended up producing less natural antibodies, meaning that they were more susceptible to germs and disease.[5]

No wonder research has shown that a happy marriage can actually improve one's health and life expectancy. Research from the National Council on Family Relations found that there was a definite correlation between the quality of study participants' marriages and their overall health. Regardless of age, if a couple reported having a happy marriage, they were more likely to have better health across the board.[6]

Psychologist and relationship expert John Gottman, whom I introduced you to in Chapter 5, has attributed a number of health and longevity benefits to a happy marriage, including better resistance to infection, reduced anxiety and mental disorders, and increased life span. He also found, in the "Love Lab" study he started in 1986, that our physiological response to our partner could be an excellent predictor of the viability of the relationship. In this study, Gottman found that couples who demonstrated a large stress response in an argument were far less likely to still be together after six years than couples who demonstrated a low stress response. I love the way he sums it up when he writes that, for these high-response couples, speaking to their partner felt like a threat to their safety. Remember, you have only one stress response, and it is the same whether you are in an argument with your partner or running away from an escaped tiger.[7]

When you think about it that way, it's no wonder that Gottman's Disaster relationships, which we discussed in Chapter 5, didn't last. The stress and strain that are created in your body when it's repeatedly thrown into a fight-or-flight state (and the impact they can have on your immunoglobulin and immune system at large) can push your body to the point where either you or your partner eventually will "fly"—right out of the relationship! On the other hand, Gottman found that his Master couples—the ones who showed low stress response when talking to their partners in an argument—were mostly still together after six years. Not only that, they were still in good health.[8]

Research has also demonstrated that married couples are less likely to develop cancer and heart disease, less likely to suffer from depression and stress, and more likely to live longer. In fact, married men live an average of 17 years longer than their unmarried peers! Some of these variables, like longevity, are definitely helped by nonbiological factors such as increased health awareness and investment in life with another person. We are more likely to take care of ourselves, or see a doctor, or stop skydiving when we have the health and happiness of our partner and family to consider (or if our partner asks us to). But I believe that it is also because a happy marriage and a strong partnership help to safeguard us against mental health issues such as depression, which in turn helps to safeguard us against conditions like heart disease and cancer.

However, if your marriage is unhappy, it can have a devastating effect on your emotional and physical well-being. In fact, there has been research to suggest that our partner's unhappiness can shorten our own lives, even if we ourselves do not suffer from depression! A huge and important study on life expectancy led by psychologist Lewis Terman found that women who were married to men who suffered from depression were more likely to be unhealthy and have shorter lives.[9]

I certainly don't mean to imply that if you have a depressed or anxious mate you should kick him to the curb because he is bringing down your vibe. However, with conscious attention you have the power to hold your own energetic frequency no matter what is happening in the environment and the people around you.

Sharing Your Vibration

The good news is that if your partner's energy is affecting yours for good or bad, the opposite is true as well. If you are living a positive, meaningful life and humming in your home frequency, you are going to emanate that energy out to the people around you, especially your partner. And, even though she might not realize it, she will be beneficially impacted by your change of vibration and will subconsciously begin to try and entrain with you at this level.

I have seen this happen with numerous couples I work with as well as with my husband and my children. I mentioned earlier how I got into a state of coherence during an argument with Sam and was able not only to stop the argument in its tracks, but also to make my very verbal and intelligent husband forget his train of thought!

The same is true with my children. Like most kids, my youngest son, Jackson, went through a phase recently where he had a very hard time falling asleep at night. This seems to happen most often between ages six and nine, which is a big developmental transition in children's lives as they start to see themselves as separate individuals with separate identities. Jackson would fight sleep, afraid of nightmares, too revved up to relax, and worrying about whatever it was that didn't go well that day or might not work out tomorrow. Getting him to calm down was nearly impossible, and it left both of us tired, frustrated, and cranky.

When my oldest went through this phase, I would sing to him, tickle his back, and sit with him for what felt like forever, cringing at the slightest creak in the floor as I tried to tiptoe out of his room at the first signs of slumber. With my second son, I started to employ positive visualizations, guiding him to hang all his troubles on a worry tree so he could let go of them until tomorrow. All of these strategies worked well, especially when combined with gentle cuddles and quiet. But it all took forever and was quite exhausting after a long day.

When Jackson started with sleep troubles, though, I was already well versed in Quantum Love. It occurred to me that if I could change my vibrational field, I might help Jackson to do the same by entraining to my frequency. Rather than trying to meet him where he was (in a state of distress, fear, and loneliness) and talk him through it, maybe I could get him to entrain with me as I held a state of unconditional love and peace.

So, the next time Jackson couldn't sleep, I got into bed and curled up next to him like I always did. But instead of just lying there comforting him, I silently did the grounding and heart-opening exercise you learned on page 56. As I held my son, I imagined the barriers of our bodies disappearing. We were no longer two separate bodies beside each other, but one powerful light with no distance between us, just as we were when he was still in my womb. I quietly held him without saying a word and imagined all the love and peace I felt in my body gently flowing into his.

And even though I had not said a single word to Jackson about what I was doing, I felt his body suddenly go limp. The tension seemed to fall away as he began to relax into me. In a matter of moments he was breathing deeply, fast asleep in my arms, without any of his usual fretting, tossing, and turning. I was shocked, and I almost couldn't believe that my own energy had anything to do with this change. Perhaps it was merely a coincidence. However, when I tested the practice again over the next several nights, I found that it was only when I was in a state of coherence that Jackson would react with such an immediate and noticeable shift. If I just held him quietly he would eventually fall asleep, but it would take much longer. Yet if I got into a state of coherence and envisioned our physical barriers slipping away, he would almost immediately fall asleep—and stay asleep.

The Heart Is an Epicenter of Coherence

One of the most surprising things I have learned in my journey into quantum physics and Quantum Love is that our body has TWO epicenters. One I already knew about: the brain, which I had always presumed ran the whole show. As it turns out, the *heart* is an energy powerhouse in itself and communicates with the brain in a two-way dialogue!

The Institute of HeartMath is one of the leading centers for research into the power of the heart-brain connection, and investigators there have learned some truly incredible things. Their research has found that the conversation between our hearts and our brains happens via four mechanisms:

- Our nervous system (neurological communication)
- Our hormones (biochemical communication)
- Pulse waves (biophysical communication)
- Electromagnetic fields (energetic communication)

Electromagnetic fields?? You might think it sounds crazy, but studies at HeartMath have shown that our hearts have a powerful electromagnetic field around them that is 60 times greater in amplitude and *5,000 times stronger* than the electrical activity produced by the brain! In fact, the energy of the heart is so strong it can be detected from several feet away.[10]

Just think about what that kind of power can mean for your body, your mind, and your frequency. Moving your heart into an open, coherent state can actually change what's going on in your brain to bring you better clarity, lowered stress, and even a heightened intuitive sensitivity.

I truly believe coherence starts in the heart. One of the easiest ways to get there is via the heart-opening exercise I taught you in Chapter 3. Coherence (or home frequency) is a loving, appreciative, heart-focused state where ego does not live. Furthermore, through the powerful field of our heart, the brain actually entrains to the high-frequency energy of our heart in coherence! A study at HeartMath found that the brain's alpha waves would increase in synchronization to a coherent heart.[11] In other words, the brain's activity changed as a result of its connection to the heart. The same study also demonstrated that bringing yourself into coherence through your heart center could increase cognitive performance. A heart in home frequency makes your brain work better!

I consider the most important takeaway from these studies to be the idea that communication and influence are a two-way street for our hearts and brains. Our brains aren't running the show, which means that if you are finding it difficult to quiet your crazy roommate ego self, it might be time to employ the power of your open heart. The mind-body connection works in both directions.

HeartMath research also shows that our powerful heart energy can impact the brains of *others* who come into our heart field. Researchers performed a study in which they hooked one person up to an electroencephalogram (EEG) and another person to an electrocardiogram (ECG) to see if one's heart could talk to another's brain. They found that the answer was *yes!* In fact, the brain waves of the person wearing the EEG synchronized with the heartbeat of the other person.[12]

What this means is that by moving your heart into an open, coherent state, you can actually physically impact another person. And as your energy moves up the Quantum Lovemap, theirs will entrain to you. By harnessing your heart's power, you will not only help keep yourself in coherence but also help your partner to reach a positive state as you move into Quantum Love.

How Our Bodies Store Emotion

Any emotion that we don't fully experience and process can get trapped in the body. Simply put, what we resist persists.

Anger, fear, sadness, blame, anxiety—these are all uncomfortable emotions that we try to avoid feeling if we can. Unfortunately, when these emotions stay stored and ignored for too long, they can actually manifest as physical pain (or worse). The body stores negative emotions in a number of different places: from our hips to our back to our jaw to our eyes, a low-frequency emotion will stick around until we allow ourselves to feel it. Sometimes, however, we might not even know it is there. Maybe our pain is so buried, or so chronic, that we don't even notice that we're carrying it around like a weight.

I was in a yoga class one day when the woman next to me burst into tears. We had been holding deep hip and pelvic stretches for several minutes. The position wasn't easy—at least not for me, as it requires a lot of flexibility. But everyone in class was doing their best to ease into and then hold the pose. This woman's breakdown started as a slow release, one I wouldn't have noticed if I hadn't been right next to her in the quiet room. A few tears escaped, then a sniffle, and then her upper body heaved with a sob as she folded her torso over her extended leg. I didn't really know what to do. *Should I help?* I looked up at the course instructor, who looked back at me with an expression that said, *This happens all the time.*

Most energy healers (and certainly yogis) know that emotions are stored in the body. Remember, our emotions are energy in action. More than that, they carry an actual energetic weight, and that weight has to be stored somewhere. This is why we feel certain emotions in certain places—tightness in our shoulders, a pain in our neck. It is believed that the hips in particular are a place where sadness is stored, especially unexpressed sadness.

My yoga instructor surely knew that as she gave me her knowing look that day. The woman next to me felt an unexpressed sadness, whether she was conscious of it or not, that was escaping as she stretched out the area that had been containing that emotion.

Knowing what I know now, I would have understood the quantum process that was happening in that class: the energy of her stored painful emotion was being dislodged, moving and releasing from where it had been held within her body. Her stretch was releasing the energy of stored sadness that she wasn't consciously allowing to pass through her.

If you hold on to the energy of your emotions for too long, it can build up, packing itself in more and more, forcing your body and spirit to carry the weight. This energy is often painful and lower-frequency energy that will interfere with your ability to get to or stay in home frequency. Energy, even the energy of your emotions, is meant to pass through your body. And as I learned during the painful time when my mom was dying, avoidance doesn't work, because the energy of those emotions stays whether you want it to or not. If you don't allow your emotions to move through you, they will simply get stored in your body, negatively affecting your frequency and your body's health.

The Body as an Emotional Translator

The amazing thing about the energy of our emotions is that the physical expression of it can bring to our attention feelings we weren't aware we were feeling. It is possible to use your body as a guide to your emotional state—your *true* emotional state. Your brain may try to rationalize how you're feeling, excusing it, mitigating it, or even trying to convince you that you feel something else. But your body will not mislead you. The tightness or pain you feel in your body holds a wisdom all its own, and that wisdom speaks not only of your physical condition but of your mental, emotional, and spiritual condition as well. It will communicate that wisdom to you in some pretty eye-opening ways.

A Finnish study published in 2013 was actually able to document all of the places in the body where different emotions are felt. The researchers gave subjects (both men and women) two silhouettes along with emotionally charged words, stories, or movie scenes that tugged at the heartstrings, or just a picture of a person making a particular facial expression. Participants were then asked to mark on the silhouettes the places in their bodies where they were feeling any physical responses of emotion (either increasing or decreasing). The results showed that the locations where emotions were felt on the body were the same nearly across the board. There were no differences running along gender or cultural lines; it was simply biological response.[13] This makes sense, of course, as our very survival has relied on our biological response to emotional stimuli for thousands of years.

When we feel fear, our hearts start pounding and our muscles tighten as we get ready to fight or run away. This fits perfectly with the reported location of anger in the Finnish study: participants reported increased response and activity in their core, especially in their heart center.

Anger looks very different from fear. We feel anger as a surge of sensation throughout the entire top part of our bodies: our head, face, arms, and shoulders. Envy is felt almost entirely in the head. Then, in what I consider the most illuminating of the emotional places, love is felt over almost our entire body, particularly in the head, heart, and genitals. It's a whole-body surge in energy. Depression, on the other hand, looks exactly the opposite. It's experienced as a diminishment in sensation all over the body, with an almost complete absence of sensation in the extremities.

If you don't know what you're feeling—and most people don't—you can tune in to your body for an answer. Look for tightness, pain, constriction, or tension in any of the places where your emotions are felt. You can often determine what you're feeling as a result.

A greater connection to your body will also yield a better sense of your energetic frequency and where you are vibrating on the Quantum Lovemap. Your awareness becomes a confluence of the body and mind, showing you not only how you're feeling emotionally but how you're feeling physically as well. This is especially helpful with people who have difficulty showing emotion. While both genders can struggle with this, I believe it's most often men who find emotional expression difficult, mostly due to how they were raised. But not always.

Alanna and George had been happily married for three years but had begun drifting apart two years after their first child was born. Now their children were more self-sufficient and George and Alanna could lift their heads up and breathe again. They came to see me because, as they did so, they discovered what felt like a valley between them. In a sense, they had turned into roommates and co-parents and the energy between them set itself accordingly; they were not enjoying the spicy, loving energy of lovers who were happily married. Alanna could feel the disconnect between them and had been trying to encourage George to share his feelings with her. She knew he was frustrated with the lack of sex in their life (she was frustrated too), but she couldn't get him to talk about it.

One of the first things I do when a couple starts seeing me is meet with them individually, at least once, to get more information about their personal history and development. Taking George's history, I learned that he grew up in a very traditional household. His father was stoic and stereotypically masculine: he didn't cry, didn't do housework, and was the sole breadwinner for the family. George's mother was very kind and loving, but from a very early age he grew up with the axiom that boys don't cry, and feelings in general were not a part of the family culture. Nobody talked about what they were feeling; they were just expected to get over things. Alanna's family, on the other hand, let it all out. They would rage, cry, speak their minds, and address any problem directly with the person they held responsible for causing it. Alanna was very attuned to how she was feeling and had a strong emotional vocabulary to go with it. She viewed emotional exchange, as many women do, as a part of bonding. George, needless to say, did not view it the same way.

George deeply loved and cared about his wife and children, and he desperately wanted to make Alanna happy. He just had no idea how. He looked at me beseechingly and said, "I can't tell you how I'm feeling. I don't even know how I'm feeling. It doesn't compute." It wasn't that he didn't want to talk to his wife about his emotional life. He didn't have a mechanism for getting there. George understood the benefits of expressing his emotions; he just didn't know how to do it.

I asked him to close his eyes, walked him through the process of grounding himself, then asked him to do a scan of his body and notice any sensations he was having physically. He said, "I feel really tight in my chest. And I feel this ache behind my eyes and in the back of my neck." *Sadness and fear with a touch of anger,* I thought. I explained to George how our body stores our emotions and how he could use those feelings in his body as biofeedback for what his emotions were. Once he identified the feeling, he could identify the thought behind the feeling. As he connected more with his emotions, it became easier and easier to express them. And as he gained greater facility in expressing feeling, that created more connection and intimacy between him and Alanna.

The other thing that really helped was teaching Alanna how to hold home frequency more consciously. While she was in touch with her emotions, she was definitely calibrating in the To Me state. There was a lot of fear and anger, judgment, hopelessness, and blame. So she started working on moving her emotional energy and changing her stories (which you will learn about in Chapter 10). As she moved herself up the Quantum Lovemap, things started to shift in their relationship.

After several months of working with the exercises I gave them, George can now easily access and identify his emotions. Best of all, both he and Alanna are modeling this behavior for their children, so their kids can see them having real emotions (including sadness and anger) and moving through them in an authentic and safe manner. And, to top it off, they report that their sex life is better than when they first met!

Our Chakras

Everything in our universe is radiating energy, from the biggest mountain or ocean, to the tiniest blade of grass, to each individual cell in our body. All of our cells emit energy in different ways, and different cells will emit different kinds of energy depending on where they are located within the body and what their job is. It should come as no surprise, then, that given the specialized nature of your body's energy, there are several different channels located on key points of the body through which energy can flow in and out in a constant stream. These are called the chakras.

The word *chakra* means "wheel" in Sanskrit, though these are not like any wheels we've ever seen. Chakra energy spins in a clockwise direction as it moves the energy of our body out into the field around us, and it spins counterclockwise to pull energy from our external world (and the people in it) into our body. It is the frequency state of our chakras that determines the direction our energy will flow as they either draw energy into our body or release it outward.

But are our chakras physical entities? Are they actual little wheels spinning in the seven key centers of our body? No. They are not made up of matter; they are energetic. But like the whirring blades of a fan, just because you can't see them doesn't mean they aren't there.

You might be wondering how we can know chakras exist if we can't actually see them. It is a valid question, and one that science has not yet found a hard answer for. It was a bit of a leap for me as a science-minded person to make when I began learning about chakras. *I'm a scientist, not a philosopher* is the resistance my ego threw at me as I started to explore what was an entirely new frontier for me.

But while the concept of chakras was new for me (and still manages to evade scientific proof), it has existed for thousands of years and across cultures. It has been studied and demonstrated time and again in the Ayurvedic and yogic traditions, as well as through the Chinese concepts of chi and meridians, and it is something that I have "proven" to myself through my own experience and in my work with my patients. The influence of our body's energy, the life force that flows through us, and the power of the quantum field itself are things that our scientific capabilities have yet to catch up with. I do believe that we will get there eventually, but until then we can only rely on our experience and the teachings of others. For more information on meridians, check out the Grace Points exercise in the Appendix.

Our chakras exist at seven points along our body (see Figure 6), each one associated with a different set of organs and systems. It shouldn't be too surprising that the locations of our chakras correspond with the places on our body where essential systems use a lot of energy. For instance, the one between the eyes sits around our visual center, of course, but also the frontal lobe of our brain. That location is the epicenter of our decision making, planning, and orientation. There is so much energy required in that region of our body that it makes perfect sense for it to have an energy outlet sitting in a handy location. The same goes for the heart chakra, which we know contains so much energy that it has its own force field and emits so much electromagnetic energy that it can be measured from several feet away. The chakras can be open or closed, overactive or underactive, depending on how well energy is able to flow through them. And that flow is determined by the open or constricted state of, you guessed it, your body.

We can further understand the energetic existence of our chakras (and their associated emotions) by understanding their color. Yes, each chakra has a color associated with it. Visible light gives off electromagnetic waves, vibrating across the field through time and space. Depending on how quickly the waves are vibrating, our eyes will pick them up as different colors. Red, for instance, is a lower-frequency wave that looks like a slow roll; purple, on the other hand, is a high-frequency wave with sharp peaks and valleys. In fact, we can measure a wave in nanometers and then determine its energetic strength! The chakras, vibrating at their different frequencies, likewise have different colors.

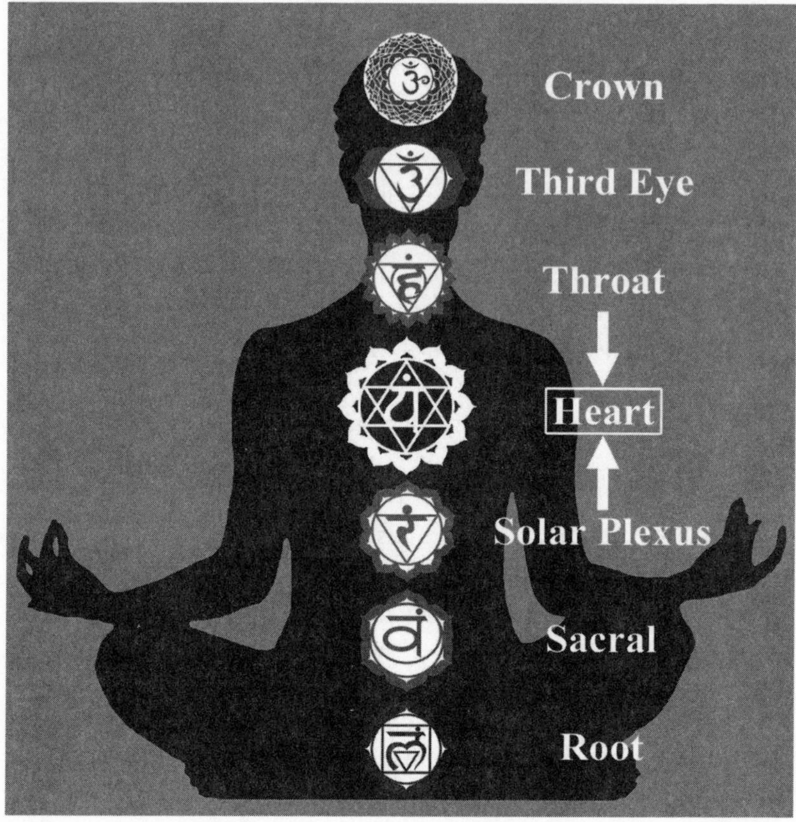

Figure 6: The Chakra System

How Does a Chakra Work, Anyway?

A chakra may be a wheel or a vortex, but it operates like a ball of energy interpenetrating the physical body. The chakras themselves are not physical; you can't see them on an X-ray. They are aspects of consciousness, and they interact with the physical body through two major vehicles, the endocrine system and the nervous system. Each of the seven chakras is associated with one of the nine endocrine glands, and also with a particular group of nerves, called a plexus. Thus, each chakra corresponds with particular parts of the body and particular functions within the body controlled by that plexus or that endocrine gland.

The chakras represent not only particular parts of your physical body, but also particular parts of your consciousness. Your consciousness, how you perceive your reality, represents everything it is possible for you to experience. All of your senses, perceptions, and possible states of awareness can be divided into seven categories, and each of these categories can be associated with a particular chakra. When you feel tension in your consciousness, you feel it in the chakra associated with the part of your consciousness experiencing the stress, and in the parts of the physical body associated with that chakra (see Figure 7). *Where* you feel the stress depends therefore on *why* you feel the stress.

When you are hurt in a relationship, you feel it in your heart. When you are nervous, your legs tremble and your bladder becomes weak. When there is tension in a particular part of your consciousness, and therefore in the chakra associated with that part of your consciousness, the tension is detected by the nerves of the plexus associated with that chakra and communicated to the parts of the body controlled by that plexus. When the tension continues over a period of time or reaches a particular degree of intensity, it creates a symptom on the physical level. Again, the symptom serves to communicate to you through your body what you have been doing to yourself in your consciousness.

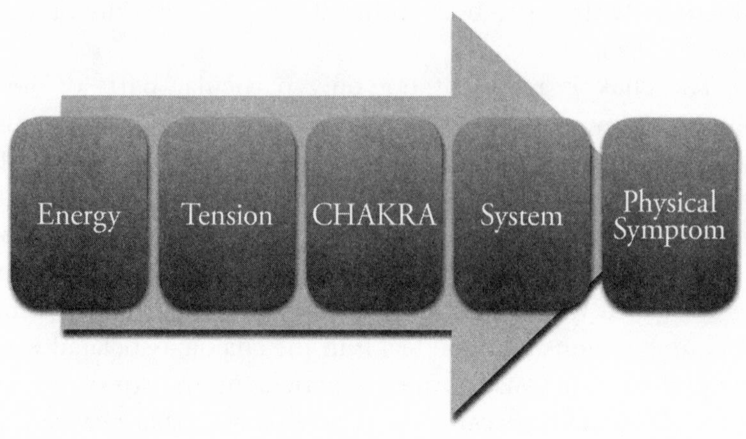

Figure 7: The Path of Energy to Physical Symptoms through the Chakras

Just like thirst (by the time you feel thirsty, you are already dehydrated), the physical symptom belies a long-standing energetic malady. In order to reverse it, physical change may be required first. This is where shift moves come in, as we'll discuss extensively in Chapter 10. When we change something about our way of *being*, we can release the stress that has been creating the symptom(s), and then we can return to our natural state of balance and health.

Opening and Closing Chakras

The opening and closing of our chakras works like an energetic defense system. A negative experience (and the low-frequency energy that comes with it) can cause the associated chakra to close in order to block that energy out. Similarly, if we are clinging to a low-calibrating feeling like blame, prolonging the emotion because we refuse to deal with or move it, we close off the chakra (the channel through which the energy would otherwise escape). Any of the emotions that sit at the lower end of the Quantum Lovemap will likely trigger a chakra constriction. I believe we feel that constriction as the tightness that comes into our mind and body when we are stressed. In the next chapter I will be teaching you a lot more about how to keep your chakras open and balanced.

As we open our chakras, energy is able to flow freely once again and things return to normal. Sometimes it's a matter of moving energy throughout our body, moving our own frequency up the Quantum Lovemap, or tackling and extracting a difficult thorn that is stressing us out. I will be teaching you these techniques in the following chapters. For now, I simply want you to understand how important it is that your chakras be open and allow energy to move through you without obstruction. Each chakra's connection to a key endocrine gland and nervous system in your body means that an energy deficiency could lead to serious physical consequences if you ignore it for too long. I often wonder if the heartbreak I experienced when my mother died suppressed my immune system enough—along with all the negative thinking, grief, and sugar (cancer cells have far more glucose receptors than do normal cells)—to allow the cancer cells that were already in my body to grow.

Balance Is Key

No one chakra is better than the others. You don't want to have extra heart chakra and less throat chakra; it simply doesn't work like that. Ideally, all seven of your chakras are balanced, open, and humming, allowing energy to flow into and out of your body. The amazing thing is that your body is going to find a way to move energy in and out (unless, of course, your ego self is telling it to hold on to something). If one of your chakras is closed or underactive, there is a very good chance that another chakra will be overactive to make up the difference.

Because your body wants to achieve energetic balance in your chakras, moving too far in either direction (underactive or overactive) in any one chakra can actually yield negative effects in your body. An underactive chakra kicks another chakra into overdrive, which in turn pulls extra energy away from that part of the body. The charts here show how you may act or feel when your chakras get knocked out of balance. The first one lists the physical systems associated with each chakra and the potential physical *symptoms* that may tell you something's out of whack.

How You May Feel or Act When Chakras Are Overactive or Underactive

Chakra	Overactive	Underactive
Root	Fearful, nervous, insecure, or ungrounded; materialistic or greedy; resistant to change	Lacking a sense of being at home or secure anywhere, codependent, unable to get into one's body, fearful of abandonment
Sacral	Overemotional, very quick to attach and invest in others, attracted to drama, moody, lacking personal boundaries	Stiff, unemotional, closed off to others, lacking self-esteem or self-worth, possibly in an abusive relationship
Navel (Solar Plexus)	Domineering, aggressive, angry, perfectionistic or overly critical of oneself or others	Passive, indecisive, timid, lacking self-control
Heart	Loving in a clingy, suffocating way; lacking a sense of self in a relationship; willing to say yes to everything; lacking boundaries, letting everyone in	Cold, distant, lonely, unable or unwilling to open up to others, grudgeful
Throat	Overly talkative, unable to listen, highly critical, verbally abusive, condescending	Introverted, shy, having difficulty speaking the truth, unable to express needs
Third Eye	Out of touch with reality, lacking good judgment, unable to focus, prone to hallucinations	Rigid in thinking, closed off to new ideas, too reliant on authority, disconnected or distrustful of inner voice, anxious, clinging to the past and fearful of the future
Crown	Addicted to spirituality, heedless of bodily needs, having difficulty controlling emotions	Not very open to spirituality, unable to set or maintain goals, lacking direction

The Chakras and Associated Glands, Organs, and Symptoms

Chakra	Associated Endocrine Glands & Organs	Physical Symptoms of Unbalanced Chakra
Root	Adrenal glands, spine, blood, and reproductive organs	Inability to sit still, restlessness, unhealthy weight (either obesity or eating disorder), constipation, cramps, fatigue or sluggishness
Sacral	Kidneys and reproductive organs: ovaries, testes, and uterus	Lower-back pain or stiffness, urinary issues, kidney pain or infection, infertility, impotence
Navel (Solar Plexus)	Central nervous system, digestive system (stomach and intestines), liver, pancreas, metabolic system	Ulcers, gas, nausea, or other digestive problems; eating disorders; asthma or other respiratory ailments; nerve pain or fibromyalgia; infection in the liver or kidneys; other organ problems
Heart	Thymus gland and immune system, heart, lungs, breasts, arms, hands	Heart and circulatory problems (high blood pressure, heart palpitations, heart attack), poor circulation or numbness, asthma or other respiratory ailments, breast cancer, stiff joints or joint problems in the hands
Throat	Thyroid, neck, throat, shoulders, ears, and mouth	Stiffness or soreness in the neck or shoulders, sore throat, hoarseness or laryngitis, earaches or infection, dental issues or TMJ, thyroid issues
Third Eye	Pituitary, eyes, brow, base of skull, biorhythms	Vision problems, headaches or migraines, insomnia or sleep disorders, seizures, nightmares (though this isn't a physical symptom per se, it is a common occurrence)
Crown	Pituitary and pineal glands, brain, hypothalamus, cerebral cortex, central nervous system	Dizziness, confusion, mental fog, neurological disorders, nerve pain, schizophrenia or other mental disorders

As you can see, a lot of these physical symptoms are not to be taken lightly! The difficult thing to remember is that the body is going to keep sending us its message—amping up the intensity if it needs to—until we pay attention. Don't let a physical symptom turn into an AFGE!

Chakras and Your Frequency: The Chicken or the Egg?

The energy of our chakras influences our physical processes via inhibition and stimulation. Remember, chakras are like wheels whose job is not only to keep energy moving, but also to constrict or close as a defense against negative energy. In order to compensate for a constricted, underactive chakra, another chakra will become overactive, sending out your low-frequency vibes at a greater rate. That in turn creates and prolongs a low-frequency reality. If your chakras are these energy centers emitting and absorbing energy, then are they the source of your frequency, or are they the result of it? Are your chakras the chicken or the egg?

I think they're both. I think the dual role of the chakras, in terms of your consciousness and your physical self, really speaks to the relationship between the mind and the body. When you work on the body, the mind comes along for the ride, and vice versa. It's the same with your frequency and your chakras. When you're in ego frequency, it affects the flow of energy within your chakras and your body as a whole. However, as you clear and clean your chakras by moving energy around, then you are also making a positive change in your frequency.

Just remember, if you're operating on a lower frequency, then 1) you're creating your reality, because your five senses are picking up what you're applying your consciousness to ("*This* is where we are, find me all the things that reinforce *that*"), and 2) your resonant frequency is what you're putting out into the quantum field and what you're drawing into yourself through your chakras, impacting your physical state. That's why it's easier to stub your toe when you're having a bad day.

In the next chapter, I will show you how to connect your chakras to your EHFI and your place on the Quantum Lovemap. I will also teach you how to move energy through your chakras and keep them balanced. Just as you can use your body's feelings to help you determine your emotional feelings, you can use your body's energy channels to help determine where your under- or overactive chakras could be making an impact in your relationship. This is just another way of tapping into your body's wisdom.

It may feel funny to think about your body as a vehicle for your energy. If anything, it may bring to mind images from a sci-fi flick or a novel that takes place in the age of the machines! I prefer to think of our bodies as vehicles from a more spiritual and metaphysical standpoint: They are the channel for the energy of our mind, soul, and spirit, and they bring it into the physical world. Our bodies allow us tangible, physical connection to others and an opportunity to experience our world through our five senses. They allow our essential self to connect with the essential selves of others in a tangible way, manifesting our quantum existence, *and Quantum Love,* in the world we experience.

CHAPTER 8

Commitment #3

I Will Take Responsibility for My Body's Energy

The day will come when after we have mastered the winds, the waves, the tides and gravity, we shall harness for God the energies of love. Then for the second time in the history of the world, man will have discovered fire.

— Teilhard de Chardin

Our bodies are veritable powerhouses of energy. From the electromagnetic field of our heart center to the whirring vortices of our chakras, energy is constantly moving in, out, all around us and within us in a dynamic dance. Our bodies' energy has the power to shape our physical experience, and through the power of our mind-body connection it can shape our mental and emotional experiences too. This is why it is so important to keep the energy of our bodies moving, rather than trapping and holding it where it can weigh us down physically and bring us down energetically into a low-frequency state.

The fact is, our bodies are a vehicle for our energy and our means for interacting with our physical world (and *creating* our world!). This is also the only body we get, at least in this lifetime. For these reasons, it is so important that we commit ourselves to doing everything we can to support the health and well-being of our bodies and become conscious caretakers of our bodies' energy. We have to bring our relationship with our bodies into Quantum Love.

In this chapter, I'm going to teach you how to manage your body's energy and care for it so that energy can keep flowing. I'm going to show you why your body image is so important to manifesting the reality that you want (or don't want) and why love, compassion, and gratitude are some of the greatest "boosters" you can give yourself. I'm also going to show you how to put your focus on what you put into your body in a way that is loving and supportive instead of self-critical or blaming.

All you have to do is make the commitment to show loving-kindness to your body. Then get curious about the wisdom it is trying to share with you. Understand that your physical state often has an important underlying message for you—and that your body will keep trying to deliver the message until you listen to it!

Working with Your Body's Energy

As we learned in the last chapter, our chakras are our body's energy channels and can have a powerful impact on our self and our reality as they open, close, constrict, and expand in an attempt to stay balanced. These energy fluctuations impact our physical health and our emotional and energetic states, and thus they shape our reality and our relationship. Understanding our emotions in the language of our body's energy can help us use the wisdom of our body to pinpoint and address the obstacles that might be keeping us out of Quantum Love.

Jane came to me feeling frustrated with her long-term relationship with Rita. She had a very thorny history. She'd had numerous difficult relationships, including a betrayal through a partner's infidelity. Her love model wasn't a strong one either: her father had cheated on her mother, and her mom knew it on some level. Jane told me it came out later that her mom had stayed in the marriage because she didn't feel she had any other options. By virtue of the stories she carried, Jane always made it her mission to be self-sufficient and was very guarded about letting other people in.

We discussed how her thorns could be manifesting themselves in her body's energy. It was clear to me that her root chakra was overactive while her heart chakra was underactive. Jane herself felt that she was seen as no-nonsense and harsh. She knew she was capable of intimacy and caring, but it could take her a long time to trust. On my recommendation, Jane asked Rita to join us for a couple of sessions so that we could discuss Jane's body's energy, learn more about Rita's, and get a sense of how they worked together to create their relationship reality.

Rita had a closed throat chakra. Growing up, she had a brother who was very difficult. He got in a lot of trouble and took up a lot of the family's attention. There was significant pressure on Rita to toe the line and not add to her parents' issues. She was a super-pleaser, saying and doing whatever she needed to say and do to keep everyone happy. She didn't feel comfortable voicing her needs, particularly in her relationship with Jane (who, with her underactive heart chakra, could sometimes lack empathy). Rita found that she often wanted to speak up but wouldn't. As a result, she had been building resentments toward Jane that were negatively impacting their relationship.

Rita had been dealing with the conflict by avoiding it and emotionally withdrawing from the relationship. Their intimacy was starting to disintegrate, and Jane, who was already very prone not to trust, was starting to feel suspicious that Rita was cheating. Rita, in turn, was feeling abandoned and started shutting down as well. It was a vicious cycle in which neither of them felt safe being openhearted. Without realizing it, each of them was sending low-frequency energy that said, "Stay away," when what they were really thinking was *Please don't hurt me.* Through this understanding of their bodies' energy and the impact it was having on their emotional states, Rita and Jane realized their different patterns and the reasons behind them. They realized, too, that they shared a tendency toward fear and had difficulty staying grounded. They each recognized that they bore 100 percent responsibility for changing things between them. And they started to spiral upward toward Quantum Love.

When it comes to your body's energy, it is key to come from a place of compassion and empathy. Remember, energy is neither good nor bad. It simply *is*. Rita and Jane were able to understand that they were each coming from a low-frequency place and that their chakras were constricting their energy flow in different places as a result. They were both in an energetic self-defense mode that was shaped around the thorns from their earlier lives. The conflicts between them, in fact, had little to do with each other and everything to do with what was going on inside them. By tapping into the wisdom of their bodies' energy, they were able to depersonalize each other's actions and move into a state of Quantum Love, first within themselves and then in their relationship.

The more you understand where your partner is coming from, the less likely you are to take conflicts with your partner personally. Another person's actions (yes, even your mate's) are never really about *you*. Just as the way you're feeling about your partner is rarely ever about *her*. If you find yourself in conflict with your partner, ask yourself: what thorn is being touched?

If you are having a hard time determining what you are feeling, turn to your body's wisdom. Do a body scan to look for any physical sign that you are storing emotion: tightness in your chest or shoulders, an ache in your neck, or even a sore throat. Look for symbolism in your symptom. If your throat hurts, ask yourself whether you are failing to express something that you need or want to say. If your shoulders are sore, ask yourself if you are carrying anger. Then get to know your chakras better.

You can use your Quantum Love Quiz results to get a good sense of whether your chakras are balanced. Each subcategory on the quiz applies to a different chakra. If your score on a particular section was between 6 and 12, that chakra is likely more closed.

If your score was between 13 and 18, that chakra is balanced, and a score of 19 to 24 indicates that chakra is likely more open. It is my experience that if you're closed or underactive in four or more chakras, you are likely operating in ego frequency.

Translating the Quantum Love Quiz Results to Your Chakra Balance

Quantum Love Quiz Category	Corresponding Chakra
Security	Root
Sexual Energy	Sacral
Worthiness/Love	Solar Plexus
Openheartedness	Heart
Self-Expression	Throat
Intuition	Third Eye
Higher Plan	Crown

If your partner has filled out a Quantum Lovemap (or if you have attempted to fill it out for him or her), you may refer to that as well to get a sense of your partner's body energy. I have found it extremely helpful to explore this with my patients and in my own life. When you understand which chakras are more open and more closed, you will better understand the issue you are dealing with in your love life as well as the energy of your partner and the energy between the two of you. Once you know which chakras are over- or underactive, many of the conflicts or struggles you are having in your love life will make much more sense. Go back to the chart in the previous chapter. You will likely find that the symptoms of your over- or underactive chakra are reflected in your relationship.

Let's look more closely at your chakras and how balance (or lack thereof) plays out in your relationship.

Root Chakra

The root chakra is what connects us to our bodies and our sense of place in the physical world. When your root chakra is in balance, you feel secure and safe and sure of yourself. When it is overactive, you may find yourself being very rigid and FMC about your routine. You may be resistant to change and even aggressive toward someone who challenges your "authority." When your root chakra is underactive, you may find yourself feeling disconnected, insecure, or even unsafe in this world. You may have a difficult time setting boundaries and find that your own energy and moods are easily changed by the moods of others. For example, if your partner is stressed out about work, you will find yourself feeling and reflecting that stress back to him or her. You will take it personally if he isn't in a good mood, and you will make his mood about you. This is dangerous because you need to be in charge of your own energy, and because this might prevent your partner from being "allowed" to be in a bad mood. He might think, "I have to put on a happy face so my wife doesn't get upset with me." Not only is this not fair to him, but that stressful energy won't disappear just because he is unable to show it. It will simmer under the surface and appear in other ways. If this sounds familiar, it's time to bring your root chakra back into balance, and grounding yourself (as described in Chapter 3) is the perfect way to do that.

Sacral Chakra

Our sacral chakra is the seat of our creativity and sexual energy. When your sacral chakra is in balance, you feel comfortable in your body and with your sexuality. Your feelings flow, you feel good about your body, and you are able to express yourself physically. When it is overactive, you may be living a drama-filled life and riding a roller coaster of emotions. When it is underactive, you may be denying yourself the things that make you feel good. You may notice that creativity doesn't really flow to you, and new ideas or out-of-the-box thinking may be difficult. You may also find that you are hyper-focused on your looks. Whether you gained half a pound or discovered a new wrinkle, all of your energy will be on desperately trying to perfect your appearance and comparing yourself with other people around you. You won't be able to enjoy your sexuality or intimacy with your partner because you will feel unhappy in your own skin.

Solar Plexus Chakra

The solar plexus chakra is where our sense of ourselves exists. It governs our self-esteem and our emotional self, and it is the home of our physical intuition in the form of our gut feelings. When your solar plexus chakra is in balance, you feel good about yourself and confident in who you are. You are also very accepting of others. Your emotional life is balanced and you trust your intuition. When it is overactive, you may find that you are overcritical of yourself or others. You may be a perfectionist and someone who is constantly putting other things, like work, before yourself. When your solar plexus chakra is underactive, you may care too much about what other people think and constantly look outside of yourself for approval and affirmation. You may not feel worthy of love or any of the other good things in this life.

Heart Chakra

As we have learned, our heart is an extremely powerful energy center. Our heart chakra governs the big feelings in this life: love and joy on one end; and sadness, anger, and fear on the other. When your heart chakra is balanced, you feel joy and love and compassion, all the juicy, feel-good feelings, and are able to give and receive love very openly. When it is overactive, you may find that you are ruled by your emotions and have difficulty setting boundaries. You may find that you are a big-time pleaser and have difficulty being happy if your partner (or anyone else, for that matter) is not content. An underactive heart chakra will make it very difficult for you to open yourself to trusting, loving, or caring for others. You may find that you naturally veer toward negative thought patterns and feelings of unworthiness. Perhaps you have walls built up around your heart that are thick and impenetrable. Many people with underactive heart chakras have a history of abuse and childhood trauma. If you weren't taught to love yourself as a child, it can be very difficult to do so as an adult unless you address that trauma and seek the help you need and deserve.

Throat Chakra

The throat chakra governs our self-expression and communication and our listening ability. When your throat chakra is balanced, you are comfortable asking for what you need or want and expressing yourself in an authentic, honest way. When it is overactive, you may find you're taking a "my way or the highway" approach to life. You may be hypercritical or even verbally abusive to others and closed off to the advice someone else might try to give you. When it is underactive, you may have a hard time speaking up for yourself, communicating your ideas in a way that others understand, or telling the truth. Women and men both suffer from closed throat chakras, typically for different reasons—women because they have been socialized to be people pleasers, and men because they have been socialized not to discuss their emotional needs. If you and your partner both have closed throat chakras, your relationship could greatly suffer as a result.

Third Eye Chakra

This is the epicenter of our ideas, our dreams, our goals, and our mental or emotional intuition. When your third eye chakra is in balance, you are able to access your intuitional sensitivities, envision what you want for your future, and let your ideas flow. When it is overactive, you may be judgmental or too much "in your head," running around in a fantasy world instead of connecting to the one you're standing in. If it is underactive, you may have difficulty accessing or trusting your intuition. You may lack empathy for others or yourself and find it difficult to connect to your more spiritual side.

Crown Chakra

It is believed that our crown chakra is our connection to our spiritual source and our highest selves. When your crown chakra is in balance, you grasp the oneness of our universe and understand that you are a part of something much bigger and grander than yourself. You know that you create your own reality and that everything that happens to you serves you. When it is overactive, you may find it hard to keep both feet in this world. It may be difficult to ground yourself and feel a connection to your body and the physical realm. If it is underactive, you may find it hard to connect with a higher consciousness or spirituality. Surrender is probably very difficult since you neither know nor trust what you are surrendering to. You may find that you struggle to know what your purpose in this life is and to connect with your partner on a deeper spiritual level.

Chakra Exercises

The key to bringing your chakras into balance is to keep your energy moving. Remember, our thoughts and emotions have energy that may become trapped in our bodies (especially if our chakras are underactive or closed) and bring our frequency down. Try the exercises here, and go to the Appendix to find even more ways to move your body's energy.

The Chakra Elevator: Going Up!

The idea behind this exercise is to help you become attuned to your energy and your chakras. If this is your first time learning about chakras, I bet you are feeling a little confused, hesitant, and skeptical. That's okay. The only purpose here is to help you get familiar with your body and the places where you might be stuck energetically. With practice, you will be amazed at how your energy will flow in those areas to which you bring awareness. Remember, where intention goes, energy flows, and that is particularly true in chakra meditations.

1. Sit comfortably with your back supported. Ground yourself as described in Chapter 3. Take some deep breaths.
2. Imagine the energy in your body in a beautiful glass elevator, all pooling at the base of your spine, your root chakra. Put all your attention on that area of your body. Imagine that you can envision the beautiful red vortex of light energy pulsating and vibrating there.
3. The elevator has the capacity to go up seven floors, through each chakra. Slowly count from one to two. As you do, imagine the beautiful, energy-filled elevator moving up one "floor" from the root chakra to the sacral chakra, shifting from a vibrating red vortex of light to an orange one.
4. Continue raising the elevator up through each chakra and just take note of sensations and images that come up along the way. You may be surprised at what you discover!

Chakra Tune-Up

This is an exercise shared in Donna Eden's wonderful book *Energy Medicine.* I really love this exercise as a general tune-up. It can also be centered on one particular chakra that you feel is over- or underactive. I will describe it here in terms of your partner doing this exercise on you, but you can do it on yourself without a partner (or do it on your partner!). It involves moving the energy around in your body in the way an energy healer might. If you stay in a state of relaxed focus, I find that you will often feel the energy moving. It may feel warm or like a gentle pulling sensation. The idea is that the hands working on the chakra act like a magnet, pulling stale or toxic energies up and out. As the chakra energies follow the energy of the hand, they start to spin in a way that allows blocks to be removed. You can also use these exercise with your friends or even your kids.

My son Sammy was particularly anxious several months ago. He was having a hard time in school and feeling socially isolated. I knew that letting that anxiety build within him wasn't doing him any favors. Even though he rolled his eyes at me, he agreed to humor me and let me try this exercise on him. I focused on the solar plexus and root chakras. He immediately calmed down and took a few moments to breathe deeply, quiet his mind, and get grounded. Yes, even young children can get grounded. I find that the overstimulation in today's world, with video games, cell phones, and constant noise and action, can really overload children, and taking just a few private, calming moments can be so beneficial, especially if it includes chakra work.

This is true for older kids as well. My friend Oscar tried it on his teenage daughter when she was anxious about starting a new high school, and they both told me that they really enjoyed it. In fact, Oscar's daughter (who is in the drama club) recently performed this exercise with a bunch of her classmates to help them deal with opening-night jitters!

1. Have the subject lie on his or her back. Vigorously shake your hands. Energy medicine practitioners believe that this clears any excess energy from their own body so they are a clean energetic instrument.
2. Begin with the root chakra. Place one or both hands about four inches over the chakra with palms down and gently begin to circle them counterclockwise, ideally for three minutes. The circles should be slow and wide, about the width of the body. Then switch to clockwise circles, doing them for about half as long as the counterclockwise circles were performed.
3. Shake your hands again and move on to the next chakra, repeating step 2. Do this for each chakra.

According to Eden, if the three minutes in the counterclockwise direction start to feel like too much for the recipient, simply reverse to clockwise, and that should restore balance. She goes on to advise that if you experience a headache while your chakras are being cleared, this is often because stagnant or toxic energies are being released. If you are prone to headaches, it doesn't hurt to start on the crown chakra and work your way down from there instead. Eden also warns that when working on a man, you should reverse the order when you get to the crown chakra, staring with the clockwise motion and ending with counterclockwise, because a man's crown chakra spins in the opposite direction from all the rest. But a woman's crown chakra spins in the usual direction.

The Sacral-Heart Hookup

I learned this exercise from Donna Eden's work as well. I find it to be extremely helpful during periods of anxiety or insecurity, especially about love, as well as when you want to build a better connection between the physical and emotional expressions of intimacy in your relationship.

First ground yourself and take five or six deep breaths in through your nose and out through your mouth. Place the middle finger of one hand on your third eye chakra and the middle finger of the other hand at your sacral chakra, right in your navel. Then gently press each finger into your skin, pulling upward as you do. Hold that for 20 seconds. It's typically a sign of a hookup when you feel the need to sigh deeply. You can really hook up any two chakras by placing your right hand on one chakra and your left on the other.

Working with Your Breath

Most of us never think twice about our breathing. And why should we? Like the beating of our heart, our breath is something we never have to consider, something that happens whether we are awake or asleep, without ever requiring any effort.

However, breathing is also at the root of all of our body's processes. When we consciously seek to slow down our breathing during a stressful event, we can feel an almost immediate effect on our body. Our heart rate slows down. Our mind becomes clearer. We feel less shaky and more in control.[1]

Yogic breathing (pranayama) is even more beneficial. Loosely translated, *pranayama* means "mastery of life force" or "removal of obstacles to free the flow of life force." In other words, it essentially brings your body into its purest essence, aligning it with your mind and clearing any obstructions that might prevent you from reaching this state.

Although it might sound intimidating, yogic breathing is quite simple. In order to practice it, simply sit in a comfortable position with your back straight and supported. Don't hunch over or otherwise obstruct your breathing. Now take a long breath in through your nose. Feel the air flowing over your lip and envision it coming into your nostrils. Now release the breath through your nose. Make the exhale at least one second longer than the inhale. (It might be helpful to count the seconds as you go.) Now repeat it again, inhaling a long breath through your nostrils, envisioning it coming into the nostrils at an even, smooth speed. Then exhale it through your nose slowly. It should sound almost like the sound of the ocean.

Yogic breathing can have amazing benefits. We so rarely breathe deeply and bring consciousness to our breath. When we do, it really is like a "breath of fresh air" for all of our organs. Not only that, deep breathing helps to establish a feeling of calm and encourages us to deeply connect with our essential self.

Breathing is also a wonderful way to help improve your communication with your partner. There's a reason why people tell you to take a few deep breaths when you are angry. When you shut your eyes and breathe deeply, it is much easier to let go of your ego and your need to be right, even for just a moment in time. You are able to step back and see the stressful event clearly, and you are able to get clear on your intention and on what you want to create in your relationship.

Yes, it can take self-control to shut your eyes (and your mouth!) to do yogic breathing when what you really want to do is yell and scream, but I guarantee if you do it just a couple of times and see the amazing results, you will want to continue doing it. Soon it will become second nature and you won't even have to force yourself to stop and breathe; it will be your immediate reaction whenever you start to notice that you are becoming overwhelmed with negative emotions.

The Square Breath

The square breath is a very simple exercise and a great way of allowing your body to hit the reset button. I find it especially useful when emotions are moving into ego frequency and the stress response is kicking in. It will bring you back to calmness and home frequency.

Square breath is a four-step process that holds a count of four for each step. You can do it anywhere, at any time. Start by inhaling slowly through your nose (counting in your mind, "One, two, three, four") and then hold your breath for another count of four. Next, exhale slowly through your mouth ("One, two, three, four") until your lungs are emptied. Hold in this state for another four seconds before slowly inhaling again. That's the pattern: In for four seconds, hold for four seconds, out for four seconds, hold for four seconds.

If you'd like to add a meditative focus to this exercise to help release tension even further, use any four-sided object—preferably a square—as a visual guide. You can even draw one on a piece of paper. Start by focusing on the top left corner of the square as you breathe in. As you hold, gently shift your focus to the top right corner. Breathing out, gently shift your focus to the bottom right corner, and as you hold your breath again, move on to the bottom left corner. If you'd like to take it a step further, you can couple this exercise with a mini-gratitude reboot by thinking of one thing you're grateful for in the moment at each step of your square breath.

The 4-7-8 Breath

Another great breathing exercise is one I learned from Dr. Andrew Weil, author and holistic health expert. It's called the 4-7-8 Breath, and it slows down the nervous system. I find it particularly useful for difficulty sleeping or falling back asleep in the middle of the night.

It is very similar to the square breath exercise. Exhale deeply through your mouth, clearing all of the air out of your lungs in one big *WHOOSH* sound. Next, slowly and deeply inhale through your nose as you mentally count to four. Then hold your breath for a count of seven. Now slowly and deeply exhale through your mouth to a count of eight, once again clearing all of the air out of your lungs in a big *WHOOSH*. Then repeat the process at least five times.

Weil also recommends using your breath as a form of meditation, which can be a great way to get into it when you are just starting. Simply sit down in a comfortable position with your head forward and eyes closed and begin to put your attention on your breath. Observe your breath, but don't try to influence or control the depth or speed of your breathing. Just be aware. After a minute or two, begin to count your exhales until you reach five, then start over. If you find that you have kept counting past five, you will know that your mind has wandered. Don't get frustrated, just steer your attention back to your breath and start again.

The Bellows Breath

The above exercises are all great ways to help you calm down and ease any stress you might be feeling, but what if what you really need is to recharge? Weil has an exercise for that too. He calls it the Bellows Breath.

Keeping your mouth closed but relaxed, start breathing quickly in and out through your nose. These aren't quiet breaths; you actually want to make noise as you try to fit three in-and-out cycles in one second! Picture your diaphragm working the way a bellows would to get a fire started—that fire is your energy!

In Chapter 11, "Quantum Sex," I will go over a number of other breathing exercises that will move your energy (and your sexual pleasure) through your entire body, so stay tuned for that!

Move Your Body

I cannot stress enough how powerful moving your body can be in keeping low-frequency emotions from getting stored for too long. As we have learned, your body is a vehicle for energy. When you take care of your body, energy can move through it more successfully. A healthy body is more energetically healthy as well, which can mean a boosted immune system, less illness, and even a slowdown (or reversal) of the degenerative aging process!

Yoga, as I mentioned earlier, will often help you get energy moving effectively and efficiently in your body. Along with myriad other benefits, it is a great way to reduce inflammation, which is becoming a key point of focus for cancer research and other immune-related diseases. I started doing yoga years ago. I was attracted to the benefits I kept reading about: flexibility, focus, and a quieting of the mind. As I started practicing yoga, I loved it immediately, recognizing an array of physical, mental, and even sexual benefits.

It wasn't long before I was recommending it to my patients, for two reasons. First, it's excellent for strengthening your pelvic floor and sexual response! It's a phenomenal way to keep connected to your body and to maintain the energy flow through it, which will become particularly important for Quantum Sex.

Second, with most forms of exercise, from running to tennis, you are constantly thinking about other things while you do them. Whether you're having an actual conversation with a running buddy or playing one out in your head, thinking about your technique or distracted in your backswing, your mind (and often your mouth) is not quiet. In yoga, it's hard to think about anything beyond your breath and where your hands and feet are. Your mind goes quiet, as you are fully present in your body.

Yoga also does wonders for helping us manage our stress levels, which is a key component of managing our body's response to stress and keeping those stress chemicals at bay. When we relax into an easy pose like Child's Pose, we are essentially telling our brain that it's okay to relax too. This pulls back on the forward thrust of the immune response system, and inflammation can diminish.

Yoga is good for our organs, too. As we twist and bend into different positions, we actually massage and stimulate our organs and increase circulation to them, which can flush out any blockages and increase oxygen flow.[2] I believe that I learned the hard way about what happens if we hold our low-frequency energy within our bodies for too long. Yoga is also an astonishingly effective way of increasing our body awareness, accessing our feelings, and tapping into our body's wisdom.

Breathing and yoga are great ways of keeping our energy moving, but it is also very important that we do what we can to keep our body a clean, open vessel for our energy. This makes it harder for the energy of our thoughts and emotions to get stuck. And the health of the body has a lot to do with what we feed it.

Feed Your Body

When I say the word *nutrition,* where does your mind go? Does it go directly to dieting and counting calories? Do you immediately start to think, "Oh, that's something I need to do better"? Or do you think of nutrition as a means of supporting and loving your body? Do you see it as showing yourself the care that you deserve? Your outlook on nutrition is shaping the reality of your body's health and well-being, and negative thoughts and low-frequency beliefs about what you eat can actually harm you.

All of this is unfortunately quite normal for our society. We live in a world that puts an emphasis on physical perfection, and we put our bodies through hoops every day as we try to fix-manage-control them to fit into that impossible mold. I used to be on that very same treadmill, and I believed that my choices were going to earn me not only a fit body but also a healthy, long life.

Of course, I found out that my body had different ideas. And as I learned more about nutrition and diet, I also discovered that some of my previous "healthy eating" choices actually were not so healthy after all—at least as far as my quantum energy went. Whereas I had previously done my best to maintain a lower-carb, high-protein diet, I soon found out that many of my staples (meat, eggs, cheese, etc.) actually took quite an energetic toll on the body. Digesting these foods meant ingesting the hormones, antibiotics, and other unnatural and harmful ingredients that are pumped into nonorganic or corn-fed meat and dairy products. I also learned that different foods require different energy to digest. For example, a meat-heavy diet requires plenty of effort and energy from the liver, as meat is high in uric acid that must be broken down as it is digested. This means that the liver has less available energy to process other toxins that are being put into the body via polluted air, chemicals in our beauty and grooming products, chemicals in our dishware, and so on.

That's not all. A diet that is heavy in meat and dairy has actually been linked to an increased likelihood of cancer. The China Study, a project led by researchers at Oxford University and Cornell University and funded by the National Institutes of Health and the American Cancer Society, found a strong relationship between a person's diet and their likelihood of developing cancer.[3] The research, which ran for 30 years and is considered one of the premier studies on cancer causation of our time, found that animal-based diets (including both meat and dairy) were linked to a higher incidence of breast cancer, while plant-based diets were linked to a lower incidence of breast cancer and a lower incidence of cancer in the digestive tract.

As a woman battling breast cancer at the time, learning this information was shocking and eye-opening. I had always known that fruits and vegetables were good for you and that a lower-fat, lower-calorie diet was the key to staying trim, but my diet still featured things like yogurt, egg-white omelets, chicken breast, and dairy-based smoothies. I was surprised to realize that many of my favorite "healthy" foods might actually be difficult for my body to break down and might even lead to cancer down the line.

We can't control our genetic predisposition to cancer, but there is growing evidence that we actually might play some role in whether or not those genes turn on and whether we get cancer again if we've already had it. Regardless of your genetic disposition, cancer cells are born every day in everyone's body. There is growing evidence supporting the idea that reducing inflammation in your cells and supporting your immune system help not only in fighting cancer but in preventing it. The cleaner you keep your body running, the stronger the flow of energy through your body can be.

Let's examine some of the keys to keeping the energy vessel that is your body strong and clear and optimized for Quantum Love. Please be sure to talk to your doctor before making any dietary or supplement changes.

Support the Liver

When the liver is stressed out with the toxic workload we've handed it, or just under stress processing the kind of food and drink that requires a lot of energy, it gets tired and inflammation occurs in the tissue. As I've mentioned, inflammation is now believed to put us at risk for cancer as well as a number of degenerative diseases. The key is to focus on foods that support liver function, such as those I'll list below. The information I am sharing with you here comes primarily from two amazing books I highly recommend: *Crazy Sexy Cancer Tips*, by cancer survivor and activist Kris Carr, and *The Beauty Detox Solution*, by nutritionist Kimberly Snyder.

Get enough vitamin B

B vitamins are liver friendly, especially B-12, which significantly reduces jaundice, serum bilirubin, and recovery from illness.

Eat lots of veggies and greens

The fiber and abundant nutrients in vegetables are great for the liver. Vegetables are essentially fat free. And they are rich in the B vitamin folic acid.

Eat less fat

Your liver normally makes 250 to 1,000 milliliters (over a quart!) of bile *daily*. Bile is a critical part of the digestive process and key to the absorption of fats and fat-soluble vitamins in the small intestines, but too much bile (often a result of eating too much fat) can cause inflammation in the cells. Most (about 80 percent) of your bile salts are reabsorbed by the intestinal tract and returned to and recycled by the liver. This is how your body, with about 3.6 grams of total bile salts in it, can secrete 4 to 8 grams of bile salts per single fatty meal. Saturated and trans fats are especially difficult for the liver to process and can cause liver damage over time, even resulting in nonalcoholic fatty liver disease, which is much more common than you would expect, affecting 25 percent of the population.

Avoid dairy

Dairy is also very difficult for the liver to process and contains some unhealthy fats. It's better to get calcium from coconut milk (which is evidently also really good for pH), almond milk, or hemp milk, as well as all the leafy greens you are eating for the reasons given above.

Stay away from sugar

Turns out cancer cells have nine times as many glucose receptors as other cells have! It's better to use stevia or agave nectar as a sweetener. Mark Hyman, the director of the UltraWellness Center and author of *The Daniel Plan* and *10-Day Detox Diet*, has a great outlook on sugar. He says that it isn't evil; we just have to treat it like a recreational drug. In other words, it's not the end of the world if you have it every now and then, but you have to be careful with it. You can make a conscious choice to eat sugar, but do so with an understanding that it's really not the best thing for your body.

Work Your Nutrition into Your Daily Routine

I have found that it is easiest for me to incorporate good nutritional support in my life if I work it into my daily routine. For example, I like to start every morning with what my kids call "Mom's Green Gloop." It's a green smoothie that includes veggies, fruit, and even fresh herbs to give my system a kick start at the beginning of my day.

Here's my favorite green smoothie recipe (from Kimberly Snyder's book *The Beauty Detox Solution*). Use organic produce and filtered water if possible! Organic is best with everything you eat and drink, if you can manage it. If cost is a concern, check out your local farmer's market or keep an eye on coupons.

Kimberly Snyder's Glowing Green Smoothie

Ingredients

1½ cups water
1 head romaine lettuce, chopped
½ large bunch of spinach
1 apple, cored and chopped
3–4 stalks celery
1 pear, cored and chopped
1 banana
Juice of ½ lemon
Optional: Any fresh herbs you like—cilantro, parsley, mint, basil, and so on—as well as spirulina, chlorella, and aloe juice, if you want!

Put the water, lettuce, and spinach in the blender and mix until smooth. Add the apple, celery, and pear. Add the fresh herbs if you are using them. Add the banana and lemon juice last.

Make it your goal to have a green smoothie every day. Not only is it delicious (yes, trust me, it really is good!), but it will make you feel awesome, energized, and satisfied. It can also help improve your skin and appearance (Snyder doesn't call it the Glowing Green Smoothie for nothing). While the digestive enzymes in the drink are most active right away, nutritionists generally agree that most of the benefits remain for a couple of days if you want to store it in (ideally) a glass container in the refrigerator. Or if you are really short on time, like me, you can make a big batch at the start of each week and store it in smaller glass containers in the freezer, then just thaw one out in the fridge overnight. Soon you will find that you start craving your smoothie—no, really! When you're feeling hungry and tired, your mind will think *smoothie* instead of *candy bar,* and when that happens, you'll know you're on the right track!

For more ideas on nutrition and supplements to support Quantum Love, go to www.drlauraberman.com/quantumlove.

Just Say No to Simple Carbs

In my journey to learn more about nutrition, I also confirmed what I had long believed about carbohydrates. As a mother, I saw firsthand how a carb-heavy diet affected my kids, especially when it involved a lot of simple carbs like sugars, fruit juice, and white bread (as compared to complex carbohydrates like whole grains and starchy vegetables, which are often rich in fiber and are processed in the body very differently). We tend to think of sugar as the big no-no when it comes to children (it gives them a big spike of energy and then a huge dip), but what many people don't realize is that simple carbs are actually chock-full of sugar. In fact, a plate of mashed potatoes or a big bowl of fettuccine Alfredo can have just as much sugar as a can of soda or a slice of cake!

Not only do carbs give us a sugar hit, they mess with our insulin and serotonin levels. After we eat a pastry, for example, our body releases insulin to mop up all the sugar we just ate and send it out of our bloodstream and into our cells. Once the insulin has done its job, we experience a drop in our blood sugar (and all the nasty, irritable feelings that come with that). Insulin doesn't just take care of sugar, though; at really high levels it also clears out all but one amino acid: tryptophan (the chemical that makes you sleepy after too much Thanksgiving turkey). And if a lot of tryptophan is present, your body will make a lot of serotonin. Now, serotonin might be a "feel-good" chemical, but in large doses it's actually not so fun. Too much serotonin can make you nervous, tense, or wired and can make it hard to control your appetite.[4] However, most of us tend to crave carb-laden comfort foods after a bad day. So we reach for pizza, pasta, and other fare when we feel bad, but shortly after eating it we feel worse than before.

The truth is that while "feel-good" foods make us happy in the moment, they come with a big cost: weight gain, decreased mood, and overall fatigue. Over time, they can even impact your libido and your sexual performance!

Start the Day Right

How do you start each day? If you're like most people, it's by hitting the snooze button a few times and then groggily making your way to the kitchen for a big mug of hot coffee. Sounds awesome, right? There is nothing wrong with coffee in moderation (and some studies have found positive associations between reduced liver cancer and coffee intake); however, you shouldn't rely on a pot of coffee to keep you upright and energized throughout the day. When that happens, your coffee goes from being a pleasure to being a crutch, and that's never good. If you're a real caffeine junkie, it probably also makes it hard for you to sleep at night (not to mention, all those Starbucks runs are probably hard on your wallet!).

Instead of going through your morning routine like a grouchy automaton who needs an IV drip of black coffee, why not bring intention and awareness to how you start your morning? This will set the tone for your mood and energy for the rest of the day.

Personally, even before drinking my smoothie, I like to start my morning with a glass of warm lemon water. Lemons have many health benefits and have been highly valued for these properties for thousands of years. Lemon juice may be acidic, but most nutritionists agree it has an alkaline effect on the body. Ironically, this means your morning lemon water helps to remove acidity from your body and flush uric acid out. In doing so, it helps aid digestion, balances your pH system, boosts your immune system, hydrates your lymph system, and acts as a natural diuretic (which in turn helps to clean your body of toxins and waste).[5] It helps keep your skin clear and your breath fresh too! It can also aid weight loss, if that is one of your goals. It's best to use organic lemons and filtered water (think one-half of a lemon per glass of water). Opt for warm, not scalding hot, water, and don't use cold water, as this takes a lot of energy for your body to digest.

Think of your lemon water time as an opportunity for you to bring awareness and intention to your body. Carve out just ten minutes (or even five) to sit quietly, sip, and breathe. Practice one of the breathing exercises on pages 188–192 and set your intention for the day. It might be "Today I want to be productive and focused" or "Today I want to be kind to myself" or "Today I want to make time to go to the gym after work." By setting your intention this way, it's almost as though you are making a promise to yourself, a promise that you will likely remember and honor throughout the day, even as you get busy. If you have a bit more time, you might want to use it to journal or to read a book that is meaningful to your healing journey.

As a side note, if you want to enjoy coffee still, you can. In fact, you should never restrict yourself from enjoying life's little pleasures, as long as you can enjoy them in a way that is not harmful to your mind or body. But if you really want to make the most of these pleasures, make sure that you do so in a *mindful* way. Don't just chug down your coffee in the morning (or your glass of wine in the evening) without thinking about it. Slow down and actually enjoy what you are doing. Smell the aroma. Notice how the mug is warm and solid in your hands. Notice how creamy your almond milk is in the dark liquid. Notice how you are drinking out of your favorite cup, the cup your kids made you for Mother's Day. Bring true awareness and gratitude to the moment. Yes, it might be a busy Monday morning and you might have a million things on your to-do list, but you have the opportunity right now to treat this moment (and your body) with care, with gratitude, and with consciousness. Doing so will not only make your coffee taste better than it ever has before, it might also help you move from ego frequency into home frequency.

Prioritizing nutrition is a way of showing care and support for the body that cares for and supports us. It is an act of love for ourselves. It sends the message that we are worthy of such attention and care. And if we think about this as a function of Quantum Love, the implications only get bigger from there.

Remember, loving and caring for yourself from a place of wholeness is the very foundation of Quantum Love. *It starts with you.* All too often we fall into the trap of judging our bodies from ego frequency. Instead of looking at our bodies as the powerhouses they are, we focus on what we consider our flaws: a roll in our stomach, a pocket of fat on our thigh, or an extra wiggle on our arms. We judge our birthmarks or acne or wrinkles as blemishes. We bring our own energy down as we feel everything *but* love for our bodies.

I think it's very important, first and foremost, to understand that our bodies *and our perspective on our bodies* move in the same natural ebb and flow pattern that our energy does. There are times of contraction and times of expansion, but it is never static. Home frequency is maintained by keeping a perspective on the ebb and flow of our bodies that is understanding, compassionate, and even grateful for these fluctuations in order to create a more positive reality and be in Quantum Love.

Love Your Body

Poet and womanist Audre Lorde once described self-care as a daring and transgressive act for a woman in today's society, and I believe there is great truth in that. Most of us rarely take time to care for ourselves, and when we do, we often feel guilty or think we have to justify our choices to other people. However, I believe great spiritual change can occur in our lives when we celebrate and attend to our own personal needs. Are you cringing right now? You might be thinking, *That sounds so selfish*. But I have to ask, what's wrong with caring for the self? What's wrong with being good to your body, even tender and indulgent at times? What is wrong with thanking your body for its strength and service and showing yourself gratitude through a yoga class, a restorative nap, or even self-stimulation? Yes, I said it! Masturbation can be an act of self-care. Anything that helps you to breathe deeper, move slower, and bask in simple pleasure is self-care in my book.

So let me ask you: what messages do you send yourself and your body in the way you take care of it? Most of us criticize or talk down to our bodies 10, 20, even 50 times a day without even realizing it. These thoughts can be so ingrained that we no longer notice when we're thinking them. So it can be extremely powerful to notice and keep track of your negative thoughts. Even if it's just for an afternoon, set an intention to really notice what you are telling yourself (especially the thoughts you have about your body). Record them in a journal or even as a note on your phone. The thoughts you see when you look back at the end of the day might surprise you in both how numerous they are and how downright *mean* they are! The things that you say to yourself are likely things that you would never say to anyone else.

Such was the case with Alexa, a good friend of mine. Alexa is the ideal specimen of American beauty: thin, large-breasted, with long, soft, honey-blond hair and deep blue eyes. However, ever since I'd met Alexa years before, all I heard about were her flaws. She would enter a room apologizing for her appearance, saying, "Oh, Laura, I'm sorry I look a mess! I just came from the gym" or "Sorry you have to see me popping out of these pants. I had too many cookies over Christmas!" Sometimes I wanted to shake her and say, "Alexa, you're beautiful! Shut up and pass the salt!" But of course I knew nothing I said would make her feel better. Her discomfort came from deep within, from a hard childhood with a pageant mother who was always focused on Alexa's looks rather than her sparkly wit and her big heart.

Then an amazing change happened in Alexa. It all started when she got pregnant. She found out she was having a daughter, whom she named Constance Anne before she even left the ultrasound visit. After doing some reading, she decided she wanted to have a home birth with a midwife, a doula, and her sweet husband, Robert. However, she was struggling with whether or not to have her mother present at the birth. Fretting to me over a salad, she said, "I don't know what to do. My mom will kill me if I don't invite her, but at the same time, I don't think I can labor in front of her. I know she will make jokes about how I look and little comments about how much weight I gained and my cellulite. What should I do?"

"I think you already answered that question," I said.

Alexa agreed and told her mother she wasn't invited to the home birth. I never really heard how the conversation went, because the next few times I saw Alexa, her energy had completely changed. Instead of fretting about her mother's disappointment or the weight she was gaining, she was full of positive energy and hopeful plans for the future.

"My midwife gave me this book of birth affirmations to read," she said. "They are all about how strong and powerful my body is. It's so strange. I have never thought of my body in terms of what it can do. I've only thought of it in terms of how it looks."

I nodded in sympathy. "I think that's true for a lot of women. So this book is helping you to change your story about yourself?"

She nodded and smiled. "You know, I let Robert see me without makeup for the first time in years. I told him, 'You are going to see me at my worst during my labor, so you might as well get used to it.' And do you know what he said?"

I shook my head.

"He said, 'Lex, are you crazy? I am going to be seeing you push our daughter into the world. I am going to be seeing you at your *best*,'" said Alexa in an awed tone.

That was the last time I saw Alexa before she went into labor. She had a marathon session of 40 hours of contractions before Constance came into the world. A few weeks later, I received a beautiful picture of mother and daughter via e-mail and this touching note: *Laura, here is my baby girl. She's beautiful, isn't she? But that is just the tip of the iceberg. She is also fierce and strong and powerful, just like her mama. I can't wait to teach her how to walk and run and swim and play. I want her to be amazed and in awe of all the things her body can do, just like I am learning to be. I want her to count stars, not calories. XO Lex*

I was so amazed and proud of how my friend had changed, at how she took back control of her body image and changed her story, not just for herself but for Constance as well. The reality is that most women are not so lucky. Most of us are like Alexa before her pregnancy, always fretting over every calorie and being ashamed of our outer appearance. When you're constantly feeding yourself these kinds of messages and thoughts, you are bringing your frequency way down. Our body image stories are no different from our thorny stories in terms of their capacity to affect our energetic state and the reality that we create for ourselves. Remember, when you're vibrating at a low frequency because of these stories you tell yourself, you're attracting more of the things that will reinforce those beliefs in your life, your awareness, and your relationship.

When you are filled with negative beliefs about your body, it gets in the way of everything: how you carry yourself, how self-conscious you are, how confident you feel getting naked in front of a partner. The way you feel about your body in front of your mate is a classic instance of creating your own reality in the logistical field through your thoughts and feelings. You feel self-conscious, so you avoid getting naked, maybe avoid sex altogether. You deflect your partner's advances because you don't feel good about yourself, but his first thought isn't going to be *Oh, she must be feeling bad about her body.* He is going to be thinking, *Why was I just rejected? I guess I won't try that move again.* Then, when he stops propositioning you, you imagine, *What I believe about myself must be true. He isn't attracted to me.* To change your relationship reality, especially when it comes to the physical and sexual side of your relationship, you have to change your perspective on your body.

The truth is, ladies, if you are naked with a man, he is *not* noticing your cellulite or any other flaws, unless you are incessantly pointing them out to him. If you want to see what he sees, stand naked in front of the mirror and just soften your vision so it becomes a little blurry. Your partner is seeing the whole silhouette. He's seeing breasts and behind and curves; he's not looking at whether your arms jiggle. What really turns your partner on is not how perfectly firm your behind is, it's how totally comfortable you are in your body.

Soul Gazing with Yourself

Not long ago I was at a women's retreat where my soul sister and life coach, Susan Hyman, was the facilitator. She put us into pairs and instructed us to simply stare into our partner's eyes . . . for three minutes. The only person I've ever done this with is my husband, so it felt extremely intimate and awkward for the first ten seconds. But my partner and I persisted, with a few little smirks and snorts. Then after about a minute, things started to change. I couldn't really see my partner's face anymore, but her irises appeared endless. While everything else became blurry, the sense of oneness and connection was very clear. Everyone could feel it.

When the three minutes were up, Susan asked us to volunteer any images, words, or ideas that had come to our minds as we stared into each other's eyes. The amazing thing is that every single one of us "got" some sort of image or idea during the exercise, and each one turned out to have tremendous meaning to the individual it described. We weren't a group of women who did this kind of thing in day-to-day life. But the images that came to our minds were metaphorically perfect and absolutely beautiful, whether it was a glow of beautiful pink love-mama energy that described a group member who was quietly struggling with maternal guilt over her busy work schedule, or a beautiful gray wall covered in lichen and moss with the ocean smashing against it, describing a woman who was ambivalent about letting a new love interest into her heart.

How often do you stare into anyone's eyes, even your partner's? When you stare into your lover's eyes, the intensity magnifies by 100. You have a bond that you don't have with your friends. It's very powerful. Soul gazing is one of my favorite things to teach people to do, especially couples seeking Quantum Love. I'll explain more about how it works in Chapter 11, "Quantum Sex." It's a powerful energy exchange and extremely intimate. But for now, I want to focus on what happens when you soul gaze with yourself! Have you ever done it? I have no doubt you've looked at yourself in the mirror a lot, and rarely with love in your eyes. When was the last time you stood in front of the mirror and looked deeply into the eyes of the one you love: *you?*

When I had my first mammogram after my cancer treatment, I was not fully aware of how scared I was. I went by myself, thinking it would be no big deal. The radiologist looked at the film and said, "Everything looks great." It was all very matter-of-fact. I went back into the dressing room to change. As I was buttoning my shirt, I looked up and saw my reflection in the mirror. I stopped and just stared into my own eyes. Without thinking or meaning to, I said out loud, "You're *okay.*" It felt like my essential self was talking to me. All of a sudden the floodgates opened. I felt overwhelmed with love, compassion, and appreciation for my body and filled with gratitude that I was well again. I was so proud of myself. And in that moment of fullness, as I looked into the mirror, I saw my mother's eyes reflected there. It was a powerful moment of connection and a beautiful reminder that she is me and I am her. Give it a try.

When we think about our bodies and everything they are capable of, it is so important to view ourselves through a lens of love, compassion, and gratitude. Our bodies are the vehicles in which we are traveling through this universe, the way we show and receive love, the way we bring the energy of our thoughts and beliefs into physical reality. Your body is a brilliant, perfect vessel that can do almost anything you ask it to do. You are whole and you are enough, exactly as you are in this moment.

We imagine (and I'm guilty of this too) that criticism is a motivator. It's not. It will show you what you're lacking and keep you in that low-frequency place of lack. Choose to see your body from a higher-frequency point of view. Compassion for your body will help you see it as the perfect vehicle that it is. Gratitude will reveal what an awesome machine it is (seriously, your circulatory system is a miracle of design in and of itself). Admire your body with a wide lens the way your partner does, and don't be afraid to use it playfully. Care for your body by giving it the nutritional and physical support it needs to run smoothly. Trust in its wisdom so it can direct you toward what you need. All of these are high-frequency states that will move your relationship with your body into a place of Quantum Love.

CHAPTER 9

Retrain Your Brain So Your Mind Can Work

If you want to find the secrets of the universe, think in terms of energy, frequency, and vibration.

Nikola Tesla

Our bodies have a powerful energy that can impact our physical state and even our emotional states through the mind-body connection. That connection works both ways, of course, and as powerful as our body is, our brain is still a big part of running the show. Our brains are made up of complex neural networks that are constantly firing in the electrical pulses of our different states of consciousness. Like the body, the brain never stops as it keeps the energy of our thoughts, beliefs, and stories flowing and moving. It is the realm of our highest consciousness and the home of our ego and our most frantic state of FMC.

The brain does so much for us, and we rely on it so heavily in everything we do, that it can be hard to remember that our brain does not control us. Our habits and emotional patterns are not set in stone. In fact, as we will discuss in this chapter, the brain is highly malleable because of what is known as neuroplasticity. It is constantly changing, and we have the ability to shape it to our (and our relationship's) benefit through the power of our own consciousness. In retraining your brain and changing your patterns, you are also changing your perception; and through changing your perception you change your energetic frequency and your reality, manifesting the Quantum Love reality you desire.

What Is the Brain? What Is the Mind?

Many people use the terms *mind* and *brain* interchangeably. However, scientists and medical professionals have long understood that the two are actually separate. So what makes them different?

Think of the brain as a physical part of your body, much like your arm, your stomach, or your toenails. The brain is the powerhouse for every process that occurs in your body, including digestion, thought, and even sexual pleasure. Your mind isn't a physical entity; it certainly can't be dissected in a laboratory. Your mind is a transcendent, limitless, unknowable powerhouse of energy. Your mind is your consciousness.

In other words, your brain is *how you think*. Your mind is *who is thinking.*

Let's do a quick exercise: Take a piece of paper (or go to your Quantum Love Journal) and write down ten words to describe yourself. What are some of the words you chose? Maybe you wrote about your personality using words such as *shy* or *outgoing* or *brave* or *sensitive.* Or maybe you wrote about professional achievements or your relationships, such as *doctor* or *husband* or *mother.* These descriptors of who you are, and what you are or are not capable of, are the voice of your mind, not your brain. Your mind is where your essential self lives.

Your brain is hard at work every day keeping all of your bodily systems on track, and it is always looking for shortcuts and ways to simplify, conserve energy, and save time. These shortcuts are our habits. However, while our brain's shortcuts might save us time, they also can cause us to become stuck in repetitive and unhealthy thinking patterns. Your brain is where that crazy roommate, your ego, likes to hang out. In addition to all the glorious purposes your brain serves, it is also where your ego's limiting, self-criticizing, and low-frequency thoughts are born.

Both your brain and your mind are speaking to you constantly, and it can be difficult sometimes to determine who is who. If you can become more aware of the character of each, you can determine whether you are listening to your ego or your essential self.

What the Brain Might Think	What the Mind Would Think
I look so fat in these jeans. I have to lose weight!	I am perfect the way I am and doing the best I can. Loving myself is the only path to looking and feeling better.
I am not initiating sex with my partner because it makes me feel awkward. I'm just not a sexy person.	I am creating my reality with my stories, thoughts, and feelings, and I can create any reality I want.
If my son doesn't start getting better grades, I will send him to military school. We don't screw up in this family.	I am not responsible for how others behave and each of us is on our own journey. I can only be a guide and inspiration.
Men are jerks. All the good ones are taken.	If I want to find love, I must remember my thoughts are powerful and play a huge role in creating my reality.
I can't believe she dumped me! Am I never going to find love?	That which is right is unfolding. I only want to be with women who see and appreciate my gifts. The right one will come.
I can't stand up for myself. I just don't have the backbone.	I don't have to believe the stories I've been told about who I am. I will imagine all the ways I am brave every day and focus on those.
My mom is so selfish. I wish I had better parents.	I am loved for no reason other than that I exist. My self-worth is not dependent on the views of others, not even my family.
I am not going to speak to my husband the rest of the night. He is going to regret screwing up again.	Each of us has 100 percent responsibility for the easy and the hard dynamics in our relationship. I wonder how I helped create this problem?
I am in a horrible mood and being such a bitch, but I can't seem to stop myself.	I am feeling anxious and just need to sit quietly for a minute and find out why.

Are you starting to get the idea? Our brain/ego is always trying to tell us who we are. It's telling us stories every minute, every day. It's trying to be helpful. It wants to keep us safe. It wants to keep us from being hurt. It's always reminding us of things that have gone wrong in the past, such as: *Remember in grade school when those girls picked on you? You aren't good at making friends, and people can't be trusted.* Or: *Remember how scared you feel when you think about heights? Better stay on the ground so you won't have to face that pain.* Or: *It really aches when you feel like your husband doesn't find you sexually attractive. You can show him. Next time he initiates sex, shut him down and see how he likes it.*

The mind is able to look at life with a more comprehensive and clear eye. It can see the brain at work and it can be interested in the brain's messages, but it is also removed. The mind says, *Aha, I see that my brain is giving me a lot of messages of fear and self-doubt right now. Where is this fear coming from? Is there wisdom in this fear? Or can I live with this fear while still taking risks?*

Moving forward on the Quantum Love journey, it is key to remember that you are not your brain or the thoughts your brain creates. Your brain is a big part of you, but it isn't your whole self, any more than your arm is or your toenails are. When you realize that, you realize you don't have to believe everything your brain may be telling you, especially about yourself and your partner.

Our Beliefs and Our Reality

One thing I know for sure is that for almost all of us, our beliefs about who we are in love are simply *not true*. Most of us are stuck with limiting To Me stories that get in the way of the truth that anything and everything is possible in our relationship when we are in Quantum Love. Our limiting beliefs about who we are and what we are capable of in the realm of love all come from the stories we have chosen to tell ourselves (mostly unconsciously) about how deserving we are of fulfilling, deep, passionate love.

The most common Quantum Love–limiting beliefs I come across include these:

- I'll never find real love.
- This (abusive, unavailable, untrustworthy, etc.) behavior is just how men (or women) are.
- As soon as I let down my defenses I'll get hurt.
- Love can't feel this good. The other shoe is going to eventually drop.
- All men (or women) leave.
- All men (or women) cheat.
- Women (or men) don't really want a nice guy (or girl).
- All the good ones are taken.
- I'll lose my power if I give in (to love, to this moment, to this argument, etc.).
- I'm just not good at being vulnerable.
- Love never lasts.

My guess is that you relate to several of the beliefs on this list, and you could probably add a few others as well. But these beliefs didn't appear out of thin air. Where do your beliefs come from? I don't mean your religious beliefs or your personal opinions (such as "I hate the color pink" or "Winter is depressing"), but your beliefs about who you are. Where did *those* beliefs come from?

Let's go back to the exercise I asked you to do earlier in the chapter, listing ten words that describe you. I guarantee you there were at least a few less-than-flattering adjectives there. Choose one or two of them and trace them back to where that message took hold in your experience. When was the first time in your life you identified as shy or lazy? When did you start to believe that nice girls aren't too assertive or that men leave? More often than not, the answer is in your childhood.

In fact, if it is a truly deeply held belief, you probably can't even remember the first time you identified in this manner. It's probably been a part of your self-perception and a facet of your role in your family system since before you were able to form lasting memories. But all of these beliefs grew out of messages you received and experiences you had in the past. They create a wealth of low-frequency thoughts and feelings that stand in the way of Quantum Love.

Typically I can trace someone's worthiness-killing stories by looking at the points of conflict in their relationship. Every couple has touchy areas in their relationship, things that drive them crazy or make them angry or launch them into a fight. As we discussed in Chapter 5, your partner is your greatest teacher and your most powerful spiritual mirror. There is so much to be learned, not only from your partner's experience and knowledge (and the experience and knowledge you pick up together) but also in the lessons he or she can teach you about yourself, especially in conflict. When you get into conflict with your partner, it is the equivalent of holding a blinking arrow that says, *Thorn here!* After counseling as many couples as I have, I believe we unconsciously choose our mates in large part because our essential self knows they will uncover and touch our thorns. And our essential self wants very much to let those thorns go.

So how do we get to the bottom of a Quantum Love–limiting belief? As an individual (or couple) I am working with tells me about a recent conflict or miscommunication, I first help him or her (or them) get clear on the specific feelings that were triggered during the incident. Then we consider the story behind the feelings, which is always a low-calibrating To Me story, often some version of one of those I listed earlier.

Abe and Joaquim came to see me because they felt like there was a huge valley between them. Kids and life had gotten in the way, and they found themselves feeling resentful toward and disconnected from each other. They came into my office and reported on a fight they'd had over the weekend. Joaquim had felt furious and sad that when they finally had an hour together,

Abe went right for the remote and turned on the television. Abe didn't really understand the depth and breadth of Joaquim's fury; he simply thought his partner was looking for something to criticize, as usual.

I call this the incident story. It's what the couple *think* they are fighting about (in this case, "I'm angry because he chose to watch television rather than hanging out with me"). But there's a greater worthiness-killing story behind it. I had learned during one of our prior sessions that Joaquim's father and mother really hadn't been there for him and hadn't shown up in the ways he deserved as a child. He was usually left with a nanny and later to his own devices while they traveled and worked outside the home. He took on the good-boy role, making great grades, not getting into trouble, taking on lots of responsibilities, all with the hope that he would get his parents' attention and win their love. The worthiness-killing belief underneath had always been (and still was) that if he had been good enough, smart enough, *worthy enough*, his parents would have been there. So as an adult he created a reality in which he had a mate who would tune him out, neither showing up nor sharing his desire to create time and space for connecting. When Abe decided to turn on the TV rather than connect with him, it touched the thorn of the emotional abandonment he experienced in childhood.

I helped Joaquim learn to ground himself and open his heart using the exercise I taught you on page 56. While he was in a state of coherence, I asked him some key questions about what he wanted from Abe and what lessons he was here to learn. It became clear that Joaquim's essential self was attracted to Abe because he wanted to feel worthy of love just for being himself. He wanted to learn to be complete in and of himself, without needing to have his worth reflected back to him by Abe or anyone else. His essential self sought to live in love for no reason.

As I uncovered Joaquim's worthiness-killing story and connected it to the thorn Abe had unwittingly touched, I anticipated that we'd discover one of three things:

1. A Quick Shift: When Abe learns of the thorn that has been touched and the worthiness-killing story behind it, he will feel deep compassion for Joaquim, and instead of feeling defensive and frustrated, he will seek to tune in to him more.
2. A Symptom of a Larger Problem: As we talk through the feelings and thoughts that led up to the incident, it will become clear that Abe's emotional withdrawal from Joaquim has been a result of their sexual connection being out of whack.
3. Mutual Thorns: It may turn out that this is an area where Joaquim and Abe's thorns complement each other, and thus they have discovered a wonderful area of mutual growth.

As often happens, Abe and Joaquim ended up with Option 3. It wasn't that they didn't need to reconnect sexually—they did. And Abe could certainly feel compassion for Joaquim, now recognizing that it wasn't so much about him as it was about the way Joaquim's parents had behaved when he was a child. But the biggest "aha" moment came when Abe and Joaquim recognized that they were touching each other's thorns in beautifully complementary ways.

Abe was raised in a family in which he never learned how to deal with stress effectively. They never talked about feelings, and there was no room for pain, sadness, fear, or anger. His parents were peaceful roommates, living separate lives. They didn't set a great standard for what a loving, intimate relationship looks like between two people who relish stolen moments they get to spend alone together. As a result, Abe learned to squelch his feelings and stoically move through life's challenges on his own. The worthiness-killing belief he developed was that he was lovable only if he had it all together and "stayed strong." To Abe, love was conditional, and it was not safe to let down his guard and really *feel*. In fact, it seemed like an insurmountable challenge to do so.

Yet a big part of the attraction for Abe in the beginning of their relationship was Joaquim's engagement with and interest in Abe's thoughts and feelings. Abe relished the fact that Joaquim was so invested in deep connection. His essential self recognized how much he wanted that kind of relationship even if he didn't know how to get there himself. As Abe grounded and opened his heart and moved into coherence, where the wisdom of the essential self can be heard, he asked himself key questions with Joaquim's and my guidance.

It became clear that Abe's essential self wanted to learn how to be fully present in life while still dealing with the inevitable stressors that show up. He had been under tremendous pressure at work. But as he'd never learned how to cope with stress, his only mechanism was losing himself in sex (which Joaquim had withdrawn from due to building resentments and anger) or distracting himself with television or video games. Joaquim was calling on him to get better at emotions so Abe could be more present with him, and Joaquim was a great teacher for Abe to learn how to experience and express deep emotional connection. If Abe's parents couldn't model it, Joaquim certainly could.

As soon as they realized this thorny connection and the worthiness-killing beliefs underneath, they were on their way to Quantum Love. In the next chapter I will lay out a process you can use to uncover your own worthiness-killing beliefs, identify the thorns that you've developed as a result, and move from the To Me into the By Me and Through Me zones, ever closer to Quantum Love.

What Quantum Physics Tells Us about Beliefs

Many beliefs are conscious, such as "I believe love conquers all" or "I believe that people are intrinsically good." Other beliefs are subconscious. They come from the messages we got growing up about love, both the ones we were given directly and the ones we read between the lines. These beliefs have tremendous power in manifesting the reality we are creating for ourselves.

Here's how it works: Your beliefs about who you are, what you are capable of, what kind of love you deserve or don't deserve, what is possible for you and what isn't, all lead to your expectations. Your expectations are the reality you expect to experience and the thoughts you have about it. Those expectations and thoughts create emotion in you, which may range from hopelessness and despair to joy and elation (refer to the Quantum Lovemap for a complete list). These emotions are the energy that creates your reality.

As we discussed in Chapter 2, quantum physics has taught us that we each create our own reality based on our expectations. Our emotions are the energetic vehicle through which this occurs. Obviously, your expectations and emotions are going to impact your experience on a practical level, in the logistical field. In the following pages I will show you that they also impact the neurological processes in your brain, which in turn affect how you see things. But on an energetic level, your expectations and emotions, which arise directly from your beliefs, are fundamental to creating Quantum Love.

So ask yourself: are your beliefs keeping you in home frequency or in ego frequency? If they are keeping you in home frequency, the reality you create is joyful and positive; if in ego frequency, the reality you create is likely more grasping and unpleasant. This is the Law of Attraction at its core, and this profound realization is something that everyone from poets to philosophers to mental health professionals to scientists to Albert Einstein himself has agreed upon.

Teachers of the Law of Attraction and people who practice it will tell you that your beliefs, particularly your unconscious beliefs, are the most important ingredient in manifesting what you want. So you can tell yourself anything you want, but if your beliefs say the opposite, you aren't going to create what you want. You can set intentions for your relationship, but if your beliefs don't match the intentions, you won't raise your frequency to create Quantum Love.

Your Lens Shapes Your Life

One of my favorite exercises to do with a big group I am teaching is to tell everyone that they have 30 seconds to look around the room and identify every brown thing that they see without taking any notes. They madly scan the room, noting every possible object that fits the description. When 30 seconds have passed, I call time. As they sit eagerly waiting for me to ask for their count, I say, "Okay, now tell me every *blue* thing you saw in this room."

It's a great example of the limitations of our five senses and the way our brain sees through the lenses we apply to it. We're only able to sense what we put our attention on. In this exercise I created the lens, the filter, but most of us have a whole collection of unconscious lenses that work the same way.

Your lens directly impacts your reality. That's why, when you are in a negative emotional state, it is as though you're wearing gray-colored glasses and your whole worldview is clouded. For example, if you lose your job and you're panicking about money and what you're going to do next, you might notice the foreclosure sign in a storefront window but you won't see the Help Wanted sign on your favorite café as you walk past. When we are stuck in beliefs that create sadness, anger, or fear, we look for (and invariably find) evidence to validate our worst feelings rather than evidence to validate our highest hopes. When our beliefs lead us to expect a certain kind of reality, then our brains look for evidence to support that. We not only miss all the evidence to the contrary, but we continue to operate in the world and in our relationship in a way that reinforces those ego-frequency beliefs.

If you believe your partner is selfish or doesn't love you, that he or she isn't enough in some way, or that you aren't, you are going to find evidence for that in every action and reaction. If you have a story that the love is gone from your relationship, you will find evidence for that in your (and your partner's) actions and deeds. And if your story is the opposite, then the lens of your consciousness will find all of the good-feeling evidence to support that. Which reality would you rather support?

Let's look at the example of Michelle, a beautiful, accomplished woman whose early experiences created the belief in her that all men cheat. As an adult, she brought that belief into her relationship with her boyfriend, Ian. Creating her reality through the lens of her belief, she had no trouble finding evidence that reinforced her suspicions of him: Ian bought a new suit, he didn't hug her the minute he walked in the door, or he didn't answer his phone in the middle of the afternoon. In reality, Ian bought a new suit for a job interview, didn't hug her because he saw the look on her face and thought she was mad at him and would reject him, and didn't answer his phone because he was in a meeting.

As I mentioned earlier, this isn't all about quantum physics and the energy of your emotions based on your beliefs, thoughts, and expectations. There is also a logistical and practical level on which your beliefs create your reality. All of us base our behavior on our beliefs every single day, even when we don't realize what those beliefs are. For example, if you believe that the world is a dangerous place, you will make decisions that are guided by that fear. You will have a lot of anxiety about interacting with strangers, you will double-check the locks on your door, and you will keep your guard up when meeting new people. This affects your entire reality in a negative way. Your life is limiting; people may be turned off by how restricted your life is and avoid you; you may carry yourself with body language that expresses anxiety and fear and have trouble being seen as open and attractive.

Your beliefs also impact the way you interact with your partner. As in Michelle's case, if you think all men will cheat if given the chance, it will impact your behavior and actually help create the reality you fear. You will be suspicious and insecure, going through his phone and throwing fits if he comes home five minutes late. You can imagine what that does for your connection and intimacy.

Or maybe you have a belief that all women should be nurturing and attentive. Then, when you are sick and your girlfriend seems too busy to take care of you, you might feel doubly hurt. Not only will you be upset that you are sick and being ignored, but your beliefs will tell you that your girlfriend is *supposed* to know what you need and *supposed* to bring you soup and offer TLC. Hence you will feel twice as let down when your sniffles go unattended.

If you really believe that the love is gone (even if you wish it otherwise), unconsciously you are not fully open to feeling the love, and your behavior communicates that. The world then responds in kind. You are closed off to the energy of change and you are shutting down opportunities to give and receive love, without even realizing it.

Fortunately, you can create a new belief system for yourself.

Creating a New Belief System

Your energy affects the energy of those around you and impacts your reality. So when you walk around feeling and (even unconsciously) emanating the energy of a negative belief, that is what you create for yourself and even what you accidentally start to inspire in other people. So it's not enough to try and "force" new beliefs on yourself. You can't wake up and say, "Today I have to feel beautiful" or "Today I have to believe in myself." (Remember: anytime you *have to* be anything, you're in FMC mode!) Changing your conscious beliefs is a fine place to start, but unless you are in home frequency and using the process of thinking-to-being to gradually address and change your subconscious beliefs, the Quantum Love reality you want to create won't manifest.

Of course, beliefs don't change overnight. It can take some time and effort to consciously coax your subconscious to join you in your conscious intentions. Greg Kuhn, thought leader in the field of living a quantum life and author of *Why Quantum Physicists Do Not Fail* and *How Quantum Physicists Build New Beliefs*, gives a great example of the process behind changing beliefs. While on a vacation in the country, Greg noticed a wild rabbit playing at the far edge of the yard. He wanted to get close to the rabbit, but he knew he couldn't just dash across the yard and grab for it. He knew he had to gain the rabbit's trust. So he set an intention that by the end of his vacation he would have the wild rabbit eating lettuce out of his hand.

Every morning Greg got up early and sat on the patio waiting for the rabbit. He put out treats for the rabbit like carrots and lettuce, first at the edge of the yard, and each day he moved the bunny treats closer and closer to the patio. The rabbit moved closer to the patio each day to munch on the veggies that Greg had set out for him. It was probably a bit intimidating at first, but the promise of fresh, delicious lettuce made it worth the risk. Soon the rabbit was almost to the deck. And then he was almost to the patio. And then he was almost next to Greg's chair. Until finally the rabbit was eating out of his hand, just as Greg intended.

Think of your unconscious beliefs as the rabbit in this scenario. The key is not to try to get the rabbit to come bounding up to the patio right away. That never works. Too often people try to change their beliefs by practicing positive affirmations such as "I am amazing" or "I am perfect" or "I am beautiful," and then they get really angry with themselves when their lives don't improve as a result. They think: "What the heck is going on? The Law of Attraction must be a load of baloney, because I have been doing affirmations for weeks and nothing has changed."

Here's why: Your subconscious doesn't really believe what you're saying. You're telling yourself that you are amazing and perfect, but your subconscious is thinking, "Yeah, right, sure you are" or "Don't you remember what happened?" or "You are kidding yourself if you think all these great things about you and your relationship are true." It doesn't matter if you look in the mirror and say, "I'm beautiful," if you are inwardly thinking the opposite. Your conscious mind can tell you, "You are wonderful" morning, noon, and night, but if your subconscious is telling you, "You stink," guess what? You are going to feel like you stink. And not only are you not going to know why, but you are going to be twice as angry and annoyed with yourself because all your hard work and affirmations didn't work—and that makes you think you stink even more.

You're trying to get your subconscious to jump to the patio without heeding the fact that it is actually cowering and scared in the grass. If your subconscious, where those core beliefs about yourself are held, is not aligned with your conscious intentions, the Law of Attraction isn't going to work. Remember, you are creating your Quantum Love reality with your thoughts and feelings, the conscious and unconscious ones. So getting clear on what those are and starting to move them up the Quantum Lovemap is the only way to reach Quantum Love. In the next chapter, I'll share with you strategies for shifting into home frequency so you can consciously move your belief system up the Quantum Lovemap with intention and clarity, giving your subconscious time to catch up with your intentions.

The next step is to wean your brain and body off of the chemicals they have become addicted to. Yes, your emotions (especially some of the lower-frequency ones) trigger chemical responses that your brain and body have become conditioned to expect, even demand. When they want the juice of your stress reactions, they'll find a way to get it, even if that means pushing you out of the driver's seat of your own thoughts and mood. But more on that in a moment.

How Our Brains Work

Let's take a closer look at how our brains work in order to better understand how we can retrain them to work for us. The brain is composed of the following parts: the cerebrum, cerebellum, limbic system, and brain stem.

Our cerebrum houses our thinking brain. It consists of four lobes—the frontal, occipital, temporal, and parietal—that house all of our higher brain functions, like thought and action. Each lobe has a different job to do. The frontal lobe is the home of our reasoning, planning, and problem-solving abilities. The occipital lobe is where we do all our visual processing, while the temporal lobe handles auditory stimuli, speech, and memory. Finally, the parietal lobe manages our movement and orientation as well as our perception and recognition.

Our frontal lobe also houses our prefrontal cortex, which is the center for all of our executive functioning and complex cognition, including social behavior, decision making, and even the expression of our personality. The prefrontal cortex, or PFC, is also the place in our brain that allows us to regulate our emotions, expectations, and anticipations in response to stimuli. Our brain perceives stimuli, assesses the emotional significance, and triggers the physiological and behavioral response.[1] When we get anxious or stressed, our PFC can't function as effectively as we need it to. Fortunately, our PFC can be taught new methods of response. This is our key to retraining our brain so our mind can work, and in the next chapter I will teach you specific shift moves for doing this, even in a stressful moment or in the midst of an AFGE.

Our cerebellum is much smaller than our cerebrum, and it is believed to be much older, in an evolutionary sense. The cerebellum, which can be thought of as our "being" brain, holds the "hardware" that governs functions like movement, posture, balance, and subconscious thought. It is the part that is active when you can repeat an experience without much conscious effort. You've memorized the action, behavior, or emotional reaction. The cerebellum stores hardwired attitudes and emotional reactions and habits along with skills you have mastered and memorized.

Our limbic system is evolutionarily older too. This is the feeling brain, and it houses our thalamus, hypothalamus, hippocampus, and amygdala. The thalamus picks up on all of the sensory and motor information that comes our way and relays it to the thinking brain. The hypothalamus, meanwhile, manages everything that's going on inside us. It is like the thermostat of our body state, determining when we are hungry, thirsty, or sleepy. It also manages our automatic nerve response (this is the part that snaps our hand away from a hot stove, no thinking required). Our hippocampus manages the conversion of short-term memories into long-term ones. It is important to note that this function exists in our feeling brain because this is in large part what makes entering into the feeling state of Quantum Love (or any of our other core desired relationship feelings) so important. It is through actually feeling what we want to feel that we engage our hippocampus in committing to a new belief.

Finally there is the amygdala, which is where our brains process fear and emotion and all of the memories and stories that contribute to and reinforce them. The amygdala is also responsible for waving the red flag to our hypothalamus to activate our body's stress response. Once the amygdala sounds the alarm, the hypothalamus triggers our sympathetic nerve system through our adrenal glands, which respond by dumping adrenaline into our bloodstream. Now we get a cascade of physical changes (increased heart rate and blood flow, for example) as the flow of oxygen and energy to our whole body increases, all before our thinking brain has fully processed what is happening. Then comes the secondary response, in which our hypothalamus triggers our adrenals to release cortisol, which will keep us in this heightened state until the perceived threat is gone. This is our only stress response, and it initiates in the same way whether we are facing an actual physical threat or just a snippy argument with our partner. To our amygdala it is all the same.[2]

The prefrontal cortex is key here—it lets us use our thinking brain to help our feeling brain control our stress response appropriately. Our PFC gives us the power to observe our own thoughts and then determine whether we want to feel something different (such as realizing that we are in ego frequency and choosing to move into home frequency). We can use the executive functioning of our PFC to create change and produce better outcomes.[3] This is the part of the brain that is at play when you are observing the way you talk to yourself in your mind and when you are monitoring your thoughts throughout the day, as I advised in Chapter 8.

A huge part of retraining your brain so your mind can work is to move from *thinking* to *being*. Through conscious mental rehearsal in the form of meditation, mindfulness, and conscious awareness, the thinking brain (called the neocortex, which is the thin layered structure surrounding the entire brain) can activate new circuits in our neural networks. Then our thought creates an experience, and via the emotional (limbic) brain, that produces a new emotion. Our thinking and feeling brains work together to either create a new experience or alter the script. Once we can get our thinking and feeling brains working together, our being brain (cerebellum) initiates a new state of physical being and starts to rewrite our subconscious thoughts and beliefs.

When you learn a new way of being and then *plan and rehearse* that new way in your mind, you are literally beginning to create a new mind. In fact, experiments considered the effectiveness of mental rehearsal (rather than physical practice) for biceps curls. And guess what? The results were the same! Mental exercises demonstrated physiological changes without ever having the physical experience! In another study leading up to the biceps experiment, one group of subjects was asked to contract and relax one finger on their left hands for five one-hour training sessions per week over the course of four weeks. The second group mentally rehearsed the same. The third group was the control group and didn't do either. The first group, in which participants did the actual exercises, exhibited 30 percent greater finger strength than the control group. But those who mentally rehearsed had an increase in strength as well! Those participants had a 22 percent increase compared with the control group.[4]

When you unlearn any emotion that has become part of your identity, you narrow the gap between how you appear and who you really are. The side effect of this phenomenon is a release of energy in the form of a stored emotion in the body. Once the power of that emotion is liberated from the body, energy is freed up into the quantum field for you to use as a co-creator.

Rather than waiting for an occasion to feel a high-frequency emotion, create the feeling ahead of the experience, even if it means thinking of something totally random that gives you joy. Convince your body that a high-frequency experience has taken place. In this way, you can kick-start the thinking-to-being process and begin to move yourself into the reality of Quantum Love.

Tell Your Body to Stop Yanking on Your Brain

Neurotransmitters, neuropeptides, and hormones are the chemicals that regulate brain activity and bodily functions. These three types of chemicals connect to and interact with cells in milliseconds. Neurotransmitters are chemical messengers that send signals between nerve cells, allowing the brain and nervous system to communicate. There are different types of neurotransmitters; some excite the brain and some slow it down. Neuropeptides are the messengers in the brain, and most are made in the hypothalamus. These chemicals pass through the pituitary gland and then release a chemical message to the body in a millisecond, with specific instructions on how to respond.

Neurotransmitters, neuropeptides, and hormones all work together. When you have a sexual fantasy, for instance, all three of these factors are called into action. First, as you start to think a few thoughts, your brain whips up some neurotransmitters that turn on a network of neurons that create pictures in your mind. These chemicals then stimulate the release of specific neuropeptides into your bloodstream. Once they reach your sexual glands, those peptides bind to the cells of those tissues; they turn on your hormonal system and, presto, things start happening. You've made your fantasy (thoughts) so real in your mind that your body starts to get prepared for an actual sexual experience (ahead of the event). That's how powerfully mind and body are related through our neurochemistry.

It's not just sexual thoughts that create a neurochemical and hormonal cascade. When you have high-frequency thoughts, you produce a series of feel-good chemicals, and the same holds true if you have low-frequency thoughts. It happens in a matter of seconds. But this is a two-way street. It's not only that your body reacts to your brain; your brain is always paying attention to how your body is feeling through chemical feedback via your neurotransmitters. Because of the messages your brain receives, it will actually generate *more* thoughts that will then produce *more* of the chemicals corresponding to the way the body is feeling, so that you first begin to feel the way you think and then think the way you feel.

In her book *Molecules of Emotion*, neuroscientist Candace Pert shares the discovery she made that over time, not only does our brain become accustomed to certain emotions, but our body's cells actually build receptors for the unique combination of neuropeptides those emotions trigger the brain to create. What Dr. Pert found was that when we feel a certain emotion, the brain releases a wash of neuropeptides across every cell in our body. Every emotion or series of emotions we experience creates an immediate cascade, a unique neuropeptide wash. When you experience a feeling state consistently over any length of time, your body's cells start to build receptors for that specific neuropeptide wash. And when your cells divide, they do so with those receptors in place! So if you have been going through a period of feeling stressed or angry, you should know that your cells likely have built receptors for the angry-stress neuropeptide wash they've grown to anticipate.

When you're trying to break out of negative thinking, be aware that your body will be looking for those neuropeptides it has grown to expect on a cellular level. Despite your best intentions, the body's cells will signal the brain to begin talking you out of your intended (conscious) goals as you unconsciously create worst-case scenarios in your mind. I often liken it to that scene in *Look Who's Talking* when the baby is pulling on the umbilical cord while in utero, demanding apple juice. Mom (played by Kirstie Alley) proceeds to gulp down an entire gallon, not exactly sure why she's craving it so. So it is that our bodies yank on our brains for the neuropeptides our cells are craving. We set an intention to be positive and peaceful with our mate, and for reasons we can't seem to explain or control, we revert to anger or despair. When you change your brain to let your mind and your essential self take the wheel, when you move into higher-frequency emotions that your body and psyche aren't used to, your brain and body are going to resist.

It's a form of chemical addiction, and when you try to break it, your body will struggle against you at first. Your brain has trained your body to expect a certain neuropeptide wash. Now you are sending in totally different neuropeptides that don't fit in the receptors, and an alarm goes off. The hypothalamus, the thermostat in the brain, signals the thinking part of the brain to go back to its old, habitual ways (*Get with the program!*). The body wants you to return to your habitual thinking self, so it influences you to think in those familiar lower-frequency ways, tempting the brain to return to its old, unconscious habit. It sort of feels good (or at least familiar) to feel bad.

What to do? Stay present and conscious. When you notice yourself drifting back to old, lower-frequency modes of thought, remember that it's likely your body yanking on your brain for the neuropeptides it's used to getting. Be patient with yourself. Remember, every thought we have is arguable. There are no absolutes in life, as much as we wish there were. You are never looking at something that is 100 percent true and undeniable. As we've discussed, you are filtering the input you are getting from your surroundings, consciously and unconsciously, through the lens of your prior experience and through your memory, which is deeply flawed and not a dependable lens at all.

Lisa tended to be stuck in fearful, low-frequency thoughts, and it was making life with her husband, Bill, very difficult. Little things made her anxious, whether it was going to the grocery store or having family over for dinner. The house could never be clean enough. The kids could never behave well enough. Most important, her husband could never live up to her expectations. He was always letting her down or offending her in some way. Essentially, she was living in a place of emotional scarcity. She came to see me in an attempt to address the mood swings she frequently experienced. With my help, she identified her core desired relationship feelings—her Quantum Love Goals—and set an intention to meet them. With newfound optimism and enthusiasm, she and Bill planned a great weekend together.

Everything was going great, but about halfway through they got into a huge fight when she started criticizing him.

They came to see me shortly after and we worked to break down the weekend, retracing their emotional and logistical steps to figure out what had caused the nosedive. I asked Lisa to ground herself and think back to before the argument blew up. "I was feeling really anxious," she told me. When I asked her why, she said, "I don't know—no reason, really. I just felt physically anxious."

"What were some of the thoughts you were having prior to that anxious feeling?" I asked.

"I was thinking about how he didn't clean the kitchen before we left even though he said that he would. It made me angry because he never does what he says he's going to do."

She could see that there was no reason to get angry or anxious in that moment of their trip. But she was in those well-worn neurologic and neuropeptide pathways that had been well trodden for years, and her body was yanking on her brain for the neuropeptide wash her cells were used to. That brought on feelings of anxiety, and then the brain started having thoughts to match. It wasn't just a matter of her mind impacting her body; her body was impacting her mind in turn. "Tell your body to stop yanking on your brain!" became a mantra that Lisa would say to herself and Bill would say to her.

So how can you get your brain to shift out of these memorized reactions, and how can you start teaching yourself to embrace new beliefs? It may seem like a colossal task, but it is much easier than you think. While our brains easily become accustomed to patterns and repetition (even creating shortcuts to help simplify and quicken frequent behaviors and routines), they are also very adaptable. The saying "You can't teach an old dog new tricks" turns out to be untrue in this case. It is certainly more difficult for a mature adult to create new pathways in the brain (as opposed to a small child, who is learning new things every minute), but that doesn't mean it is impossible. It's all based on neuroplasticity, which is a fancy term that really just means your brain's ability to manage new ideas and learn new skills. The more "plastic" your brain is, the better able you will be to adapt to new things and embrace new ideas.

More on that in the next chapter. For now, just know that the brain is very forgiving. Once you apply consciousness to your daily routine and try to implement new ideas, your brain slowly but surely catches on. And when you change your brain, your mind can get to work on Quantum Love.

Our Brains Are Trained to Upper Limits

So what do we call it when we find ourselves looking for reasons to be in a bad mood? When we feel unsettled but aren't sure why, so we start looking around for things to nitpick? Maybe it's something your partner did or didn't do, maybe it's your messy house, maybe it's something that happened at work, but whatever it is, when you want something to be upset about, it's easy to find a reason.

This is what I call our upper limit, a term first popularized by psychologist, personal empowerment coach, and author Gay Hendricks. It's the point at which our brains start reverting to negative emotions because it's what they've been taught to expect. For instance, if you are prone to stress, you might find yourself getting really upset and stressed out on a Saturday afternoon even during an otherwise pleasant weekend. You are unconsciously looking for things to be worried about because that's where your body has become most comfortable. In the midst of a great weekend of relaxation and pleasure, you've reached your upper limit of joy, and your brain and body are trying to trick you into a negative mood because they're not accustomed to being happy and stress-free for so long.

There has been a lot of exciting research on how you can actually teach your brain to embrace joy and other high-calibrating emotions. For example, instead of teaching your brain to crave stress, you can teach it to crave gratitude. Studies have shown that people who keep a daily gratitude journal are happier and less stressed than their ungrateful counterparts even though that's the only change they have made in their lives.[5]

Your Brain on Stress

Our stress response system has helped ensure our survival for eons, but it has not yet evolved to fit with our modern lives, and that works against us on a neurochemical level. It is in our DNA to be quickly triggered to fight-or-flight. This puts the body into a stress reaction, with all the neurochemicals that go along with it. When we were cave people, that worked, but it doesn't really serve us anymore. In fight-or-flight, the sympathetic nervous system, part of the autonomic nervous system, which maintains the body's automatic functions such as digestion, temperature, and blood sugar level, is activated. So is the sympathetic nervous system, which automatically activates the adrenal glands to mobilize enormous amounts of energy. This is the stress response. We have the ability to turn on this response by thought alone, even in thoughts about a future event.

I believe, from my work with so many stressed-out people and from learning as much as I have about the brain and the energy of our thoughts, that we get unconsciously addicted to the adrenaline high of anger and stress. I think the majority of us are addicted to the problems and conditions of our lives that create the stress we experience. Our identity gets wrapped up in this part of who we are (the stressful job, troubled kids, difficult relationship). We become physically addicted to the neurochemicals that come with those negative stories; our bodies yank on our brains when they need a fix.

Maybe this is also why so many of us have "frenemies" or spend time with people who we know make us feel bad about ourselves. And maybe it's why we stay in negative relationship patterns, always picking the same fight over and over again or looking for all the ways our partner lets us down.

Stress is terrible for us on an energetic level too. When we're chronically stressed, we become more stuck in ego frequency and it is harder to move out of it. An overproduction of stress hormones creates anger, fear, envy, hatred, and aggression and often leads to a sense of frustration, anxiety, insecurity, sadness, depression, and hopelessness. In other words, stress sends you straight into To Me!

The better we manage stress in our lives, the more we are able to stay in home frequency. One of my favorite questions to ask clients, which always comes up at some point in our work together, is, "What's the worst that can happen if this problem is *fixed*?" You are reading this book because you want more out of your love relationship. You want a deeper connection. Maybe you are in a dissatisfying, disconnected relationship. But my guess is, as much as you want it to change, the pain you are in is serving you in some way. There is always fear with change, even good change, and that can sometimes hold you back.

Your Brain on Fear

Fear is the antithesis of Quantum Love. Let's go back to the Quantum Lovemap for a moment. Remember, until you are calibrating energetically at 200 or above (hopeful and courageous), you aren't in the Quantum Love zone. While shame and guilt calibrate the lowest (20), fear calibrates at 100. In my mind, when I am engaging in therapy with individuals and couples, I actually see shame and guilt as an incarnation of fear. When you feel shame and guilt, you are blaming yourself and feeling fearful from the stories you are telling yourself as a result: you are a bad person, insensitive, selfish, etc. You imagine that you are going to lose the person you are feeling guilty toward or lose the love or admiration of others in general.

Fear serves us in many ways: the prickling hairs on the back of our neck tell us when something is not right, the stomach drop is a fear sign we can't ignore, and the tension in our muscles prepares our body to fight for itself or flee danger. But when fear is our constant companion, especially in our relationships, Quantum Love is impossible. It's not about never being fearful. It's about changing the habit of fear in your relationship and learning how to recognize whether the fear is a reflection of the ego self or the essential self.

Marianne Williamson in *A Return to Love* writes, "Love is what we are born with. Fear is what we learn. The spiritual journey is the unlearning of fear and prejudices and the acceptance of love back in our hearts." But in order to start this journey, much less master it, you must pause to understand your fear and what it is trying to tell you. That's how you will know how to shift into a higher-frequency emotion and move into the By Me and Through Me states. Obviously this doesn't apply if you are facing an immediate physical threat; in that case you should get yourself to safety as soon as possible. I am talking here about the more insidious fear that keeps you in a place of guilt, shame, and anxiety.

Consider Figure 8. Fear can be about your physical well-being or your emotional well-being (and sometimes both). Maybe you feel fear emotionally in the form of worries or anxiety, or in the avoidance of certain situations or thoughts or of your partner in general. Or maybe you experience fear in terms of your physical well-being and this keeps you from taking risks, trying new things, or living your life to the fullest. Emotional fear typically arises because a worthiness-killing story has kicked in and a thorn has been triggered that leads to fears of abandonment, abuse, or powerlessness. Physical fear is usually rooted in worries about injury, illness, or death. Paranoia and phobias, as well as milder avoidant behaviors that grow out of fear for one's physical safety, can be very effectively treated with cognitive behavioral therapy, which has been well established as a viable treatment in this area. This kind of therapy systematically challenges your stories and assumptions and calls on you to slowly desensitize to your fear.

While physical fear is important, I want to spend some time talking about emotional fear, because that comes into play in a big way in your relationship.

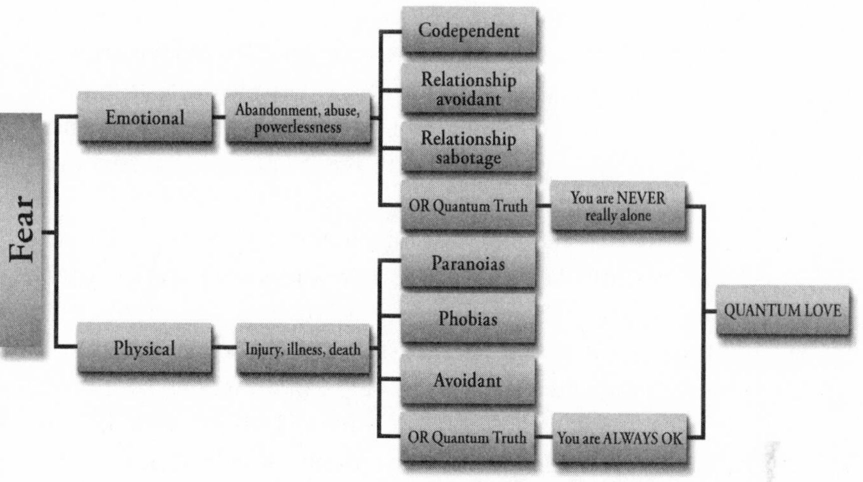

Figure 8: From Fear to Quantum Love

When you are in emotional fear, you are at risk of falling prey to what I call the Quantum Love Busters: codependence, relationship sabotage, and relationship avoidance. These are all solidly entrenched in To Me frequency, but they take different forms.

In codependence, you can't really get your needs met because you're so externally directed. You're focused on everyone else's needs and making sure you are behaving in a way that will keep you from being abandoned. You're desperately clinging to your relationship from a place of fear and FMC.

In relationship sabotage, you take steps to drive your partner away and end the relationship. Usually early on, as things are getting intimate and you are approaching the attachment stage, or as soon as you feel like your partner could be a keeper, you start to find a lot of faults in him or her. You fabricate problems or flaws, or you cheat or pick fights.

In relationship avoidance, you tend not to get serious with anyone. You come up with all sorts of excuses: "I have to work" or "I have to wait until my kids are grown up" or "I'm not ready." You don't get close enough to experience codependence and you don't stay long enough to feel the need to sabotage.

Obviously there are times when fear is good, like when you are putting your life in mortal danger. But the bottom line is that allowing yourself to be controlled by your fears keeps you in the To Me state on the Quantum Lovemap. You don't recognize your power, and you aren't vibrating at a frequency that supports Quantum Love.

Remember in Chapter 5 we talked about how the only way to get to Quantum Love with another is to get to it with yourself first? We talked about loving for no reason and tapping into the endless well of love that suffuses us all and connects us and binds us all via our essential selves. But so often we can't get there because we are too afraid of pain, physical or emotional. This is what leads to the relationship avoidance and sabotage, to the fears and paranoia that stand in the way of our happiness.

But here's the truth. Regardless of how afraid you are of being left, having your heart broken, or being made a fool, no matter what happens, you will be fine. The Quantum Truth is that no matter what happens, how many times you are abandoned, have your heart broken, or are disappointed in love, you will survive. If your current partner dumps you or betrays you or dies on you, of course it will hurt. You will be devastated. You will likely curl up in a ball for a while (literally or figuratively) and lick your wounds. It will be a whopper AFGE. You will be in some emotional pain. But the pain will pass. The tsunamis of grief will get smaller and gentler, and the waves will come less frequently. And you will be stronger and wiser and clearer on your strength, your power, and, most important, what you want in a romantic partner and from love in general.

Don't be scared of heartbreak or you won't fully experience the joy of the heart. Remember, energy cannot be decreased or destroyed. You are always okay. You are never alone. When you really hold these thoughts and allow them to become part of your energetic state, fear will lose its grip on you. You will still experience fearful thoughts, but they will pass through you rather than becoming part of your belief system and how you view the world. All emotions come through the same channel: joy, sorrow, anger, and fear. You have to be open to it all and trust and remember that everything is for you, even the AFGEs.

CHAPTER 10

Commitment #4

I Will Realize When I Am Stuck and Shift from Brain to Mind

Life is a process of becoming, a combination of states we have to go through. Where people fail is that they wish to elect a state and remain in it. This is a kind of death.

— Anaïs Nin

Some days you just wake up feeling in a funk. You're not really sure why you feel that way; you just do. You set an intention to look at your partner through a positive lens, but you just can't seem to execute. Or you can for a moment, but you just keep sliding back into an old pattern.

Or maybe a fight with your partner has you digging in your heels, feeling convinced that you are right, and it has thrown you into ego frequency. You know intellectually that you want to move back to home, but you can't seem to shift.

These are the two primary ways in which we tend to get stuck in a relationship. Whether it's an acute issue, like a charged argument with your partner, or chronic, like a funky mood or an ongoing disconnect, you are simply *stuck*. Your energy isn't flowing or humming; you're knocked out of home frequency and the voice of your ego self is speaking loud and clear. Your low-frequency energy is dragging down your reality, your partner, and your relationship.

By getting unstuck, you can reshape your reality into the one you want for yourself and your relationship. Instead of feeling scared, frustrated, or angry, you can get closer to feeling your core desired relationship feelings and move back into Quantum Love.

In these times, there is only one person who has the power to shift you into home frequency and move you back up the Quantum Lovemap: you.

Take Off the Emotional Weight Vest

In Chapter 7, we discussed how chakras are the channels through which energy flows into and out of our bodies. You also learned that our energy can be stored in our bodies—even the energy of our emotions—and can build up over time. Eventually, this buildup can clog the channels so that energy starts to move more slowly. As the energy flow slows, our frequency drops. This is the quantum process at the core of being stuck.

Sometimes closing our energetic channels is a conscious choice, one we make out of fear. I've known for many years in my work with patients that you can't squelch one emotion (refuse to feel anger, for instance) without squelching others. If you never give yourself permission to express anger because your stories tell you it's not okay, you're going to be constraining yourself. You'll be tightening your muscles, locking your jaw, flaring your nostrils; your brain is going to be ruminating on these things in your quiet moments. You will blame yourself (or someone else) or come up with other lower-frequency thoughts and feelings that can keep you from really feeling the anger that wants to come out of you. You're making your mind, body, and spirit work so hard to avoid feeling your feelings that it is hard to experience the emotions you *do* want. Many spiritual teachers believe that all of our emotions move through the same energetic channels, so you can't block the channel for anger, sadness, or fear and expect juicy emotions like joy, gratitude, and sexual feelings to come through fully.

The problem is that the feelings don't go away, no matter how much you deny them. They're still there, and they are heavy. All of our emotions have an energetic weight, and if we let our heavier emotions build up inside us, then we have to expend a lot of energy to carry the load. When we allow ourselves to feel our feelings, we release the energetic weight we've been carrying. That's why when you have a good cry or you let out your rage, you typically feel spent but also so much lighter.

The truth is it only takes about 30 to 90 seconds for an authentic emotion to pass through you. Often you will be able to shift into home frequency simply by allowing the emotion to pass through. Feel the waves of energy move through you and the field of energy and consciousness of which you are a part. There are waves that bring new frequencies of energy and information. The same waves move energy and information away as they pass through you. All you have to do is notice it, experience it, and allow it to pass. Then, once it has, you will often find that the wave had information for you about the best way to shift and move forward.

If you trust that a higher intelligence is directing the flow, and that the universe is a friendly place and everything is *for* you (and this is where faith has to come in), the frequency of your body, emotions, and mind will rise to meet you. In the pages ahead, I'll outline some techniques to help you make the shift.

Get Off the Drama Triangle

The Drama Triangle (see Figure 9) I am going to share with you here was adapted from Dr. Steven Karpman's Drama Triangle, developed in 1968. It's a social and psychological model to help us understand the ways we get stuck in our interactions with others, and I have found it extremely helpful in my own life and in my work with couples.

In essence, when you are "on the Triangle" you are in ego frequency. The problem is that most of us spend more than half our time on the Triangle and don't even realize it. Here's how it works: There are three corners of the Triangle: "victim," "villain," and "hero." We all slip into these roles from time to time, often combining a couple of roles at once (victim and villain at the same time, for instance). But we tend to have favored roles we slip into when a thorn is touched. Often this is during an argument, but it can happen at any time.

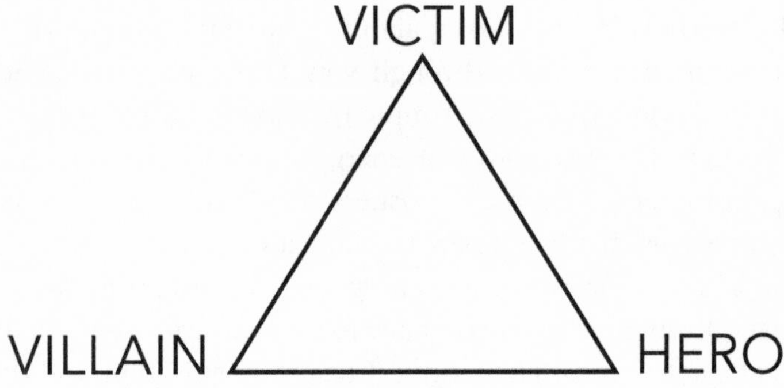

Figure 9: The Drama Triangle

The Victim

The victim sees her- or himself as "at the effect" of someone, something, or some situation and is stuck in the To Me state. There are lots of "If only" sentences in the victim role. The victim tends to be:

Passive-aggressive: The victim has a hard time overtly expressing anger. For instance, when asked where he wants to eat dinner, the victim will say he doesn't really care. But then he will feel angry and unloved when his partner doesn't choose his favorite restaurant, pouting through the meal or making snarky comments about the food or service.

Easily injured: The victim finds hidden insults, often needs to be comforted, and requires lots of apologies. The victim's partner may ask her if she'd like to go for a run, and the victim will interpret this as meaning the partner thinks she is fat.

Helpless: Victims have lots of "I can't" and "I need" statements in their vocabulary. Of course there's nothing wrong with asking for help when you need it, but victims often avoid taking responsibility for their own lives.

The Villain

The villain is typically critical, sarcastic, and blaming. Usually a villain takes on this role to hide insecurities. Rather than showing vulnerability and expressing hurt or fear, the villain attacks a partner with words and shouts. The villain tends to:

Attack the partner for things out of the partner's control: If delayed on the way to a party because of an accident farther down the highway, the villain will start shouting that his partner should have been ready to leave earlier.

Criticize the partner's character: Instead of expressing anger and frustration toward the partner's actions when the villain is upset with her, he will generalize and attack her personality. If she didn't get the right cheese at the market, the villain will call her irresponsible or untrustworthy rather than consider it a miscommunication or innocent mistake.

Try to make the partner feel inferior: Rather than take responsibility for her actions when she has let her partner down, the villain will turn it around. If she doesn't understand why her partner is upset, the villain will get exasperated instead of trying to understand, angrily throwing up her hands and saying she just never knows what her partner wants.

Refuse to admit wrongdoing or drop an argument: The villain has a hard time letting things go. The argument can be over, but the villain will have to say, "I just hope you got my point. You really upset me and I'm still in shock over this."

The Hero

The hero feels responsible for everyone else's happiness and is willing to do what it takes to make others comfortable, at any cost. This, as you can imagine, is a common role for women who are too focused on meeting the needs of everyone else in the family before their own. But men often play the hero too. The hero will often:

Take on way more than she can handle: In an effort to keep those around her happy and calm, the hero will say yes to way too much and won't ask for help. For example, the hero will come home from a long day of work, clean the kitchen, and make lunches, and, when her partner asks if she needs any help, will refuse.

Allow the partner to forgo responsibility in the relationship: The hero will take on all the responsibility for all that is wrong in the relationship. If his partner blows up in an argument, he will say, "Well, I shouldn't have pushed her so much. I should have just let things go sooner."

Treat the partner as incompetent: The hero believes she is the only responsible one. When the hero is out of town, for instance, instead of trusting her partner, she will leave endless lists, call every hour to check in, and control the family's activities from afar.

You can see how many of us can fall into more than one role at once. When the hero mother reloads the dishwasher after her husband has loaded it, while juggling homework and bath time all at once, muttering under her breath, "If I want it done right, I have to do it myself," she is also acting as a villain in the way she communicates to her partner that he is incompetent.

We can't be in Quantum Love when on the Drama Triangle because any time we are on it, we are in ego frequency. We are in fear or anger, calibrating below 200, which as you know is *not* home frequency. The only way to experience Quantum Love in your relationship, and stay there, is to recognize when you are on the Drama Triangle and get off it! Don't worry, I'm about to show you how.

First of all, how do you know when you are on the Drama Triangle? I can sum it up in five words: *You think you are right.* Yes, you read me correctly. Any time you are convinced that your position is fully justified, your partner is the only wrong one, or your position is the only sane one, you are on the Triangle!

Take Your 100 Percent

We've touched on this concept a bit in previous chapters: the most effective way to break out of the blame game is to fully own up to your part in the conflict. You have to take your 100 percent ownership, not only for your reactions to your partner, but also for the energy that you bring to it. When you recognize your part in the conflict, it's very hard to remain in the role of victim, villain, or hero.

So often, we automatically point the finger of blame at our partner for hurting us, letting us down, or not showing up in the way we want. We rarely consider *our* part in the issue. But we always play a part in whatever has occurred in our field. For instance, if you want more romance in your relationship, what are the ways you haven't been romantic yourself or haven't behaved so as to inspire romance in your partner? If you imagine your mate is being selfish, in what ways have *you* been selfish or self-centered? How much appreciation or motivation have you been providing for more altruistic and giving behaviors in your partner? When you take the critical lens off your partner and place a curious one on yourself, you will be surprised what wisdom is available for you to see.

Speak Unarguably

When you are speaking unarguably, you are speaking truths that apply only to you. You are not projecting anything onto your partner, nor are you making assumptions (or accusations) about how he or she is thinking or feeling. You are speaking unarguably because what you're saying is your truth. When you are speaking unarguably, you are off the Triangle.

There are four steps to speaking unarguably:

1. Share a physical feeling: "I feel sick to my stomach" or "I feel tightness in my shoulders."
2. Share an emotion behind the physical feeling—joy, anger, fear, sadness, or sexual attraction: "I feel sick to my stomach and tightness in my shoulders because I feel sad and scared."
3. Share your "story," the thoughts that inspire those feelings: "I feel sick to my stomach and tightness in my shoulders because I'm sad and scared. I have a story that you'd rather be out with your friends than home with me tonight."
4. State what you want: "I feel sick to my stomach and tightness in my shoulders because I'm sad and scared. I have a story that you'd rather be out with your friends than home with me tonight. I would like it if we could spend the weekend with just each other."

Note that these are all "I" statements. Keep the focus of what you're saying on yourself, your feelings, your stories, and your desires. Do not flip these into "You" statements ("You make me feel sad and scared") or you will only throw yourself further onto the Triangle and into ego frequency.

Playing with Your Personas

When you're stuck on the Triangle, especially in an area of conflict in your relationship, or even when you simply find yourself in a low-frequency state, you may notice yourself slipping into one of your personas. And when that happens, you're *definitely* on the Triangle.

Personas themselves aren't a bad thing. I like to think of them as coats. It's okay to wear them when they will serve you. I have a persona that I assume when I'm about to go speak to a 1,000-person audience: "Professional Doctor-Chick." She's someone you're going to pay attention to, someone who knows her stuff. This isn't my essential self by any means, nor is it a persona I wear when I'm being a goof with my friends or hanging with my husband and kids; it's a persona that helps me do my job better. The key is that *you* are in the driver's seat. You put the persona *on*; the persona does not attach itself to *you*.

The second key is to learn more about each of your personas. Who is he or she, or even it? When does the persona typically make an appearance? What does the persona want? When you are able to get to know your personas, they can actually lead you to greater self-awareness of what is going on in your mental and emotional state.

Love Thy Personas

A good way to release a persona's hold on you is to *love* it. Recognize all the ways in which it serves you. Two of my personas, Dire Mama and the Homework Nazi, love to stomp around the house and manage my kids. And while they may make life around the house a little unpleasant when they show up (especially during homework time), I know that they're not all bad. The Homework Nazi makes sure my kids are learning and are turning in their assignments on time. Dire Mama makes sure they aren't melting their brains with television. Each one comes from a place of love and protection, highly invested in my children and their well-being and their growth. They just tend to be really controlling and driven by fear. The Homework Nazi can get, well, pushy, while Dire Mama is dramatic and even catastrophic. But I know that if I want these personas to loosen their grip on me, I have to attach to the good parts of them.

When you name your personas—like the three of mine I've just shared with you—you are immediately moving into the role of observer. You are taking your 100 percent. Once you've done that, it often helps to go hyperbolic with it, delivering an award-winning performance of the persona in which you are stuck.

If I realize I'm in the clutches of the Homework Nazi, I start stomping around the room with my chest puffed up, saying, "This homework is only halfway complete! That's it! I'm calling college and telling them you're not coming!" By acting out the role in which I am stuck, I am able to see and feel that it's a little bit ridiculous. Better still, it changes the energy of the room and, in most cases, dispels the tension. My sons start laughing with me and playing along. I'm showing them that my reaction has more to do with me than with anything they've done. I'm also showing my commitment to freeing myself from the Homework Nazi's hold. By playing out your persona, you loosen its grip on you and get the added benefit of making your partner or your children your allies as you shift up the Quantum Lovemap.

Shake It Up

Here are some great ways to shake yourself out of a low-frequency state that's keeping you stuck. First, once you have noticed that you're on the Triangle, pay attention to your body language. Are you tense? Are your arms crossed over your body, closing you off from your partner? Or are you taking an aggressive stance, with your hands on your hips, making your anger big? If so, it's time to get moving, if only by changing your position—uncrossing your arms or dropping your hands to your sides.

If you want to take it a step further, consider some creative joint play. This is one of my go-to shift moves because it takes you out of your current position (which I think is helpful even on its own in starting to shift your energy) and gets your body moving. It's very simple to do: stand up and start moving every joint in your body in all different directions. You'll be doing a full-body wiggle and you might feel crazy at first, but it's a great way to shake off the negative feeling state that just a minute before was making your body uncomfortable. It's also next to impossible to stay stuck in a low-frequency emotion when you are moving this way. In fact, it's hard not to crack up.

Another fun way to shift through play, if you're having an argument, is to conduct the argument as if your hand is doing the talking. Hold up your hand like a puppet and have it "talk." I find this is particularly helpful in counteracting "I know I'm right" thinking because any point you're trying to make is going to sound silly when it's coming out of your hand. It also creates a little bit of distance between you and what you're saying and can make room for objectivity to kick back in.

Or try changing your environment. If you're standing in the bedroom having an argument with your partner, or if you're sitting on the couch having trouble shaking a blue mood, get up and get outta there. Go out into nature or even just move into another room. Change your view and you can change your viewpoint: sometimes getting a different visual perspective can actually help you shift to a different emotional perspective.

Table It

"I know that I'm stuck and I need to table this conversation for twenty minutes."

Sometimes this is the most productive thing you can say in the midst of an argument with your partner. If you find that you're so stuck on the Triangle you can't move forward, or if the argument is charged enough that it is firing up your body's stress response, then the best thing might be to take a break.

If I am in an argument with my husband and realize that I am solidly on the Triangle, I tell him so. I ask for 30 minutes and he's supportive of that. I go shake it off, get into coherence, or just watch some stupid television, and then I come back to him with an open heart. And that's when I can speak openly and calmly (and unarguably) about what I think or what I want.

Sometimes I'll go back to him and say, "You were right." Once I'm back in home frequency, I'm able to see both sides. I understand that the one with the most power is the one who gives in.

I also use this time to ask myself: What do I really want? What is my core desired relationship feeling? *What I want is a joyful, loving connection.* Is this argument worth moving away from what I really want? *No.* At this point, I usually decide that I'm going to surrender. I'd rather build trust and put points in the connection bank. When I surrender my need to be right, it creates more connection and a better platform for resolving our issues. It turns conflict into an opportunity to draw closer together.

To use this move, tell your partner what is happening: "I'm so convinced that I'm right, I know that I'm stuck. I really want to table this and come back to it later." Then set a specific time—20 minutes, an hour, two hours later—when you will reconvene. It's amazing the difference even a little bit of calm-down time can have on your clarity and ability to communicate.

A word on these shift moves: Not every partner will buy into your breaking into a funny dance or speaking in a silly voice in the middle of an argument. I recommend getting them on board with the idea ahead of time, explaining what it's all about and that it doesn't mean you aren't taking the argument (or their side of the argument) seriously. Then set a phrase that one or both of you can say before jumping into a play shift move. Something as simple as "I'm on the Triangle and want to shift" will let your partner know what you are about to do.

Rewrite Your Thorny Stories

If you wave at your neighbor and she doesn't wave back as you drive down the street, you could make up several stories: "Jane must not have seen me wave" or "Jane must be having a really busy day" or "Jane is such a jerk" or "I knew Jane never liked me!" From there, you will continue to build stories: "Mary is right about Jane—she is stuck up, and I bet it was no accident that I was the last person to be asked to join the neighborhood book club, and I hate this whole street! I miss our old neighborhood, where people were actually friendly."

See what I mean? All it takes is one small incident (a neglected wave) and your brain starts churning out stories and thoughts. Largely, these stories will be based on your belief systems. As we've discussed, if you believe the world is a scary place, a lot of your thoughts will likely be fear based. Or, if you believe the world is a unwelcoming place or that you are "less than" other people, you might be more insecure and more apt to read insult ("Jane purposely didn't wave to me"), whereas a more confident person might see it differently ("Jane seems busy; I will stop by and visit with her later"). You will be much less likely to get stuck in ego frequency when you become aware of your thorny stories.

It's crucial to understand that other people's thoughts about you are not under your control and that ultimately, these thoughts have very little to do with you. They are more about the person's own perception and their own history and belief system. You could make yourself crazy trying to make everyone happy, and at the end of the day, that wouldn't be a very worthwhile endeavor. Nor would you ever really know if you succeeded.

Author and thought leader Byron Katie offers a simple system for unsticking ourselves from our negative stories: a list of four questions designed to help us challenge and reconstruct our patterns and create new pathways. I have created a variation of my own based on her four questions. I highly recommend her book *Loving What Is* if you want to explore this further.

Begin by grounding yourself and opening your heart. Then try to get really clear on your story.

Then, once you are clear on the story, ask four questions:

1. *What is the story I am telling myself behind these feelings?* Get to the message at the very root of your thoughts. Break it down as much as you can.
2. *Can I absolutely know that my story is true?* Hint: the answer is ultimately, if you are honest, no. How can you be absolutely, definitely sure that any thought is true? Every single thought is arguable. You have

chosen to attach to this thought that is creating these emotions in you, but it is just as likely the opposite thought is true.

3. *What would the opposite story, or a better-feeling story, be?* To get to this idea, you might need to run through a heart-opening exercise again. Once you do, you may have the thought that instead of simply being a jerk or not liking you, perhaps the person who has you upset is just going through a rough time. Or maybe she's feeling angry and grumpy about something that has nothing to do with you.
4. *Who would I be and what would I feel right now if the opposite story were the truth?* Really feel into that different story and allow your frequency to increase. Don't just have the thought casually. Wade into it and feel how that story changes you, both physically and emotionally.

When you apply these questions to your thoughts, whether it's something small ("That cashier was rude to me") or something large ("My husband doesn't love me"), you might be surprised to find that things you think are true are actually generally false, or at least wholly subjective and greatly exaggerated.

The Thorny Story Time Line

As we've discussed several times in this book, the concept of thorns comes from Michael Singer in his book *The Untethered Soul*. He compares the issues, wounds, and painful experiences you have never dealt with to a thorn buried in your body, close to a nerve. When the thorn gets touched, it sends a shock wave of pain through your entire body. Singer says that eventually you will have to make a choice between doing everything you can to make sure the thorn never gets touched (essentially letting your biggest fears dictate your life) or doing everything you can to remove the thorn so you can move forward unimpeded.

We all have emotional thorns that can trigger us into ego frequency. I believe that those thorns are almost always the result of worthiness-killing stories to which we have unconsciously become attached. The Thorny Story Time Line exercise is a wonderful way to look at and perhaps reconsider the experiences in your life that have shaped your worthiness-killing stories about love, how love works, and how safe it is to open your heart.

Think of the points of conflict in your relationship or negative patterns in your love life that you find you can't stop repeating. Maybe you get involved with men who aren't fully available to you, or perhaps you find yourself repeatedly dumped after the first or second date. In your relationship, you may find that most of your fights come when you feel your partner is being controlling, or maybe you tend to see your partner as not caring enough, romantic enough, or present enough in your relationship. In order to get to Quantum Love, we must identify our worthiness-killing stories and loosen their grip on our thinking patterns.

Angel and Stella came to see me because Stella had told Angel that she wanted to end their marriage. They had been together 20 years, since they were 16, and Angel was completely blindsided. Stella had been telling Angel for years that he needed to be more romantic, spend more time with her, and be more present in their relationship. Angel had heard her complaints and tried his best, but work and the demands of their children often got in the way. He didn't realize things had deteriorated as far as they had.

First I spent time with each of them individually to get a sense of their histories and perspectives on the relationship. Angel's life had been pretty uneventful. He had two parents who were loving and kind toward each other, their children, and a large extended family. He had had two less serious relationships before Stella, where he was the one who did the dumping. Angel's main issues were that he needed to get clearer on what romance means to a woman (Stella in particular), how to prioritize time, and how to connect heart to heart with his wife.

Stella was a different story. Her parents had divorced when she was quite young, and she never had a model of what a loving relationship looked and felt like. After her dad moved out, she spent quality time with him regularly. But when he remarried, he became much less available to her. Once he had a couple of children with his new wife, Stella saw her dad even less. Later Stella had a serious relationship with a young man who cheated on her with her best friend. Some major thorns were showing themselves to me, so I had Stella do the Thorny Story Time Line exercise.

I asked Stella to plot out key events in her childhood and early adulthood that had taught her about love and what to expect from romance and from men. I then asked her to write the headlines of the thorny stories she developed from each experience underneath. Look at Stella's Thorny Story Time Line in Figure 10, then try this exercise yourself to make your own. You can write it out using the steps below, or go to www.drlauraberman.com/quantumlove for an electronic version. If you haven't been with the same person since the age of 16, like Stella, your time line of key events will be longer. But you can use the same process for getting to the worthiness-killing stories behind the ego-frequency beliefs that are keeping you stuck.

Steps to Make Your Thorny Story Time Line

1. Take some deep breaths, ground yourself, and open your heart. Now you are in coherence.
2. Start your time line. What is your earliest memory of someone not showing up for you, letting you down, hurting you, abandoning you (literally or emotionally)? Close your eyes and go back to that time. See the events unfolding. What were you thinking? What were you feeling? Write it down.
3. Know that every single child sees the world as revolving around him or her. It is a developmental truth. From your child's-eye view, the things the adults you loved did to each other and to you appeared to you as resulting from your own actions,

deeds, or lack of worthiness. So chances are, as you go back there from your current state of coherence, you will discover some stories you've developed along the way reflecting self-blame, self-doubt, and a sense of not being good enough or lovable enough. Write down all the milestones you remember on your time line, along with the approximate age you were when they occurred.

4. Now plot the experience and emotions of the event below each milestone event on your Thorny Story Time Line. These thorny stories may seem a little extreme to your adult ears. Don't judge; just go for it. You may be surprised by what comes out.

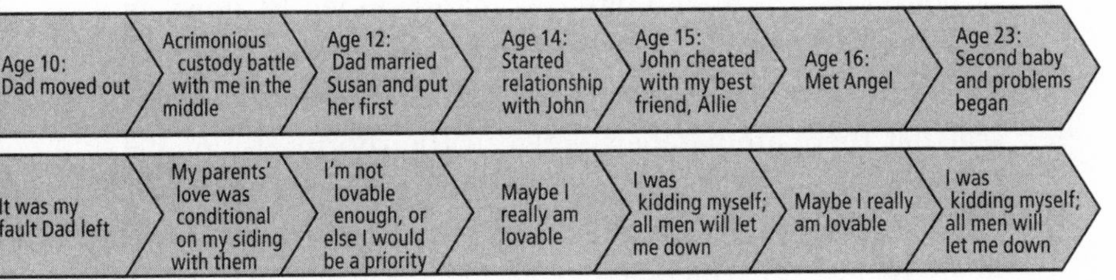

Figure 10: Stella's Thorny Story Time Line

Consider Your Thorny Legacy

Another important piece of solving this puzzle is to consider the Thorny Story Time Line of your parents, and of their parents, and of *their* parents. Yes, we're made of the genetic material of our ancestors, but I think it goes deeper than that. On a quantum level, we are carrying their energy—and if that energy is painful, we will carry their pain, which does not exist in time or space; it simply *is*. If we heal that pain and let go of that energy, then it is healed and released for us and for those who came before us.

Imagine superimposing the Thorny Story Time Line of your mother and father on top of yours. Most likely the same events didn't happen at exactly the same time in their early lives, but I can bet you their thorny stories are very similar to yours. And the same will be true for their parents and *their* parents before them, back beyond anyone's memory.

In Stella's case, her mother, Rosanna, had had a childhood experience similar to hers. Rosanna's parents came with her to the United States from Mexico when she was a young child, but her father left them with family in Chicago while he went to another state to work. He was gone for most of her childhood, and when he came home, he and her mother fought most of the time. Rosanna's mother was working full time and trying to raise four kids with no husband to help. Although Rosanna had aunts and uncles and cousins around her for support, she never felt like she had the attention of her mom. Most of Rosanna's memories of her mother were of a bitter woman who felt let down by her man and not loved enough.

Stella wasn't as familiar with her father's story, but you can see that there are parallels between the thorny stories she and her mother told themselves. If we look at this from a Quantum Love perspective, Stella came from a line of women who were let down by love and the men in their lives. They lived in the To Me ego frequency when it came to love, feeling afraid, abandoned, and unworthy. Stella had inherited these thorny stories through a series of direct messages her parents gave her as well as from the relationship dynamics they modeled for her and with her as she was growing up.

When you see how your painful milestones and stories align with those of your parents and even the generations before them, you may find that you view these stories in a new light. You may discover, like Stella did, that you feel empathy and forgiveness rather than anger and fear. Those things people did to you weren't because you were unworthy, but often because *they felt* unworthy.

This kind of empathetic awareness allows you to be a loving observer of your story. It allows you to feel empathy for the child that you were and to recognize with your adult mind that just because your mother was emotionally withholding or your father walked out on the family, this doesn't mean you have to attach to the worthiness-killing belief "If I were good enough, smart enough, and well behaved enough, these things would not have happened to me." You can look back on those things and understand, "No, they weren't my fault."

Now that you've identified them, it's time to start lovingly detaching from your thorny stories so you can move on from being stuck in ego frequency when those thorns get touched. Below are three strategies that will help you release the hold those negative stories have on you and shift to Quantum Love.

Strategy 1: The Power of Self-Awareness

When you are conscious of your thorny stories, it drastically changes the lens through which you view your partner and your points of conflict. The next time you feel yourself negatively reacting to your mate, take some deep breaths, ground yourself, open your heart, and ask yourself, "What thorny story is being triggered?" Almost always, once you have successfully done a Thorny Story Time Line, you will be able to identify not only the specific thorn that just got touched, but also the worthiness-killing story behind its triggering. Then you will realize it's no longer about your partner's behavior as much as the stories you are attaching to it. You can look at the situation more objectively, from a place of coherence and openheartedness, and from that place anything is possible.

Strategy 2: The Power of Forgiveness

Releasing the hold that worthiness-killing stories have on you and your reactions to your mate also involves forgiving those who wittingly or unwittingly hurt you. This can be a biggie and may take some time. What I do know for sure is that we are all on this planet, just doing the best we can. Some of us are misguided or more damaged than others. Some of us do horrible things to each other. But whatever happened to you, holding on to anger and resentment hurts you more than it hurts those with whom you are still angry.

Certainly if there was significant abuse or trauma, therapy may be needed to really reach a point of healing. But as I once heard Oprah Winfrey say, forgiveness is simply accepting that you can't change the past. You don't have to forget what happened and how you have been hurt, but looking at it objectively through the eyes of the adult you are now, you can choose to release its hold on you.

Can you look at your life with your adult, home frequency mind? Can you see that your parents, and their parents and *their* parents, were all struggling with worthiness-killing stories themselves? Those stories led them to act in ways that helped create your own. By understanding and feeling your own pain, can you empathize with theirs?

Strategy 3: Release the Family Worthiness-Killing Stories

When you can lovingly forgive, detach from, and observe the events on your Thorny Story Time Line from the coherent perspective of home frequency, then you can release them and let that energy go. Here is an exercise that you can use to help you do just that. I suggest you do this every day for as long as it takes to release the hold those worthiness-killing beliefs have on you. You will find that after a few weeks you will no longer be triggered the same way by your partner—or anyone, for that matter—and when you *are* triggered, you will notice it immediately and will be able to easily shift back into home frequency.

1. Take some deep breaths, ground yourself, open your heart, and close your eyes.
2. As you take deep breaths in through your nose, imagine a beautiful, healing, sparkling green light flowing in through the top of your head and into every corner of your body, filling every cell, every organ, every vein and vessel. Imagine that the light is healing and full of love, infusing any areas of pain

with peace, and feelings of loss with fullness. As you breathe out through your mouth, imagine all the stress and pain in your heart and mind flowing out of you. Spend five deep breaths doing this and feel the peace, wholeness, and coherence created in your body.

3. Say to yourself, "I have a worthiness-killing story that tells me [fill in the blank]. As the whole, powerful, and centered adult I am now, I no longer choose to believe that story. It no longer serves me. I bless it and I let it go."
4. Take a deep breath in, and slowly but forcefully breathe out. As you do, imagine the worthiness-killing story and the hold it has on you flowing out of you with your breath.
5. Slowly open your eyes.

Repeat tomorrow if necessary! You can do this for each worthiness-killing belief you have identified. In no time, you will be in the driver's seat, creating Quantum Love.

The Art of Changing Beliefs

As we discussed in the last chapter, your subconscious beliefs are typically way behind your conscious intentions of Quantum Love. Much of that has to do with the fact that your subconscious beliefs are a result of the thorny stories you have been unconsciously (and consciously) carrying with you for so long. You have learned new ways to release their hold, but let's also consider a practical way of allowing your authentic beliefs about your core desired love goals to match your intentions. Greg Kuhn summarizes this process very well in *How Quantum Physicists Build New Beliefs*. Remember, as we saw in Chapter 9, the idea is to coax your ego along, like the scared rabbit on the other side of the yard. Moving up one calibration at a time, you will get your ego eating carrots out of the hand of your essential self.

Here's how it works:

1. Pick out one of your Quantum Love Goals that you feel is particularly hard for you to achieve. Consult the Quantum Lovemap and start at the far left, lowest-calibrating emotional state: shame and humiliation. This is the feeling state you are going to wallow in around your core desired relationship goal or feeling. Even if you feel your emotions around your relationship desire are not nearly as low-frequency as shame, it doesn't matter. In this process you start from the ground up. Embrace it. Be there. For instance, maybe your goal is to find a partner. Your lowest-calibrating belief may be "I am humiliated that I don't have a partner yet, and I believe all the good ones are taken and I will always be alone." I want you to interact with this belief; journal about it, and even let yourself wallow in that negative space. Write down, say to yourself, and breathe into this: "I know I am now in a belief system of shame and humiliation around [fill in the blank], but I believe that can change, and I am open to a higher-calibrating belief."
2. The next day (or week, if you want), move a step up the Quantum Lovemap. Live there for a day or several days, journaling and accepting yourself in that place. And honestly locate what feeling you attach to it on the Quantum Lovemap. Get clear on where you are right now and accept it. Admit that your whole brain isn't on board yet. Let that be okay. Repeat the belief statement laid out above, but with the next-highest-calibrating belief.

You may wonder why I want you to start with the lowest-calibrating belief rather than where you are, worrying that you are going to create a worse reality for yourself with the low frequency of these stories. I can promise you that is not the case.

First of all, my experience has taught me that you are already likely calibrating much lower than you think. You will often find that when you try on that lowest-frequency belief, as yucky as it feels, it isn't unfamiliar. You certainly don't have to stay there long if it doesn't truly fit; just move on up to the next-highest-calibrating feeling or belief.

At the same time, you may find yourself needing to stay in one emotional spot for more than one day, and that's okay too. Just commit yourself to slowly moving up the Quantum Lovemap. As you do, your home frequency will start to take over, and your relationship reality will reflect exactly what you long to experience in love.

When the Pain Is Too Big: Sometimes the Only Way Around It Is Through It

What happens when you are going through a really tough time and the pain feels just too wide and deep to shift out of? Sometimes, especially during one of life's AFGEs, we are deep in the trenches, having a "dark night of the soul" (originally the title of a poem written by 16th-century Spanish poet and Roman Catholic mystic Saint John of the Cross). You feel adrift in a sea of pain, feeling waves of anger, sadness, and fear wash over you in wave after wave. It can seem impossible to shift into home frequency during those times, much less maintain it for any length of time. There are two key strategies involved in getting unstuck and moving into home frequency during a dark night of the soul: timing and letting pain be your teacher.

Timing Is Everything

When going through a particularly tough time in your life when your emotions feel out of control, it's crucial for your mind and body *not* to squelch them. But there is a time and a place to feel them. If emotions are taking you over at the wrong time, you can try a strategy I learned from a wonderful energy healer, Linda Hall, that works amazingly well.

First, take some deep breaths, close your eyes, and ground yourself. Visualize a container of some sort that has a cover. It can be a box, a jar with a lid, even a Tupperware container! Say to yourself: "I am putting these feelings in this container." Imagine putting them inside and closing the lid. Then make an appointment, literally: "Tonight at [give specific time] I am going to feel these feelings and let them pass through me."

You must honor your appointment. If something unexpected comes up and gets in the way of your scheduled feeling time, reschedule it. But don't get sneaky, continually rescheduling your appointment with yourself. At the appointed time, go to a place that feels safe for you where you can let it all hang out. Ground yourself again and, this time, *open your heart*, reminding yourself that you are safe. Let the feelings pass through you. If you aren't feeling anything low frequency at the time of your set appointment, do a body scan. Bring your awareness to every part of your body from head to toe. As you notice the first area of tightness or pain, breathe into it. Focus your awareness on that part of your body. The feelings will simply flow out of you. It will last only a few minutes, and you will have kept your energetic flow open and moved easily back into home frequency.

Go Through the Pain to the Stillness on the Other Side

Sometimes when pain, especially grief, is too wide and deep, the only way around the pain may be through it. This can certainly be effectively achieved through therapy with a trained clinician. But here is one very useful strategy to help you connect to a quantum or energetic level of healing inside yourself.

The most unexpected part of learning that my mother had terminal cancer was the full-body aftershocks that would rack me every time I remembered the truth of her diagnosis. I have since learned that this is a very common experience in trauma, especially where loss is concerned. I'd be busy working or with my husband and kids, and I would suddenly experience a stomach-dropping wave of shock and pain rolling through my entire being as I remembered again what I had momentarily forgotten. I asked my friend, life coach Diana Chapman, for some advice. She asked, "What would happen if instead of resisting the waves of shock, you just went with it, surrendered to it, and went all the way *into* the feeling?" I was terrified I might sink so far into it that I couldn't pull myself out of it, but at the next shock wave, I closed my eyes and breathed into the pain. I didn't fight against it but instead stayed with it. I felt like I was falling down a well of pain, but I was determined to keep trusting.

Going all the way into my grief led me to my first deep, adult spiritual epiphany. It felt like I was spiraling down a drain. But all of a sudden, after about 30 seconds, I felt filled with light in a place of pure peace and nothingness. It was a kind of emptiness, but the emptiness wasn't at all empty. I felt filled with and surrounded by intense, pure love.

In that moment, I suddenly knew that regardless of whether she was here in physical form or not, what my mother was to me and provided me was already *in me*.

In quantum terms, we are all one, made of the same energy, and energy never dies. Nor would the energy of my mother's essential self ever be gone, even when her body was no longer here. But I also knew that all those things she was to me and gave to me, I already could be *for myself*. She was me and I was her. It was an insanely deep and powerful experience to connect with the energy of my mother and to realize that it would always be here. I could keep it forever.

So, what can your pain teach you? Maybe it is a reminder that you are a survivor—that you are unbreakable and can handle life's crises. Maybe it is a lesson that acting from a place of ego, anger, and control is dangerous and hurtful. Maybe it will help you to deepen your empathy and compassion when speaking to your partner. Maybe you can store the memory of your pain away as a reminder to be gentle and forgiving with other people in the world because they, too, likely have their own stories of hurt and abuse. Or maybe you can use this memory as a reminder that you deserve to be treated with care, respect, and unconditional love, not only by other people, but also by yourself.

Remember What Coherence Feels Like

Once you have experienced your home frequency and caught glimpses of higher By Me and Through Me states, you know that it is where you want to be. It is important to remember that your essential self and your home frequency are immutable and indestructible, like the inside of a mountain. No matter what is going on around it, this essential part of you is in there. And it's waiting for you to find it again.

Feels Like Home

A great way to stay connected to home frequency is to remember times, no matter how big or small, when you have been in a state of coherence, and write them down in a "Feels Like Home" list. Anything positive, loving, satisfying, calming, or centering should be included. For example, you might list times when:

- You held your child in your arms for the first time.
- You experienced a soul connection with your partner.
- You achieved a goal you had set for yourself.
- You had mind-blowing sex.
- You pushed past what you believed were the limits of your ability.
- You snuggled with your dog.
- You were in such a great mood all day that nothing could bring you down.
- You felt that the universe was truly working for you.

- Your partner's act of kindness or consideration made your heart swell.
- You did something truly altruistic, with no expectation of repayment or recognition.
- You were in a flow state and totally "on a roll."

Once you have completed your list, select a few favorites and write down the feelings you had during that time. You can use your list of core desired feelings and the Quantum Lovemap to help you pick out the ones that fit your experiences best.

Now close your eyes and imagine yourself back in these experiences. See them from your first-person perspective as if they are happening right now. Feel those same feelings in your mind and body. This is your coherent state. It is inside you still, a place to which you can always return.

The wHolyShift

The wHolyShift, an exercise created by life coach Jackie Lesser, is a powerful, transformational navigation process you can use to make decisions that get you on the right path. When you're not sure what to do or where to turn in a particular situation in your life—a job, a relationship, a major decision, even a disappointment—and you feel stuck, you can use this exercise to get some clarity. The wHolyShift is an amazing way to retrain your brain to move away from ego frequency feeling states and to shift yourself back into home frequency.

With the wHolyShift you are reunited with your nature as a creative, resourceful, and whole being making your way in the world. The wHolyShift helps you access strategy and regain objectivity during these times of inner turmoil. It brings you home to yourself so you can move through chaos into calm and navigate easily and gracefully through whatever change you're going through in your life.

To listen to a guided audio version of Jackie Lesser's wHolyShift meditation, go to www.drlauraberman.com/quantumlove.

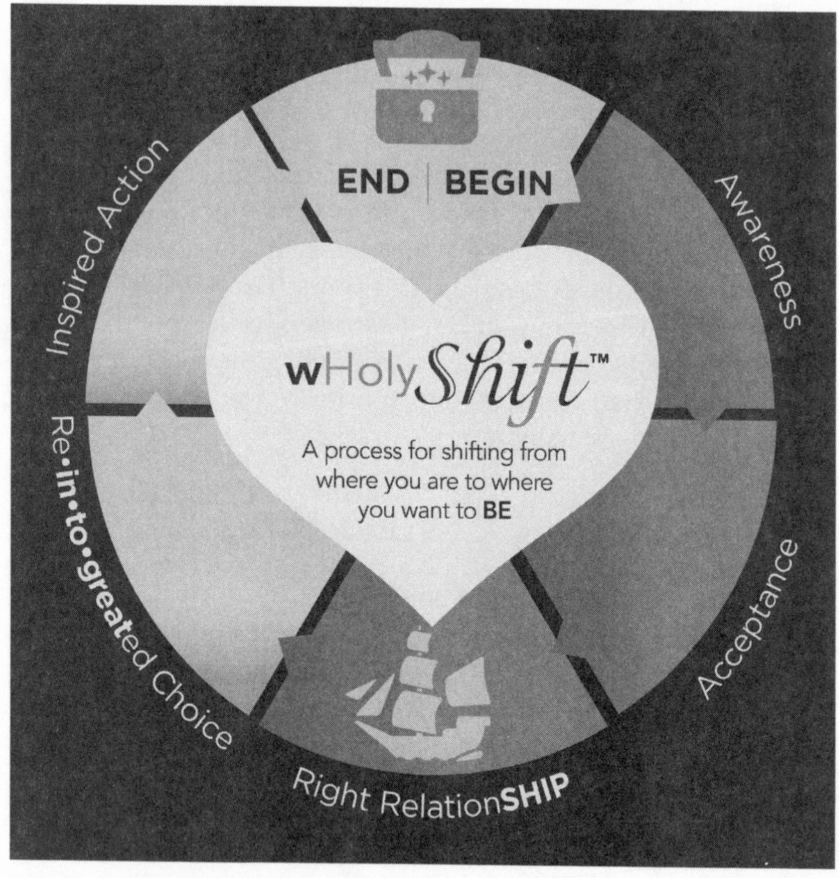

Figure 11: The wHolyShift

The wHolyShift is a seven-step process:

1. Breathe. Breathing is essential to bringing yourself into this process. You're breathing to draw your attention into the present moment.

2. Determine how you want to feel. You're entering the wHolyShift in the beginning with the end in mind. Right now you're feeling like you need new direction; you're panicked and you're feeling chaos. But ask yourself, "When this is done, how do I want to feel?"
3. Honor your observer. Realize: "Wow, there is a part of me that is feeling chaos and powerlessness and panic. But it is just a part of me. It is not *all* of me." The very fact that you are aware of how you are feeling—you are able to observe it—means that this bad feeling exists in only a part of you.
4. Accept how you feel about the facts of what *is*. And then offer yourself the same compassion that you would offer to a small child, to a loved one, to someone you really care about, like a good friend.
5. Move into "right relationship." Once you become aware that it's just a part of you that's feeling out of peace, and once you accept the facts of the situation, you've brought that part of yourself back into the fold. Now you're in what Jackie calls "right relationship," a loving relationship with yourself. You haven't tried to eject or reject that part of you that is feeling chaotic.
6. Make an "integrated choice." Now that you're in right relationship, in home frequency, you become wholly available to choose again: "How do I want to see the situation? What's another perspective that I can take?"
7. Take inspired action. What are the thoughtful steps that you feel inspired to take because of your new perspective? Sometimes they come to you as quickly as the new perspective does: You choose a new perspective and then BOOM, you know what to do or what not to do. And you will notice that the feeling that you chose to have in the beginning is what you are feeling now.

The wHolyShift is not a linear process, but it is a powerful one. You will really want to practice this with almost everything you encounter. When you get in your car, you wouldn't think of going anywhere new without plugging in your GPS. Well, you wouldn't want to take any action without knowing the truth of who you are. The wHolyShift can be a kind of GPS for your ego self to stay connected to your essential self.

Go Out into Nature

What if I told you that one of the hot new relaxation treatments at luxury spas across the country is something you can do on your own for free? It's not a masque or special massage technique; it's a simple walk through nature.

Forest bathing, as it's called, is a mindful walk through a forest (or even a park) that relaxes you as you breathe in the wood-scented air, hear the rustle of leaves or pine needles, and feel the sunlight dapple your skin as it filters through the treetops. The practice of forest bathing began in Japan, where it is known as *shinrin-yoku*. Its restorative benefits are often attributed to sensory awareness and time outside, away from the incessant noise of technology. However, budding quantum theorists that we are, we know that the positive benefit from forest bathing starts with our personal energy entraining to the pure, powerful energy of nature.

Nature vibrates at a clean, high-calibrating home frequency. It doesn't have an ego. While nature is highly complex, everything within it is perfectly aligned, balanced, and harmonious. This is why it is so calming and restorative to our bodies, minds, and spirits, raising our energy frequency as we entrain to it.

Unlike people, nature holds its own immutable frequency and will not entrain to us. But when we're in nature, we can't help but feel its effect. In relationships you entrain to your partner, your partner entrains to you, and you both influence each other's energy in a continuous cycle. With the stresses of life, work, family, bills, and all the logistical challenges—not to mention all our personal thorns that are being triggered along the way—it can be easy to get stuck. Think of going out into nature as the energetic equivalent of hitting the reset button.

Now that I know about the powerful quantum impact nature can have on our personal energy, I utilize it in my counseling whenever I can. It works wonders for couples who are really struggling and stuck in ego frequency individually or together. I have started running couples retreats in beautiful, peaceful, natural locations. During these retreats, we do guided meditations, couples and group sessions, and one-on-one work. I show them the different ways arguments happen in ego versus home frequency, and I show them how sometimes just going outside and allowing nature's restorative energy to do its thing can make all the difference.

Here's how you can get some nature therapy yourself:

Go outside: You can go to a park, to the beach, or even just out into your backyard.

Interact: Take your shoes off if you can. Sit against a tree or lie down in the sand. Use your five senses to take in your environment. Feel the warmth of the sun on your face or the coolness of the shaded ground beneath you. Listen to the sound of the moving leaves or grass as the wind moves through it. Breathe in the clean air; smell and taste it.

Notice the effect in your body: You may feel (as I do) a change in your physical self right away. Notice as your shoulders relax or as your face softens. Stretch out your arms and spread your fingers wide. It feels good to be out in nature, and putting your consciousness on that good feeling and the sensory experience of where you are will allow you to further entrain with nature's powerful, clean energy.

Note: This is a great way to reenergize yourself in the middle of the day. If you've been sitting for a while, get up and go outside for ten minutes. You will find that you feel much better when you walk back into your office.

Get Lubed Up: Strategies to Make Yourself Less Sticky

You've just learned some concrete shift moves that are great tools for changing your energy and getting unstuck in the moment. Now I want to focus on some strategies that are more like lubricants for getting and keeping your mind "unsticky" in the first place.

Change Your Brain, Change Your Life: The Effect of Neuroplasticity

Neuroplasticity describes the ability of your brain to change as the result of what you experience. Your brain is constantly reorganizing the information it holds. As new information comes in by virtue of your environment, relationships, behavior, thorny stories, AFGEs, and other experiences, your brain shuffles everything around to accommodate it, creating new neural pathways and altering existing ones. This is how you learn new things, build or break your habits, form memories, and write your stories.

As we get older, the brain becomes a curator of information. In what neuroscientists call "pruning" or "sprouting," it strengthens certain neural pathways while ignoring others. Unused neurons eventually die. This process is what helps us adapt to our changing environment as we grow and face different kinds of experiences. The amazing thing is that we can *consciously* use neuroplasticity to change our brains, and meditation is one of the best ways to do that.

Meditation

Meditation allows your mind to be more porous and able to move more quickly. It allows your cognitive functions to be more flexible. It teaches you how to reach and stay in home frequency. Even a brief meditation every day will produce these incredible changes inside your brain and body. It will also "lubricate" your brain so you are less likely to stay stuck in emotional states that don't serve you. If you have a low-frequency thought or belief in your mind, it's going to be much stickier in a brain that doesn't meditate than in one that does. If you can meditate, you will physiologically and neurologically shift into a better place, and you'll often find that your essential self has some wisdom to share with you when you're in that place.

When you meditate, you initiate positive change on a physical, psychological, and energetic level. When you restfully pay attention and concentrate and focus in a relaxed manner, you are activating the frontal lobe, which reduces activity in the neocortex. When your neocortex has less to analyze, it quiets down and your brain naturally recalibrates itself to a more orderly, coherent pattern. Those quiet moments, in which you allow your brain and body to reboot, will prime you to be more connected to your intuition and your essential self, even when you're not meditating.

There are many kinds of meditation, but I want to focus on those that I have found to be most helpful in keeping energy flowing. I will discuss them briefly here, and then, if you choose, you may refer to the Appendix to learn more about different types of meditation as well as some guided meditations you can try. There are also numerous guided meditations you can read or listen to at www.drlauraberman.com/quantumlove.

Transcendental Meditation

Transcendental Meditation is in the midst of a resurgence in the United States and around the world. This meditation is like taking some very necessary downtime for your brain.[1] There is a process to it, but it is extremely easy.

The process of "transcending" involves moving past the barrier of your analytical mind and into the loving, conscious space of your essential self. This often comes with a feeling of expansion as the perceived barriers fall away. It's a very relaxing state that is highly beneficial to both your brain and your body. Transcendental Meditation has been shown to reduce blood pressure and physical signs of stress, to improve the body's ability to repair itself, and even to improve brain function.[2] The award-winning director David Lynch, who has been practicing TM for decades, told me in an interview once that it's his way of "mining for gold." It is through meditation that he discovers his most inspiring creative ideas.

To learn how to do Transcendental Meditation, you can take a course, either privately or in a group. See the Quantum Love Resources section to find out more.

Loving-Kindness Meditation

Loving-kindness is essentially the practice of altruistic love. Often practiced by Buddhist meditators, it is the commitment to counteracting negative experiences with a loving perspective. I believe this really connects to the generosity of Quantum Love as you choose to believe the best of your partner and see even difficult experiences as a gift.

Loving-kindness meditation is built on the foundation that there are four kinds of love: compassion, friendliness, appreciative joy, and equanimity. It is centered on practicing these four types of love with four kinds of people: a respected beloved (a spiritual teacher or coach), a dearly beloved (your partner, a family member, or close friend), a neutral person (someone you encounter but don't really know), and a hostile person (someone you are having difficulty with). It begins with placing focus on yourself and then mentally dissolving the barriers between yourself and the other person—in other words, recognizing the Quantum Truth that we are all one.

Loving-kindness meditation is a wonderful way to train your brain to see your partner through the lens of Quantum Love. As your loving perception informs your relationship reality, so too will your energy state create even more opportunities to strengthen and solidify that reality. Go to the Appendix to read a guided loving-kindness meditation.

Guided Meditation and Visualization

Guided meditation and visualization have been proven to be extremely powerful arbiters of change in your mental and physical state. You may have heard of the power of visualization in training your body to do something. It is widely used in the sports world as basketball players envision their free throws going into the basket, swimmers envision their bodies executing the perfect butterfly stroke, and Olympic skiers mentally practice how they will move down the course. This meditative technique is so effective because your brain can't tell the difference between something you are actually experiencing and something you are imagining. (Note: This is also why choosing to believe the best in your partner is such an important facet of Quantum Love. To your brain, perception and reality are the same thing!) Because your brain thinks you are actually experiencing the goal of your guided meditation, it initiates physiological responses to what it believes is happening to you. Guided meditation can activate your muscles, raise or lower your body temperature, even change your cells over time.

Then there are the positive changes it can create in the brain. As we learned in Chapter 9, when you have any experience, good or bad, the neural pathways in your brain change to store the new information for future use. Guided meditation takes this one step further by not only giving the brain what it thinks is a real-life experience (and thus changing the neural pathways accordingly), but changing the perception of the experience.

This is especially useful as a way to address the thorny stories we tell ourselves. If we have experienced trauma, betrayal, or even a full-blown AFGE in our relationship, our brain's neural pathways have been changed not only to say, "I can't trust," but to attach pain to the stored information: "I can't trust because I will get hurt."

By using guided meditation and visualization, you can reframe or even change those beliefs. And in doing so, you can change your brain. The wHolyShift that you learned earlier in this chapter is a great example of a guided meditation. For others, I encourage you to either create your own imagery or visit a website that offers free guided meditations. The UCLA Mindful Awareness Research Center website has several good ones, as does the Chopra Center website.

Mindfulness Meditation

Unlike guided meditation, mindfulness meditation doesn't have a set goal or endpoint. It is a place of quiet reflection and self-observation and awareness that offers a very powerful way to access the wisdom and clarity of your essential self.

The key to mindfulness meditation is to leave all judgment at the door. You are an observer, lovingly detached from your thoughts as they enter and flow through your mind. You may find it difficult, when you are first getting started, to withhold any judgment of the thoughts that come. This will get easier over time and yield some amazing benefits along the way.

Mindfulness meditation can be a powerful tool for strengthening our brain's ability to manage negative emotions—and this, of course, makes it a very powerful tool for shifting. Dr. Richard J. Davidson, a prominent neuroscientist and professor at the University of Wisconsin–Madison, has led the charge in researching how we can train our minds to function better. He has found that mindfulness meditation "strengthens the neurological circuits that calm a part of the brain that acts as a trigger for fear and anger." In fact, he found that mindfulness meditation not only makes it easier for us to manage difficult emotions, but also activates the parts of our brains that form positive emotions.[3]

In addition to helping us manage our emotions, mindfulness meditation has been shown to lower stress, help us objectively analyze ourselves, make us more aware of and present in our bodies, and make us more compassionate—all of which is helpful in making us less "sticky" to negative emotions and in making it easier to shift out of negative feeling states. Beyond that, I believe that mindfulness is an aspirational state in one's day-to-day life. We've already established that our memories of past experiences are flawed and that we can't predict the future. *The only thing that is absolutely real is right now. And right now is where every possibility exists in Quantum terms.*

If you'd like to give mindfulness meditation a try, refer to the Appendix to find guided meditations, or go to www.drlauraberman.com/quantumlove.

Taoist Meditation

Meditation is a key part of the way in Taoism. It connects you to the larger energy of the universe, gets you into the flow, and helps relieve stress and heal the body. I have also found that it is an amazing way to calm and relax your body and mind, opening yourself to the gifts of peace and clarity from your essential self.

I have found that Taoist meditation, particularly the Inner Smile meditation, is an excellent tool for shifting and staying in home frequency as well as moving energy through the body. It seems a little weird at first, but I promise it feels wonderful—and it's very hard to stay stuck after doing it.

If you'd like to try the Inner Smile meditation, go to the Chapter 8 section of the Appendix.

Yoga

Yoga is a wonderful way of getting back into your body. When we're in a lower-frequency emotion, especially fear, one of the first things to happen is that we disconnect from our bodies. That's why you often hear people say they had an "out-of-body experience" when a crisis occurred. But it doesn't have to be a crisis that throws you out of whack energetically. Most of us aren't in tune with our bodies or the energy flowing through us. When we are, we can use our bodies to move and shift into home frequency.

Any kind of physical exercise not only will get you emotionally and spiritually back in your body, but will release lots of feel-good chemicals (endorphins) that make you feel better almost immediately. Those nerve-calming endorphins work wonders on your mood, help you sleep better, and renew your mind (literally and figuratively) so it functions properly.

Yoga has amazing physical effects on your body, as we've discussed; it also has a tremendous effect on your mind. In fact, after attending a yoga class with his father, neuroscientist Alex Korb reports that he realized it was the act of learning to keep your brain calm while twisting your body into stressful positions that created "yoga's greatest neurobiological benefit."[4]

As we've learned, your prefrontal cortex and limbic system are pretty trigger-happy when it comes to initiating stress response in your brain and body. These days, we don't have to worry too much about predators, but our survival instincts have yet to figure that out. Our prefrontal cortex and limbic system will kick-start the release of stress hormones, the muscle tension, and the changes to our breathing and heart rate whether we are arguing with our partner in the kitchen, trying to hold a painful or difficult yoga pose, or being chased by an escaped tiger.

The good news is that when you learn to manage your stress response in a safe environment, one in which a soft-spoken yoga instructor reminds you to return to your breath and relax your body, you can apply those techniques in more charged situations. And, over time, you can train your brain to take its finger off the red button and stop launching into stress response at the first sign of discomfort.

Remember, where the body goes the mind follows. I believe what makes practicing yoga such an effective strategy for being less "sticky" is that it teaches you to manage your brain through your body (and vice versa) and increases your awareness of just how powerful the connection between the two is. In just a short span of time, the length of a class, you will have at least one opportunity to feel your stress response get turned on and then practice pulling yourself back out of it. This kind of practice, on top of its myriad other benefits, makes yoga an incredibly effective strategy for managing your energy flow and getting unstuck.

We are responsible for the energy we bring into our relationship. We are responsible for the caretaking of our body's energy. And we are responsible for realizing when we are stuck in a low-frequency state and shifting out of it. Our energy will create and shape and impact our reality, our relationships, our health, and our happiness whether we are conscious of it or not. The real key lies in our commitment to *choosing home frequency.*

Now you have the ability to catch yourself when you're getting stuck, to know your triggers, your thorns. This knowledge is going to prove so powerful and so helpful as you move forward and get better and better at understanding what being stuck will do to your relationship. You have the tools now to be a conscious caretaker of your energy. I cannot say this enough: Use them!

CHAPTER 11

Quantum Sex

The purpose of intimacy is to massage the heart, soften the muscles around our hardened places, and keep pliant the places where we're deep and strong.

— Marianne Williamson

If you have read any of my past work or seen me on any television programs, you know that I often help couples tackle their sexual challenges. Whether it is low desire, mismatched libidos, early ejaculation, or difficulty reaching orgasm, I have devoted much of my career to helping people treat these common issues. Like the Florence Nightingale of bad sex, I am always there in the trenches, helping couples figure out how to fix their issues and improve their sex lives.

This book is different. I am not going to discuss sexual problems here (though if you are interested, you can check out other books of mine, such as *Real Sex for Real Women* or *The Passion Prescription*). This chapter on Quantum Sex, instead, is going to help you learn how to harness your energy in order to have the best sex of your life. I want you to get in touch with your sexual chi and discover how to have spiritual, mood-altering, relationship-changing sex. And, yes, that includes plenty of orgasms! But that is not the whole point here: I want you to embrace the journey, not the destination, and I also want you to understand that the journey is about much more than pleasure. It's about Quantum Love.

You might be thinking, "What the heck is sexual chi? It sounds like a bad R&B song. And what journey is she talking about? I am lucky if I can have sex with my partner once a week. The only journey we take is to dreamland after our usual routine." Stay with me! All will be revealed.

First things first: according to Chinese medicine, chi (or life-force energy) originates in our very bone marrow. In Chinese medicine, the sexual organs, the reproductive organs, and the secondary sex organs are believed to be part of our chi. Taoist philosophy believes chi to have a bonding force: like superglue, it "sticks" you to your sexual partner (and your partner's energy sticks to you). When the chi is in alignment, you will enjoy its benefits across the board. And when you harness that energy, you can have Quantum Sex.

This is where breath comes in. Breath is crucial for moving energy through the body. There is a hatha yoga text that says, "When the breath wanders, the mind is also unsteady. But when the breath is calmed, the mind too will be still." Something amazing happens when you simply sit and calmly breathe in and out. Your mind slows down. Tension evaporates. You feel lighter. Your heart feels stronger and more serene. You connect back to your essential self.

When you're using your breath to move energy around your body, you're increasing the circulation in your body, relaxing your muscles, and promoting blood flow, all of which is going to enhance your physical arousal. That is why many of the exercises I am going to give you incorporate breath and help you learn to use it along with intention to move your sexual energy.

For most of us, sex and all the sensations that come with it are felt in the pelvic region. We may have some tingling in our hands and feet and maybe a full flush as a result of orgasm, but the sensation of arousal and of sex (and even the release that comes with orgasm) are mostly centered in the genitals. What these breathing and energy-moving exercises teach you to do is to pull your sexual energy *and the sensations that come with sex* throughout your whole body. If you get good at these exercises, your orgasms will be more intense, full-body, and beyond powerful.

The Quantum Sex Experience

Ultimate passion is the expression of two energies merging into one. As with Neale Donald Walsch's description of TomMary that we talked about in Chapter 5, your energy and that of your partner meet in the quantum field and merge to create your shared sexual field. You are constantly feeding energy into your shared field, and the energy created in that field is being fed back to you. While we might not be able to *see* it, we can certainly *feel* it . . . as long as we let ourselves.

All too often we hold ourselves back by heeding the warnings of our thorny stories or worthiness-killing beliefs. We listen to our egos instead of our essential selves. Even as we walk around thinking, "I am so lonely!" we wall off our hearts and resist the desire of our essential selves to throw ourselves head first into communion with our partner's essential self. When you hold yourself back and cling to your separateness, it's really hard to feel that oneness. In other words, if Mary clings to "Mary" instead of consciously experiencing "TomMary," she's not having Quantum Sex. But when you are in communion with your lover and yourself, Quantum Love can start to express itself in sexual form. This is the foundation of passion, for your partner and for life itself.

As you've now learned, we are, at our core, pure energy, each of us vibrating at a different frequency. Individuals in our field, especially those closest to us, are vibrating at a frequency harmonious with ours; when our frequency is low due to our body's health or our thoughts, beliefs, or feelings, it impacts not only our reality, but that of the people around us as well. And the closer we are to each other, the greater our entrainment becomes. When two people have sex together, sharing their bodies in a physical way, entrainment is taken to a whole new level. Your bodies *and* your energy are intertwined and blended. Any kind of sexual exchange is an exchange of energy, but intercourse is especially so. It is, after all, the only time part of our body is encompassing or being encompassed by part of another body.

Most of us aren't conscious of our increased entrainment to our partner during sex, thanks to the limitations of our five senses and the fact that our attention is focused elsewhere. We are worried about our cellulite, whether the kids will wake up, if we are pleasing our partner or lasting long enough, or even if the laundry is almost done. But imagine how it would feel to be *conscious* of your body's energy as you merge it with another's in such an intimate way.

Whether it's by yourself or with someone else, sex is the most tangible way to sense your energy (physical exercise comes in a distant second). The intensity of energy that sexual arousal brings is like none other. From desire to arousal to orgasm, your body's energy is intense and the volume is set to *loud*. Whether or not you use sex as a way of moving and harnessing your body's energy, sex is great. But mind-blowing sex comes when you are conscious, in the right frequency, exchanging energy and moving it purposefully around in your body, feeling your own energy as well as your partner's as it moves into and through each of you.

Quantum Sex is a source of creative life energy, and I don't just mean that sex creates life. I mean that when you are having this kind of sex, it is something that feeds into and from your creativity, not another item on your to-do list or a way to simply release stress. Remember, the sacral chakra, the seat of your sexuality, is also the seat of your creativity. That is not an accident. When you harness this energy, boy, is anything possible. Your ability to manifest what you most desire in your romantic connection is cemented in physical form as you and your partner become energetically one.

This is Quantum Sex, and it's all yours if you're ready for it.

Why Do You Want to Have Sex?

As I am sure you have caught on by now, every key to Quantum Love starts with *you*. And Quantum Sex is no different. Before we get into the exercises and techniques that will help you have mind-blowing sex, we have to get into your mind a little bit.

Quantum Sex, like Quantum Love, exists in the By Me and Through Me states of home frequency. It simply isn't a place we can reach if we are in the low-frequency To Me zone. But it is possible to approach sex from different points on the Quantum Lovemap. Your intention for sex sets the frequency at which you're entering into it.

The interesting thing about sexual energy is that when you are in the flow, you can have great sex, even from a low-frequency place. You can have ego sex, revenge sex, hateful sex, and it'll often still feel really good. But trusting and surrendered sex comes from a much higher frequency and is therefore a very different experience.

Researchers Cindy Meston, Ph.D., and David Buss, Ph.D., asked 203 men and 241 women to list the primary reasons why they had sex. They then compiled a list of 237 reasons and presented it to another group, asking them to rank how often those reasons had motivated their own sex lives. What resulted was a ranked list of the main reasons why people had sex.[1] I've listed some of the common reasons in the table below. You can see where these motivations fall in the To Me, By Me, and Through Me states. Some of them can fall into more than one category, depending on the nuances of the motivations involved.

Sexual Motivations

Motivation	To Me	By Me	Through Me
I was attracted to the person		✓	
I wanted to experience the physical pleasure		✓	
I wanted to show my affection to the person		✓	✓
I wanted to please my partner	✓	✓	

Motivation	To Me	By Me	Through Me
I wanted to harm another person (my partner, rival, or a stranger)	✓		
I wanted to enhance my social status	✓		
I wanted to express my love for the person		✓	✓
I wanted to return a favor	✓	✓	
I wanted to feel a connection to my body		✓	✓
Someone dared me	✓		
It was out of duty or under pressure	✓		

Sex approached from different places on the Quantum Lovemap will make you feel totally different, create completely unique kinds of sexual experiences, and create more or less of the reality you want. If we look at the list here, we see a whole range of intentions that originate from different frequencies. Some, like "I wanted to express my love for the person," are loving and high-calibrating frequencies (Love and Openness). Others definitely calibrate below 200, like "I wanted to harm another person" (Anger) or "It was out of duty" (Guilt). There are any number of beliefs that might go along with these differently calibrating intentions, from "Sex is an amazing way to connect with my partner" all the way to "I'm not worthy of the love I desire."

A Glimpse of Enlightenment

No matter what your frequency is when you start out having sex, I view orgasm as a shortcut to the feeling state of *bliss,* calibrating at 600 on the Quantum Lovemap, and major Through Me energy. I find that you get a huge spike and feel the rush of that energy as you climax, giving you a glimpse into full-blown Through Me. But whether you stay there or go back to a lower-frequency state is in large part up to you. It can be a quick blip, like a spike on a heart monitor, or it can reset the bar and help you maintain or set a new bar for your coherent state of being. And the bliss found with orgasm moves even higher when it comes from a state of Quantum Love.

Take a look back at your Quantum Love Quiz, paying special attention to the sections pertaining to the root and sacral chakras. Are you calibrating in a lower frequency in either (or both) of those areas of your relationship in general? If so, you can take a giant leap forward in your sex life simply by doing some of the chakra work we discussed in Chapter 8 (and addressing some thorny stories if necessary, as we discussed in Chapter 10) to bring your frequency up. You will also find several of the exercises I describe in this chapter helpful for clearing and balancing all your chakras, but especially the root and sacral chakras. Remember, the root chakra governs our sense of being in our bodies and that is so, *so* important to having great sex. And, given the creative and playful nature of great sex, our sacral chakra has to be balanced as well. That doesn't mean you have to wait for your chakras to come into balance to have great sex, of course. You can still have Quantum Sex by having it in home frequency and setting intentions from a place of Quantum Love.

Let's talk for a minute about the importance of having sex in home frequency. It's not just about amping up the joy, passion, and physical experience of sexual connection. When you have sex with another person, you take his or her energy into you (more on that in a moment), which can then affect your own energy for better or worse. In other words, by having sex with someone who is calibrating at a low frequency, you might bring your own frequency down (especially if your intention for sex is also calibrating near 200 or below). Those with strong internal balance, who can drop into and stay in home frequency, can take in that low-frequency energy without bringing their own energy down. This is a great reason to get into home frequency before having sex. Then, even if your partner is in a low-frequency vibration, you can use your powerful home frequency sexual energy to equalize your partner's and transform it to home frequency.

Sex is one of the most powerful ways to get your partner's energy to entrain with yours, moving you into Quantum Love together.

What Kind of Sex Do You Want to Have?

The messages we get about great sex in our culture are often about titillation: the next kinky thing to try or a new way to spice things up. It's the reason why *Fifty Shades of Grey* sold millions of copies. Novelty is fun, but it isn't enough. As I've mentioned to you already, I could offer you 365 new things to try in your sex life and one year later you would be coming back to me looking for more. Novelty isn't what we actually want; what we are really looking for is *intensity.*

What makes for an intense sexual experience is, first and foremost, *intent. What is your intention with your sex life in general? With each specific sexual encounter?* There are all kinds of sex: quick or slow, sensual or mindless, a simple release or a soul-to-soul connection. It all has to do with our conscious intention and the frequency we are holding as we move into a sexual encounter.

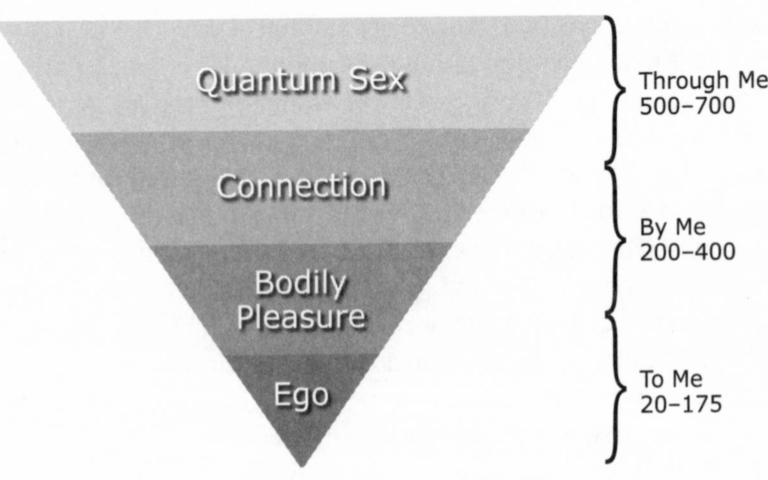

Figure 12: The Potentials of Sex

Consider Figure 12. At the bottom is ego sex. It's squarely in the To Me frequency. Ego sex occurs when we use sex to remind ourselves that we are worthy or attractive or to control our partners, keep them from leaving us, manipulate them into doing something we want them to do, and so on. That may be our conscious intention, or we may just be unconsciously vibrating at a calibration below 200 as we engage in a sexual encounter. This could be due to any number of thorns or triggers in our self, our environment, or our relationship.

Bodily-pleasure sex happens when we use sex to relieve stress, when we are just horny, or when we see someone or something that arouses us. This kind of sex can be in either the To Me or the By Me frequency, depending on internal motivation and where you are calibrating at the time of sex. For instance, if you are in a state of love and appreciation for your mate, getting along and feeling connected, and you just need a release, that would be sex for bodily pleasure in the By Me state. If you are disconnected and angry at your mate, carrying resentment and feeling apathetic toward your partner and your relationship, then the sex for bodily pleasure you are having is going to be more in the To Me zone, in ego frequency. There's nothing wrong with ego frequency sex, provided that we understand it for what it is. However, with ego frequency sex it's harder to sustain a deep and abiding connection in a long-term relationship, especially if that's the only kind of sex you have.

Sex for connection can be in the By Me or Through Me state. Here, sex is not just about release or reminding yourself you are worthy of love and desire. It is about joining your body with another with whom you feel emotionally and physically intimate. Sex is an expression of your connection to each other. You can have sex for the purposes of connection from an emotional state of acceptance or understanding, for instance (By Me), or as an expression of love and reverence for your mate (Through Me).

But Quantum Sex? That's purely in Through Me. That's sex that provides both release and deep, *deep* connection. You are in home frequency when you start the encounter, and your intentions arise from love, joy, and peace, even bliss. Quantum Sex is a merger of sexual and spiritual energy. It is supercharged, but there is also a stillness and a sacredness as you and your partner open your whole selves to each other, tune in to each other's rhythms, and eliminate the boundaries you perceive are between you. Quantum Sex feels like a powerful spiritual experience, and it begins with intention.

Sacred Sexuality

In the traditions of tantric and Taoist sexology, texts documenting the intertwining of energy and sex go back thousands of years. The ideas of merging energy, oneness, spiritual union through sex, and even sex as a spiritual, blissful glimpse into Through Me energy have been practiced for centuries, and their goals are the same now as they were in the beginning.

The Taoist perspective views sex as transformative, taking sexual energy and using it to heal and restore the body, mind, and spirit. Taoists see sexual energy as the fuel behind chi, our life-force energy. Tantra, meanwhile, teaches that sexuality is our means of deepening intimacy with our partner and expanding our consciousness beyond our perceived boundaries. I view these two perspectives as two halves of a whole. Tantra teaches the art and Taoism the science. Tantra speaks to consciousness while Taoist principles focus on the body. Both move and play with energy. Taken together, I believe these two sacred sexualities embody Quantum Sex, and their ancient teachings can inform our present and future relationships.

The Art of Manifesting Quantum Sex

Just as we talked about your core desired relationship feelings earlier, let's talk about core desired sexual feelings. If you could snap your fingers and have whatever you wanted, how would your sex life feel?

Would it be exciting and playful? Sensual and deeply connected? Would it be passionate and intense? The feelings you desire might vary depending on your mood at any given time.

That is why it is so important to set your intention for sex. If you want to feel excited and playful, then you need to make sure that you are moving your own energy into an excited and playful place.

Moving sexual energy also opens you up physically in a way that leaves your energetic channels clearer. This is partly why I think it's important to regularly self-stimulate if you don't have a sexual partner (and even if you do). I am going to be sharing many techniques for experiencing Quantum Sex in the following pages. It's a good idea to practice on your own with self-stimulation first, with less pressure, and then try it with a partner.

In my book *It's Not Him, It's You!* I list a whole collection of reasons why self-stimulation is important, including getting to know your body and what works for you, being able to communicate that to your partner, and learning to relax and enjoy pleasure without feeling low-calibrating self-consciousness. In fact (for women especially), self-stimulation is the foundation for owning your body and leading a happy, healthy, orgasmic life. And, as an added bonus, it also keeps your energy high and in home frequency.

The Intention Blessing

If you want to have a wonderful, *quantum* sexual experience, you must set your intention to do so. I advise actually saying a kind of brief blessing in the form of an intention, if only in your mind, before starting a sexual encounter. You can do it consciously and openly, even out loud, during soul gazing, for instance (more on that later). Or you can do it quietly and unobtrusively while your partner is out of the room or when you know sex is coming.

1. Take some deep breaths, ground yourself, and open your heart.
2. Say to yourself: "I am in home frequency, filled with anticipation and ready to share and merge my loving

energy with my partner. My intention for this sexual experience is [state a core desired sexual feeling]."

3. Say to yourself: "Let me take any negative energy from him/her and transform it to positive energy. Let my body be a source of pleasure, love, and fulfillment for myself and my partner."

Move yourself into the feeling state of a deep, fulfilling, loving, energetic connection. This will be key to manifesting Quantum Sex.

The Energy of Infidelity

While we are discussing the importance of determining *why* we have sex, *what kind* of sex we want to have, and how to create the experience using our intention, I would be remiss if I glossed over what happens when we have sex outside of our relationship and the energetic impact it yields.

There are all sorts of infidelities that can occur in a monogamous relationship. It could be emotional cheating, in which you are investing emotional energy in another person, having intimate or flirtatious or sexual conversations, or sharing personal things (sometimes in lieu of or before sharing them with your partner). Or it could be a physical affair, which might or might not include actual consummation. The bottom line is if you are in what is understood to be a monogamous relationship and you are speaking, writing, or behaving in a way you wouldn't if your partner were right there, you are redirecting your energy away from Quantum Love.

I don't care how good it feels in the beginning. When you cheat you are scattering and deflecting your energy. This is true whether you are sexually flirting with lots of different people or directing all that energy toward a specific person with whom you are having an emotional or physical affair. And when you do have sex in an affair, your energy isn't all there either, because some of it is with your monogamous partner. When you are juggling more than one sexual partner, especially when accompanied by the low-frequency emotions that go with secrecy and lies, nobody is getting to Quantum Love or Quantum Sex.

I find that cheating is almost always about a worthiness-killing story. The cheater is rarely cheating for purely sexual reasons. Usually it has to do with the need for validation, feeling loved, feeling attractive or good enough. As for the partner, on some level, *always,* his or her essential self signed up for this. Don't beat me up yet! Believe me, I've been cheated on as much as the next person and understand how painful it is. Goodness knows I've counseled hundreds of individuals and couples through healing after an affair. And I can tell you that it almost always becomes clear that on some level the partner knew the cheater might be cheating, or wasn't being completely honest, or wasn't fully present in the relationship. Sometimes a partner will admit that he was the one who shut down first. He either put up with a partner's disconnect or disconnected himself because he didn't really believe he was worthy of love. At his core was a belief that said, "I don't want to be alone," or "Maybe one day she will love me the way I want if I can just be [more or less of something]," or "I'm not strong enough to deal with the issues in this relationship, so I'm just going to emotionally check out."

Taking couples through the process of repairing after an affair is one of the most rewarding parts of my clinical practice. In large part this is because when both partners are willing to look at themselves and do the work it takes to shift things, they invariably end up with a much deeper, more profound connection than they ever would have had if the affair hadn't happened. The affair is their AFGE.

Remember, your partner is your greatest teacher. Exploring this in therapy while repairing your relationship after an affair is like a master's program in Quantum Love. Both partners learn so much about themselves, their triggers, and their worthiness-killing stories. More often than not, as we look back on when the divide first began (typically way before the affair started), we can see that these issues were at play and led to their disconnection, moving them away from Quantum Love and toward the infidelity.

A Note on Sexual Boredom

The most common complaint I get from couples all over the world about their long-term relationships is that their sex life has gotten "stale" or "boring." They want tips and tools, new ways to "spice it up." There's nothing wrong with that, of course; a creative spirit is very important in a good sex life. But as I've said, you are going to run out of tips eventually. The real intensity of sex comes from the frequency of your energetic state and your Quantum Love intentions. You could have sex in the exact same position at the same time of day every day for a week, and if each day you set a different *intention*, you would have seven different sexual experiences.

Sexual boredom is really, at its root, a persona. I have found that almost every time you are bored in your relationship and feel stuck, you're on the Drama Triangle. The villain says, "I'm bored with my sex life!" and points the finger of blame at his or her partner for not being adventurous enough, willing enough, or passionate enough. The victim, too, may be bored, feeling at the effect of a partner's lack of adventure or willingness. (Once again you can see how you can have a foot in victim as well as villain on the Triangle, can't you?)

Here are some ways to get out of Boredom Persona:

1. Take your 100 percent. I have found that this is the most effective way to bust out of this persona. What have you done to keep yourself engaged? How can you engage yourself further? How can *you* take responsibility for spicing things up on an *energetic* level?
2. Make a list of core desired sexual feelings. Do you want to feel sensual, adored, playful? It can be anything, but you have to determine what you want in order to create it.
3. Feel appreciation. What can you focus on that *is* working? What does your partner do that you

love or find adventurous? Put your awareness and gratitude there. Praise it and build on it.

4. Make sure you aren't directing your energy elsewhere (whether it's to an affair or to something else, such as your kids or your to-do list) or energetically shutting down.
5. Get playful and try something new.

Sexual boredom is combatted with high-frequency intentions, home frequency states, and a creative mind. By busting out of boredom persona, you will move into a higher frequency and, from that place, have amazing sex.

The Intention of Surrender

In Quantum Sex there is no room for holding on to control. It is as simple as that. Just as you cannot move into Quantum Love from ego frequency, you cannot have Quantum Sex if you are in FMC mode.

Control plays a huge role in our sexual awareness and experience:

Control over the physical experience (orgasm is a release of control).

Control over the power in our relationship (using sex as a means to an end).

Control over our emotional experience (holding on to intrusive negative thoughts about our bodies, our history, and all the *shoulds* of sex).

But if you want to have Quantum Sex, you want to be focusing on *surrender.* Your sexual pleasure will also be largely impacted by your state of mind and your energetic connection, your exchange of emotions, with your partner.

Unfortunately, many people experience low-frequency emotions when it comes to sex. From a very early age, most of us were given negative messages about our bodies and our sexuality. We were made to feel ashamed of our sexual desires and embarrassed about how our bodies looked. Many of us still unconsciously carry these stories, especially women, who were often raised with lots of *shoulds* around their sexuality and ideas about what nice girls "do" or "don't do." Many women were expected to squelch sexual feelings until marriage, at which time they were supposed to suddenly turn on their sexuality and enjoy it. This is very difficult to do. After decades of avoiding sex and thinking of it as dirty and bad, it's hard to suddenly start enjoying sexual pleasure without inhibition. The same is true for men who were raised in very conservative or religiously observant households. When you are stuck in guilt- or shame-inducing negative stories about your body or sexuality, it can be hard to relax into a sexual scenario, be fully present, and surrender to the sensations.

Men have another unique struggle. Unlike women, men are socialized to believe that they are supposed to be sexual at all times. They should always be raring to go, with high libidos and frequent, powerful erections that appear at a moment's notice. However, the truth is that men aren't automatons with just one thing on their minds. Just like women, they can often struggle to get in the mood. Work stress especially can deplete their desire, and anxiety over sexual performance can also complicate their erectile ability. These fears and anxieties, like shame and guilt, are low vibrating and in ego frequency, standing in the way of our ability to release the control necessary to move into Quantum Love, much less Quantum Sex.

The good news is that if you are following the guidance and exercises I have given you thus far in this book, you are already priming yourself for great flowing energy and Quantum Sex. If you are struggling with something, whether performance anxiety, difficulty with your sexual response, low desire, shame over your sexuality, or embarrassment over your body, use the techniques in the previous chapters to challenge your assumptions, get your body healthy, and surrender, reconnecting to your body and your partner in a coherent state that allows for Quantum Sex.

The Secret of the Pink Sparkly Vagina

Toni came to see me because she was struggling with her sex life. Her partner, Alex, had difficulty reaching orgasm; it would take him a very long time to climax. As a result, their sex life was often stressful. He felt unhappy about how difficult it was to respond, and she wanted to make him happy while ensuring that her needs were also met. It was hard for her not to internalize his delayed ejaculation as her lack of attractiveness. "It's got to factor in there somewhere, right?" she asked me. It was clear to me we needed to work on changing her stories and moving to a higher-frequency emotional state, especially before and during sex.

As part of our work together, I taught Toni the secret of the Pink Sparkly Vagina. It's a visualization that creates a deep energetic connection with your body as well as with your partner. She looked more than a little skeptical when I introduced the idea: "I'm sorry, *what?*"

I smiled and continued. "Here's how it works. During sex, close your eyes and imagine that the walls of your vagina are made of beautiful, sparkling pink light energy, pulsing and shining brightly. Imagine the light flowing all around your partner's genitals, in this case, Alex's penis." I told Toni to imagine that pink sparkly vagina holding Alex in a state of love, passion, and acceptance. "You don't even have to tell him what you are doing," I added. "Ideally we don't want to create more pressure for him."

Toni put her "homework" to practice almost immediately. She simply shifted her energy out of trying to fix, manage, and control. Before starting their sexual encounter she moved into coherence as I had taught her. In her words, she "just waded into a deep pool of love and peace and focused on channeling that message of acceptance to Alex."

During sex, Toni imagined her pink, sparkling vagina surrounding Alex's genitals and spreading into and around their entire bodies. She didn't do anything different physically, only shifted the thoughts, emotions, and visualizations. And then a wonderful thing happened. Her husband reached climax with almost none of his usual difficulty! Not to mention, her own sexual response was through the roof! Even though he had no idea what she was doing, she was able to change the tone and quality of their sexual connection, simply by changing her energetic state and getting into Quantum Love.

Give this exercise a try the next time you and your partner are having sex. You don't have to picture a pink sparkly vagina (unless you want to!). Instead, choose an image that speaks to you and makes you feel at peace and connected to your mate. You might picture your vagina as a rose, unfolding petal by petal for your partner as he dips into it like a happily buzzing bee. Or you might picture your vagina as a warm, salty ocean and your partner as waves moving quietly and powerfully through it.

And, guys, you can do the same thing, of course! Visualize your penis as an anchor connecting you to your partner, as a golden cord of light that helps unite you deeply to the person with whom you are sharing your body. Use whatever visualization works best for you. And yes, it's okay to find this exercise a little silly at first! Smiling at the idea of a pink sparkly vagina is only natural.

Yin and Yang

Even if you're not familiar with Taoist principles, I'm willing to bet that you've heard of *yin* and *yang,* two balanced halves of a whole, a combination of light and shadow constantly changing together and transforming each other. It is an interdependent duality, as one would not exist without the other, something that I think is very fun to contemplate when you have a spare ten minutes. The concept of yin and yang energy is also very important in terms of sex, as the balance of yin and yang is different in every person and in every relationship.

We tend to think of yin energy as more passive and yang as more active, of women as yin and men as yang. But we all have both in us, and our respective yin and yang energies shape our relationship in different ways.

In your relationship, ideally one of you will be more yin (and it doesn't have to be the woman) and the other more yang. You balance each other out. It can be tricky, however, when both of you lean heavily toward the same side. If both you and your partner are more yin, you may find that while very giving, neither of you are very assertive sexually. That kind of couple may find that sexual desire and shared sexual frequency are an issue. A couple that are both yang might have a lot more sex but also struggle with sexual roles: who is the top and who is the bottom, who is the giver and who the receiver?

There are still significant gender biases about how men and women are *supposed* to act sexually, but we're moving into a place where gender identity is becoming more fluid. It is no longer the expectation that men should be heavily yang and women heavily yin. Here's how I prefer to look at it: people who are more heavily yin tend to be creative, emotional, and in touch with their intuition, while those who are more heavily yang are very logical, structured, and organized. I like to think of yin's inward-moving energy not as passivity but as receptivity and magnetism, and very powerful in its own right.

The Yin and Yang of Our Sexuality

Sex is a powerful energy exchange. And there is a nature and a tone to that exchange. I prefer to talk about our sexual energy as yin or yang rather than masculine or feminine because anyone can be anything. Quantum Love should take you to a place of communion and passion where your energy is not limited by stereotypes. A man should be in touch with his emotions and a woman should be able to step into her own power. At the same time, there is a yin and yang to masculine and feminine energy that is part societal, part biological, and part energetic. Real intimacy comes when you can be in your own home frequency and consciously intertwine your energy with your partner's to create Quantum Sex.

It is yang energy that initiates sex, while yin energy receives and responds. Yang energy tends to move up, and yin down. In terms of sex, this means that people who are more yang tend to be turned on by direct stimulation of genitals, with the energy flowing up from genitals to heart; those who are more yin generally need to have their heart attended to first before the energy moves to the genitals. Yin energy is slowing and needs more foreplay to get aroused, while yang tends to get aroused quickly and burn through sexual energy faster. In heterosexual relationships it is usually (but not always) the men who are more yang and women more yin. In same-sex relationships, either partner can lean toward either kind of energy. The key is that you want a balance of both.

In a relationship between yin and yang, each has to attend to the other's energy flow. To attend to yin energy, stoke the flames every day with words of love and appreciation, spend (technology-free) time together, and kiss with no other intention than simply connecting. And to attend to yang energy, remember that the yang partner's ability and desire to hurry is not a lack of caring, but a burning energy of passion that wants to be released. Don't be offended, and if you are game, go along with it from time to time. Much energy and passion can be found in a quickie, especially when it's created from home frequency.

Finding the Yin-Yang Balance

But what happens if a quickie isn't giving you what you desire? Such was the case with Audra and Logan. They had frequent sex, but Audra felt that it wasn't always fulfilling.

"It's over so fast," she complained. "I wish Logan would tend more to my needs and slow down, but she's already reached orgasm before I can even get aroused, and then she never wants to keep going."

Logan confessed that she often lost interest once she climaxed, finding it difficult to maintain arousal afterward. When asked about trying to prolong the time before her orgasm, Logan maintained, "I've tried, but it feels so good, I just go for it." She continued, "But at the same time, there have been times I've stretched it out longer than normal. And Audra still doesn't seem satisfied."

"Audra," I asked, "why do you want her to last a long time? What are you really looking for? I bet it isn't just minutes on the clock. So what is it, really?"

"I guess I am looking for that buildup of excitement. You know, that feeling of becoming aroused and gradually getting more and more into it. And then the release, even better together," she said.

"Well, I think you can do two things. I think Logan can work more on slowing down her style." I shared a variety of strategies for stretching out the arousal process. "But," I went on, " I also think you have a piece in this, Audra. If you want to feel that buildup, you need to bring that energy into the bedroom."

"How?" she asked.

"Start working on that excitement long before you hit the sheets. Fantasize during the day. Send an erotic text to Logan. Wear something that makes you feel sexy and desirable. Really own your responsibility when it comes to creating that energy," I said. "Then, when you are in the act, try to get into the state of coherence we talked about. Feel that powerful energy and that bottomless love and desire. Don't watch the clock. Don't hold Logan to a certain standard of performance. Just be there with her. Feel what's happening in your body. Don't chase orgasm, or try to slow it down, or try to force anything. Just exist in a state of love and intimacy."

Since working with Audra and Logan, I am happy to report that they have both changed the way they approach sex. Logan is more than happy to serve Audra's needs and has widened her focus beyond her own desire. Audra no longer times Logan or stresses over what's going to happen next. They are both present and connected, and they say sex has never been better!

Building the Fire of Sexual Energy

Most of us are lucky if we fit sex into our lives at all, much less engage in a prolonged sexual and erotic experience in which we are connecting soul to soul. I definitely support the idea of a quickie as maintenance sex, allowing a yin-yang energy exchange that keeps you connected and keeps your relationship outside of the "roommates and co-parents" realm. But I also encourage you, at least twice a month (preferably four times), to try one of the exercises in this chapter to keep building your sexual energy in a more intentional way.

Building the Fire: The Energy of Kissing

The Taoists claim that kissing is a way for two people to connect energetically and a wonderful way to exchange chi. It stimulates yin as well as yang. In a physical sense, hormones and other chemicals are exchanged during kissing, and these are good for your body on many levels! In fact, studies found that kissing decreased levels of cortisol and increased levels of oxytocin in study participants, compared with participants who only held hands.[2] I also did a study of my own several years ago with K-Y, the well-known lubricant brand, that looked at predictors of sexual and emotional intimacy in love relationships. We found that couples who kiss and cuddle regularly are one-eighth as likely to be stressed and depressed as couples who don't!

As one of the best ways to get sexual energy flowing between you and your partner, kissing can be a highly erotic part of foreplay and an even more powerful libido enhancer. Here are some kissing exercises to try. I encourage you to make it a weekly practice to do at least one of these exercises, but if nothing else, kiss simply for kissing's sake. Spend 10 to 15 minutes (schedule it on your calendar if you have to) kissing and cuddling *without* moving on to any other sexual activity. This builds the sexual energy between you and is a great way to increase libido in one or both partners.

Yin-Yang of Kissing

In this exercise I want you to take turns. First, kiss your partner the way you most love to be kissed. Kiss that way for a while. Then your partner should kiss you the way he or she most loves to be kissed, and kiss that way for a while. Do this for ten minutes. You will be amazed at what you learn and how good it feels.

Kissing with Intent

When you are kissing your partner, whether it is just for its own sake, as part of foreplay, or during sex, build a clear intent into the kiss. The best way to try this at first is when you are kissing just for kissing's sake (because then you can really concentrate). As you kiss your partner, imagine sending messages of love, connection, and attraction through your lips to his or hers. When you are on the receiving end of this kind of kiss, you can really feel it!

Kissing add-ons:

- Create a physical connection beyond your lips. Try kissing your partner's shoulders, back of the neck, hair, and face. Use your hands to stroke (or even pull) his or her hair, or cup his or her head or cheek.
- Make eye contact. You can incorporate soul gazing (described later) or just stare into each other's eyes and communicate what you are feeling with your gaze. According to Chinese medicine, the eyes are connected to the genitals.
- Kiss heart to heart. If you lean your head to the left a little as you kiss, your hearts will be touching, which will make that electromagnetic communication even greater!

Building the Fire: Soul Gazing

Soul gazing with your partner is a wonderful way to ground your energy together and create an emotional intimacy that is often beyond words. In fact, while you are doing this exercise there should be no talking. It is like consciously connecting your essential selves. You can soul gaze with your partner fully clothed, but it's even better when fully undressed. You can do the exercise by itself, or use it as a way to get completely present and connected on every level before you are sexual together—as part of or preceding foreplay.

Soul gazing should last at least two minutes, which I promise will feel like a *very* long time at first. Often people feel uncomfortable when they try it the first time, but don't be discouraged. It may feel awkward in the beginning, maybe a bit silly. You may want to giggle a little—and let yourself, if you need to—but know that it is just from nervousness around how unaccustomed you are to this level of deep intimacy. It's normal, and it will pass.

1. Sit comfortably facing each other, cross-legged on the bed or some other comfortable surface, maybe supporting yourself with some pillows. You can also try a position known as *Yab Yum*. Here the larger partner is sitting up straight with back supported and arms embracing the other partner, face to face. The other partner is sitting in the first partner's lap, supported by the embrace, wrapping his or her legs around the partner's waist.
2. Take a few moments to ground yourselves and open your hearts, as described in Chapter 3. If your partner doesn't know how to do this, you can explain it. If he or she enjoys this, grounding and opening your hearts together as a daily practice (at any time) can bring a new level of connection to your daily life together and help you resolve an argument quickly and effectively.

3. Place your right hand over your partner's heart, and have your partner do the same. Put your awareness on your partner's heartbeat. Can you feel it? Imagine your heartbeats synchronizing and entraining. Take some deep breaths together.
4. As you keep your hand over your partner's heart, stare deeply into his or her left eye (directly above the heart). Imagine you can send all your love into your partner's eyes, and visualize it traveling like energetic light through your partner's whole body.
5. Now start to synchronize your breath, taking slow, deep breaths in and out while continuing to gaze into your partner's left eye.

If you'd like to, you can add another level to soul gazing by incorporating circular breath. In this case, you should be in the *Yab Yum* position with your faces close together. The idea is to create a circular, continuous flow of breath with no break or pause between inhale and exhale.

1. Breathe gently through your mouth, keeping your face, mouth, and jaw relaxed. Let the back of your throat relax and, without pushing out your breath, let it simply fall out of you.
2. Breathe in and out in a continuous circle. Do this on your own and then—the key of this exercise—do it with your partner, synchronizing your breath. In the *Yab Yum* position, stare into your partner's eyes and breathe the circular breath into each other's mouths, both of you breathing out at the same time. (Hint: make sure you don't eat a garlicky or heavy meal before this, and brush your teeth!)

Soul gazing during the act of sex not only makes the experience phenomenally more rich and deep but also slows things down in a good way. Once you have mastered soul gazing during foreplay, I encourage you to try it during intercourse if you are engaged in a position that is face to face. You continue penetration in this position but stay perfectly still during soul gazing. You will be amazed at how intense and arousing it can be.

Building the Fire: Sensual Touching

Just as you can communicate tremendous love and high-frequency energy to your partner during soul gazing, you can also send energy physically through sensual touching. This exercise should be done with both of you completely nude; it can be part of foreplay or just to connect with each other in a deep, physical way. There should be little to no talking. The key here is to train your senses on the physical sensations you are creating.

1. Take turns being the giver and the receiver. The receiver lies face down first and the giver focuses on sensually touching the receiver head to toe. Use long, sensual strokes and circles with the focused intention to communicate loving energy through your hands. You can use a massage oil if you wish. However, the touch should not be massagelike or intended to relax your partner. Your intention is to send high-frequency energy from your body into your partner's through touch.
2. After 5 to 10 minutes, the receiver flips over and the giver continues touching the same way, head to toe, on the front side of the body. The receiver should do nothing but stay intensely focused on receiving, noticing if it's possible to feel the love and high-frequency energy flowing from the giver's hands.
3. Then the receiver becomes the giver and the giver the receiver.
4. Sensual touching can include breast and genital touching, but it doesn't have to. Chances are, once you get into the exercise, you will both be so aroused that sex will happen regardless!

Building the Fire: Working Your Kegels

I can never talk about sex without mentioning the Kegels. That's how important they are! These are the muscles named after Dr. Arnold Kegel, a gynecologist who first highlighted the importance of strengthening them. Your Kegels run in a figure eight (sort of like an EHFI!) around the vagina or scrotum and the anus. Performing Kegel exercises regularly will keep your pelvic floor strong. The pelvic floor (or pelvic bowl, as I like to think of it, due to its shape) is a group of muscles in your pelvis, essentially forming a sling that holds up all the reproductive organs. Think of them as a large, shallow bowl that reaches between your hips and from the front of your body to your spine.

The Kegels are also key muscles for your orgasmic potential, as physiologically an orgasm is an intense contraction and release of muscle tension. I view the Kegels as a sexual powerhouse, a momentum-creating energetic pump, especially when you use them in some of the exercises I will outline later in this chapter. Kegel exercises can supercharge your sexual experience, giving it a boost of power. From a physiologic standpoint, Kegel exercises increase blood flow, create nerve stimulation, and yield more friction on a woman's G-spot and a man's penis. In addition to being an energetic pump, Kegels are also a punctuation mark: a comma, not a period, moving your energy flow forward.

Kegel exercises are very simple to do. You can identify the Kegels as the muscles you would use to stop the flow of urine. Squeeze these muscles while leaving your anus relaxed. It takes a little practice, but once you've located them, make it a habit to exercise them with at least 100 to 200 contractions a day. Don't balk! You can do Kegel exercises anywhere (in the car, at the office, at the movies). Contract the muscles for five seconds and then release for five seconds. Your sexual response will thank you, I promise. You can also use Kegels to create pools of energy in your pelvis in the following exercise.

Pelvic Bowl Energy Builder

This is a great exercise to use when you want to build physical sexual energy and arousal in the genitals before sex, and it's great exercise for your Kegels as well. You can do it alone or with your partner.

1. Ground yourself and open your heart.
2. Take some deep breaths in and out. After a few breaths, imagine that as you breathe in, a beautiful light (you choose the color) is coming in through the top of your head and flowing down your spine toward your pelvic bowl.
3. With each breath in, imagine the light flowing in and down your spine. With each breath out, squeeze your Kegels and imagine all that light pooling in the pelvic bowl.
4. Breathe in, pull the light down, breathe out, and squeeze the Kegels seven to ten times.

You will notice a sense of fullness and physical arousal in your genitals. The energy will build the longer you practice.

The Bottom Breath

This is another great exercise for building internal pelvic sexual energy. Bottom breath moves energy around the genitals and around the body in general, and it's very easy to do.

1. Sit on the floor with crossed legs or on a chair with feet on the floor.
2. Place your hands on your belly and relax them there. Let your belly be mushy and soft and rounded.
3. Push/exhale all the air out of your lungs.

4. Inhale, and as you do, gently push out your anal sphincter—the way I have heard it described (forgive me here) is to imagine your anus kissing the floor or the seat of the chair.
5. As you exhale, simply relax and let go.
6. Repeat several times.

Time to Make Sex Electric!

In the pages ahead are exercises that will allow you to practice moving sexual energy, or chi, around your body. When you master them and use them during sex, I can promise you that you will find enhanced sensation, deeper connection, and easier and more intense orgasms. The energy movement techniques I will teach you work in four key ways:

- They generate more chi and distribute energy around the body.
- They increase pelvic blood flow, which enhances engorgement and sensation.
- When used during sex, they distribute sexual energy and enhance it, making orgasm a whole-body experience.
- They help strengthen pelvic floor muscles!

Ideally you should try these exercises first during self-stimulation, then try them with a partner. It's better to get really comfortable with the sequence of the exercise before using it during sex so it doesn't become a distraction rather than an enhancement.

Some of these exercises involve the chakras, so see Figure 13 for a quick reminder of which chakras are where.

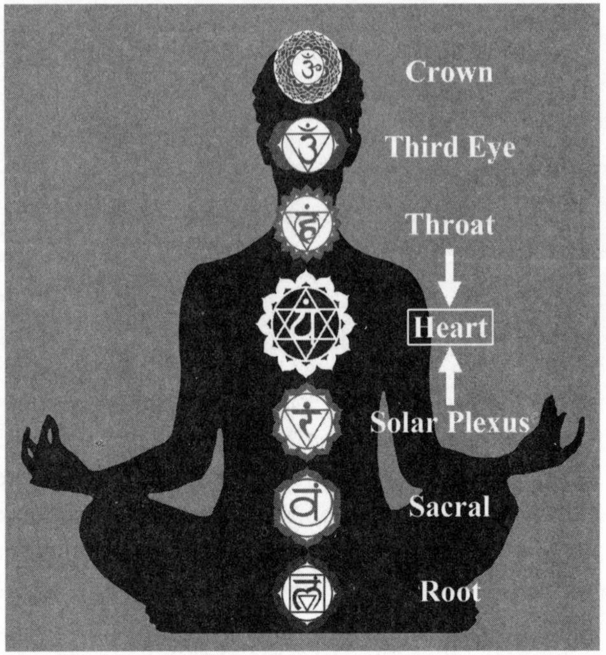

Figure 13: The Chakra System

Sexpiration Meditation

This is the perfect exercise for when you want to create more desire, greater response, and deeper creative inspiration. If you do this as a regular practice, you will find that it significantly facilitates living in By Me and Through Me, not only sexually but in the rest of your relationship. You can do this alone or during sex with a partner. (If you'd like to hear a guided Sexpiration meditation, go to www.drlauraberman.com/quantumlove.)

Start by placing your focus on your breath. Slowly breathe in through your nose and out through your mouth.

1. Connect with your essential self by saying "Hello" to yourself. Remember, your essential self is the self that hears your hello.

2. Ground yourself and open your heart.
3. After a few more breaths, start to imagine a beautiful, bright light pouring in through the top of your head and flowing through your entire body, permeating the cells, the muscles, the organs. The light is healing and beautiful, and it can be any color you choose. As you breathe in, visualize the light flowing into your body. As you breathe out, visualize the light spreading out like a wave from your head to your toes.
4. Now put your attention on your heart. As you breathe in the light, send it to your heart. Notice how the left side of your body expands and relaxes as you inhale. Imagine the beautiful, healing light filling your heart, relaxing it and illuminating it. As you breathe in, the light becomes more intense. As you breathe out, the heart is relaxing, opening and expanding like a flower. As your heart expands and opens, you can send your light out to another person—someone you love, want to connect with, or want to heal. Maybe for now you just keep the light centered on your own heart.
5. Your body is filled with and flowing with light. Now put your awareness on the pelvic bowl. As you breathe in, imagine the light flowing in through your head as the bowl lengthens out to receive it. As you breathe out, squeeze the Kegel muscles and imagine the bowl settling snugly into your pelvis, with light pooling in it, just like in the Pelvic Bowl Energy Builder. Do this for several breaths.
6. Now let's try looping the energy. Imagine the pool of light in your pelvic bowl. It is sparkling and bright and almost like a precious oil of light. Imagine that your spine is like a straw. This time as you breathe in, tighten the Kegels and imagine

sucking the light up the straw, all the way up the spine to your brow chakra. As you breathe out, imagine the light pouring up and around, through your third eye, down through the front of your body back into the pelvic bowl. Repeat this several times.

The Microcosmic Orbit

The Microcosmic Orbit was created as a breath-centered meditation. As it turns out, it is an extremely powerful sexual meditation too. Like the Sexpiration meditation, and like the Tantra exercises that I will be describing later in this chapter, it is a method of moving sexual energy around your body.

1. The first time, it helps to sit comfortably in a chair or with your back supported, alone. Once you get the hang of it, you can do this lying down or in any sexual position you wish!
2. Rest your hand between your navel and pubic bone (which is the front part of the sacral chakra, the sexual center of your body's energy).
3. Now focus on your sacrum, which is where the spine meets the pelvic bowl in the lower part of your back. Move your hand there. This is the back part of the sacral chakra.
4. As you breathe in, imagine pulling strong, clear, beautiful energy from the front part of your sacral chakra to the back part and bathing all your sexual organs and your pelvic floor in that beautiful energy.
5. Then, as you breathe out, move your hand back to the spot beneath your navel and pull the energy forward again. Move your hand from one spot to the other, sending energy back and forth as you breathe deeply in and out.

6. Now it's time to create a sacral circle of energy. As you breathe in, imagine moving the energy up to the top of the sacral chakra, and as you exhale, imagine moving energy back down to the bottom. Breathe in as you move the energy to the back of the sacral chakra, and breathe out as you move it to the front. You are creating little circles with your breath.
7. Move your pelvis back and forth as you breathe in and out.

Note: When you do this exercise during sex or self-stimulation, you will obviously not be using your hands to guide your energy, but the sensations and effects will be the same or even better!

The Three-Zone Approach

You can use the Three-Zone Approach to warm up your body and get the energy flowing, especially to your genitals. According to Chinese medicine, we have three levels of erogenous zones. The lips, breasts/nipples, and genitals are the *primary zones. Secondary zones* include earlobes, nape of the neck, small of the back, buttocks, inner thighs, and the backs of the knees. The *tertiary zones* include the palms, navel, edges of the pinkie fingers, nostrils, ear openings, anus, soles of the feet, and big toes.

Who knew that the outside of the pinkie was an erogenous zone?

Try this during self-stimulation or with a partner. If with a partner, you can take turns! First focus on the secondary zones. As the Taoists insisted (and I heartily agree), foreplay should not begin with the genitals! Next focus on the primary zones, and *then* move into the tertiary. I know it seems counterintuitive, but you'll be surprised at the intensity of the sensations that this order creates. As you approach each area, begin with a touch or kiss, then breathe or blow gently on it. Circular, light strokes are better. The Taoists believed this approach arouses sexual energy slowly (yin), and then there is a little release (yang), and then arousal can continue to build. When you start on the secondary zone, you can build erotic energy for full-body experience.

Nine Is the Magic Number

In Taoism, sex is seen primarily as a joining of energy, and Taoist writings describe many techniques for working with this energy. One of the most famous is the Nine Thrusts technique. Basically, this involves a pattern of thrusting during sex that builds sexual energy and stimulates the external sensitive areas of the woman's genitals and the frenulum (underside tip) of the penis as well as the G-spot and the shaft of the penis. This technique can also work with anal penetration, and it can be done either with a male partner or with a phallic sex toy.

First, make sure you are in a position that allows for the male partner to fully control the depth of penetration. It's also a great idea to have extra lubricant on hand. I always recommend organic coconut oil, a phenomenal lubricant that's all natural and wonderful for your body and skin.

The Nine Thrusts technique combines shallower thrusts (which are yang-oriented) and deeper strokes (which are more yin). The sequence goes like this:

1. 9:1 Shallow to Deep: To start with, the man inserts only the head of his penis into the vagina (or anus). He does this nine times. Then he inserts the entire penis in a deep thrust, just once.
2. 8:2 Shallow to Deep: Next, the man uses eight shallow strokes followed by two deep strokes. He then goes on in this way, decreasing the number of shallow strokes by one and increasing the deep strokes by one.
3. 7:3 Shallow to Deep
4. 6:4 Shallow to Deep
5. 5:5 Shallow to Deep
6. 4:6 Shallow to Deep

7. 3:7 Shallow to Deep
8. 2:8 Shallow to Deep
9. 1:9 Shallow to Deep

That's right! Ninety strokes! You can choose the pace, but slower is better. The varying strokes build sexual tension and intensify the experience. To add another level, the woman can squeeze her Kegels, contracting them during the deep strokes or during withdrawals. Don't worry if you lose count. Practice makes perfect!

Orgasmic Meditation

Orgasmic meditation has received a lot of hype. Given that it's a practice of giving 15 minutes of undivided attention to your genitals, it's no surprise that people are taking notice.

The idea was brought into the mainstream by Nicole Daedone, author of *Slow Sex,* who views orgasm as a renewable and regenerative resource rooted in our fundamental need for physical connection and refers to the practice as OM.

In a TEDx talk, she tells the story of how she discovered OM, focused awareness and intention combined with nonsexual stimulation. After just a few minutes, she says, the "traffic jam of my mind broke open." She was able to access the innate desire for human connection, what she calls the hunger underneath all hunger.

Note that while this practice can be performed with partners of either sex, OM is largely focused on female arousal. However, the practice is not intended to be goal-oriented, and orgasm may or may not occur. Think of it as a mindfulness exercise for your clitoris! If you are two women in a relationship, determine who is the giver and who is the receiver before you begin. If you're in a heterosexual relationship, don't worry, guys, you will have your turn, but this exercise is all about her!

The instructions that follow are adapted from OneTaste, the organization that Nicole Daedone founded, which trains people in the practice of OM. These instructions are much more general than OneTaste's training. For more information, check out the organization's website, which you'll find in the Quantum Love Resources section.

To do OM, the receiver lies down, unclothed at least from the waist down, while the giver stays fully clothed. The giver then uses his or her index finger to slowly, lightly, and deliberately stroke the clitoris of the receiver for 15 minutes. During this time, both partners focus their attention specifically on the receiver's clitoris and the sensations or feelings that are arising. After 15 minutes, each partner shares his or her experience and what was felt and observed.

Testicular Breathing

Guys, I didn't forget about you. Testicular Breathing is both a great exercise for men who want to extend their staying power and a way to move and build sexual energy. To do it:

1. Sit on the edge of a chair, with your back straight but relaxed. Your weight should be distributed mainly on your buttocks and feet. You do not want your genitals to be in contact with the chair itself.
2. Scan your body for any tension. If you feel tension, get up and move around or go for a walk until it is gone, then return to the exercise.
3. Now bring your attention to your scrotum. Inhale slowly and contract your pelvic muscles so that your testicles are drawn to your body. While inhaling, visualize your breath as a flow of energy that fills your testes. Hold your breath for as long as you feel comfortable, then let it fall out of your body as you release the muscles in your pelvis.
4. Repeat this series for nine breaths, then take a break. Perform another three to six sets before moving on to step 5.

5. Now, as you breathe in, begin to pull the energy up along the spine, from the testicles to the perineum (root chakra), then to the lower back (sacral chakra). Breathe out each time you've raised your energy up a chakra, and breathe in as you pull it up another level. Visualize each chakra center filling up with energy before continuing to move the energy up your spine.
6. Keep moving your energy up your body using these breaths, through the solar plexus chakra to the heart chakra, throat chakra, third eye chakra, until you reach the top of your head, your crown chakra.
7. Finally, bring the sexual energy from the testicles to the head during one inhalation only.

You can do this exercise several times or just once—whatever feels good to you.

Fire Breath Orgasm

This exercise is a chakra-oriented orgasmic meditation named by a Cherokee medicine man, Harley Swiftdeer. You will be breathing into each of your chakras and, as you do so, imagining the colors of that chakra illuminating with bright, healing light. As you continue to breathe, you will move this beautiful energy up your body in circles, and by the time it reaches your upper chakras it will feel like it has taken on a life of its own. It's a wonderful way to move energy *and* combine it with intimacy and pleasure.

Fire Breath is extremely relaxing and rejuvenating, but it can also yield some unexpected discoveries. Big emotions may move through you, often emotions you weren't even aware you were holding. You may want to release tears or express anger. While it can absolutely be done with your partner, I suggest doing it on your own first. Try it initially as a breath exercise, with no sexual stimulation. Then you may want to do it during self-stimulation.

Finally you can practice with your partner. Many of my patients report that they *and* their partners feel the intensity rise as they are pulling the energy upward. I'll describe the full Fire Breath meditation first (it's called Fire Breath 2), then I'll share Fire Breath 1, an abridged version. Take a look at the illustrations in Figures 14 and 15, and take your time mastering the steps. Your energy and your sex life will thank you!

Fire Breath 2

1. Drop any expectations and put yourself in the mind-set and energy state of the feeling you desire. Let go of any attachment or expectation with regard to outcome.
2. Lie on your back with your knees up and feet flat on the floor (or bed). Relax your jaw. Breathe in through your nose and exhale through your mouth.
3. Imagine your breath filling up your belly like a balloon. As you exhale, flatten your lower back to the floor. There should be a gentle rocking in your pelvis as you do this.
4. Squeeze your Kegels as you exhale.
5. As you breathe in, imagine pulling energy from your root chakra—your perineum. You don't have to push or pull the energy. It will follow your thoughts.
6. Next, inhale your energy from your root chakra up to your sacral chakra. Then exhale, circulating the energy back down to the root. Continue moving your energy between the root and sacral chakras by breathing in and feeling it rise, breathing out and letting it go back to the root. Repeat several times and you will notice it feels like the energy is moving easily and almost on its own.

7. Now enlarge the circle by breathing energy from your root chakra up to your solar plexus chakra, squeezing your Kegel muscles as you breathe out. Repeat this several times as well. When this feels complete, reduce the circle so that the energy goes between your sacral chakra and your solar plexus.
8. As you continue breathing and squeezing your Kegels, enlarge the circle of energy so that it moves between your sacral chakra and your heart. When this feels complete, reduce the circle so that the energy goes between your solar plexus and your heart center. You are moving your energy from sacral to heart and solar plexus to heart.
9. Next, make a circle of energy between the solar plexus and throat, followed by a smaller circle between heart and throat. When you reach the throat, make some sounds if you aren't already doing so, anything from sighs to moans to "aahs." This is liberating and helps move energy. The energy may start moving up the chakras in circles on its own as the momentum gets building.
10. Breathe in, moving energy from the heart to the third eye, and breathe out and back down to the heart. Do this several times, followed by a smaller circle between the throat and the third eye. When you're sending energy into your third eye, roll your eyes up (keeping them closed) as if you can see out the top of your head. This will help your energy rise.
11. The next circle is from the throat to the crown followed by a smaller circle between the third eye and the crown chakra.
12. Keep breathing and moving your hips and moving the energy in circles.

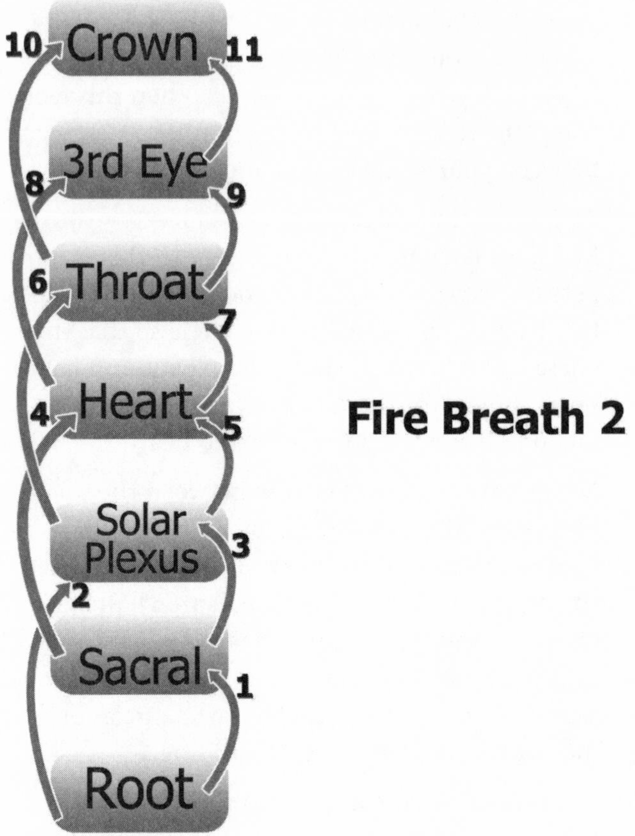

Figure 14: Fire Breath 2

Fire Breath 1

This is a simpler version of the Fire Breath exercise, in which you just move up the chakras in order. Follow steps 1 through 6 of Fire Breath 2. Then, simply move between two chakras at a time: root to sacral, sacral to solar plexus, solar plexus to heart, heart to throat, throat to third eye, and third eye to crown. Keep breathing and moving your hips as the energy circles.

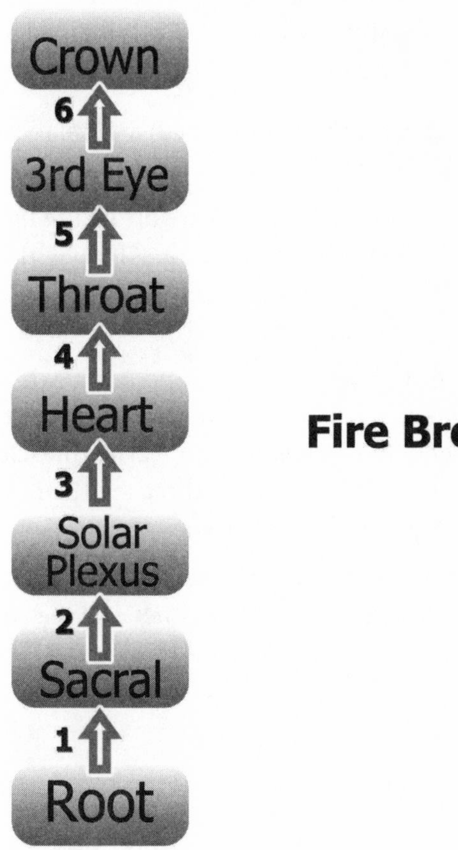

Figure 15: Fire Breath 1

The Clench and Hold

This is a Taoist technique as well. It is another breath-oriented, energy-moving sexual experience that plays with the expansion and contraction that we discussed in Chapter 3. The Taoist explanation for why the Clench and Hold works is that when you build lots of energy through breathing and then suddenly stop and constrict your muscles, there is nowhere for your energy to go but through your central energy channel, which is called the Inner Flute, and out the top of your head. Thus many describe the Clench and Hold as a kind of inward "blasting off."

1. Sit comfortably on the floor (or bed) and relax your face and jaw.
2. Breathe in, imagining that you are breathing light into and around your heart chakra. Fill up with as much breath as you can, then gently let it pour out of you completely and fully. Do this two times.
3. After the third breath in, hold it and don't exhale! Instead, clench your abdominal muscles, Kegels, and anus. It may help to squeeze all the other muscles in your body as well, but those three are the most important. Squeeze as hard as you can.
4. Hold for 15 seconds, then release, relaxing completely. Repeat three to five times and see what happens. You may find you want to continue!

Tantric Sex

If all you know about tantric sex is that Sting used to boast about how it helped his long-lasting prowess, you are in for a treat. There is so much more to tantric sex than marathon sex sessions (although they can be awesome too!).

First, you must understand that according to tantric philosophy, sex is sacred. Sexual fluids are considered a precious offering. Sex created us. It's a huge part of who we are and why we are. It's nothing to hide or be ashamed of. But neither is it something to abuse or treat lightly. Tantra teaches us that when we have sex, we are communing with another person's soul. We are not just bodies. We are beings with no space between us, two forces melding into one, creating a perfect unity of spirit and flesh.

How sad to consider that many people now use sex as a way to escape themselves, as a way to forget their pain or distract themselves from their hurts. This is the very opposite of tantric teachings. Tantra teaches us that sex isn't a Band-Aid for our soul-scrapes or a way to numb our heart's pain, but a way to be fully present with and seen by another person, and by extension, the universe or God or whatever you want to think of that power as. In Tantra, sex isn't for distraction. It is for transformation.

Circling Your Sexual Energy

In Tantra, it is believed that during a sexual encounter between a man and a woman, energy comes in through a woman's heart and out through the genitals, while for men it comes in through the genitals and out through the heart. It becomes an endless energetic loop that continues to build, creating more intense arousal and orgasms. When a man and woman are being sexual together, it is extremely powerful to imagine this circle of energy.

In my work with couples, I have found a tremendous connection between this circle of sexual energy and the role sex plays in relationships, particularly heterosexual relationships. For most men, sex is the vehicle by which they reach emotional intimacy. Women, on the other hand, need an emotional connection in order to be inspired to have sex. This parallels the tantric view of the way energy flows in the sexual exchange. High-frequency emotions come from the man's heart via his genitals, and sexual energy develops in the woman through high-frequency, heart-centered thoughts and feelings.

When we are talking about same-sex unions, the same yin and yang energy is there. Sometimes the partners balance each other out intuitively. Other times one partner fulfills more of the yin or the yang. It varies by the individual and the relationship.

Here's how you can work with this dynamic:

For women having sex with men: During sex, imagine beautiful, loving sexual energy and light coming into your heart from your partner's heart. For several breaths, imagine the light flowing down through your chakras to your sacral and root chakras and the pelvic bowl, building in intensity as it goes. Then as you breathe out, imagine the light flowing straight out your (pink sparkly?) vagina and into your partner's genitals. Imagine a loop of energy between you, coming into you through your partner's heart and flowing out through your genitals into his.

For men having sex with women: Imagine taking energy or light from your partner's genitals into yours. For several breaths, imagine the light flowing through your root and sacral chakras all the way up to your heart chakra. Let it pool and build there. On an out-breath, send the beautiful light energy out of your heart and into your partner's heart. Imagine a loop of energy between you, coming in through your partner's genitals into yours and flowing up and out through your heart into hers.

For women having sex with women and men having sex with men: You can experiment with what feels best. Some couples I have worked with enjoy circling the energy back and forth between their genitals, or back and forth between their hearts, the latter creating much more emotional as well as physical intensity. You can also take turns being the heart starter or genital starter, unless one of you enjoys one direction more than the other.

Triple Lock

The Triple Lock is a tantric exercise that was originally conceived for use in men, but it is extremely powerful for women too. It draws energy from the top of the body down to the pelvis.

The three "locks" include neck, abdominal, and anal muscles, which you contract in a key order at key times. Sit comfortably with your back and shoulders straight and supported. Hold your head upright, looking straight ahead, and then do the following steps:

1. Throat lock comes first. Take a deep breath in, then tighten your throat muscles by pulling your chin toward your chest, as if you are pinching a pencil between your chin and neck. Hold this for a count

of three, then slowly relax, raising your head and releasing your breath.

2. Abdominal lock comes next. Take a breath and draw your abdomen in, as if you are trying to touch your spine with your belly button. Hold for a count of three, then release.
3. Anal lock is last and just involves contracting the muscles that you would use if you were holding in a bowel movement. Breathe in, hold briefly, and then squeeze more firmly still. Hold this tightest squeeze for a count of three, and then relax.

Once you have familiarized yourself with each of the three locks, you can try squeezing them all consecutively, but without releasing the previous locks: squeeze the throat, keep it squeezed while you add your abdominals, and as those two stay contracted, add the anal lock. Hold your breath as long as you can and then exhale.

To deepen orgasm, use the Triple Lock just as you feel orgasm approaching.

Kundalini Meditation

Kundalini meditation is a tantric yoga practice. Kundalini is considered to be a huge volume of energy that lies coiled in the base of the spine (sometimes it is represented as a snake). It is believed that a person's Kundalini can be awakened via meditation, yoga, or other spiritual practices. When it is awakened, the person will experience feelings of tingling along the spine along with enhanced energy, creativity, and bliss. Some even say that they have transcendental experiences.

Kundalini meditation can help a person to become receptive of loving energy as well as more prepared for deep sexual connection. In order to perform Kundalini meditation, sit cross-legged in a quiet room with your eyes shut. (You can do this alone or with your partner.) Holding your hands still and keeping your face soft, breathe in through your nose and out through your mouth. Now visualize the base of your spine and the energy coiled there. If you aren't a snake person, you can visualize something different—perhaps a glowing rainbow or silver bubbles. With each breath, you pull more and more bubbles out of the base of your spine. The bubbles travel along your spine, humming with energy. Each bubble is filled with pure loving potential. Each bubble offers an opportunity for connection, sexual and otherwise. If you are doing this with your partner, you can visualize his Kundalini growing in strength as well. Do this exercise before sex for a truly mind-blowing connection.

The Energy Hangover of Sex

As with all things in a relationship, not all energy shared in the sexual realm is going to be positive. When we have sex, we are vulnerable to our partner's negative energy. Ever since I started to pay attention to and ask about this, I find I often hear from couples that when one partner is in a bad mood and they have sex, the mood is often transferred to the other partner.

Marla Henderson is a wellness coach and intuitive who works in a holistic manner with people who are dealing with chronic medical struggles. She has shared with me that she often counsels people who are left with the negative, or even toxic, energy of their sexual partners inside their bodies. This is certainly the case with rape or trauma, but it extends even to our past experiences and thorny stories. I view the cases she has worked with as an extension of the body's wisdom (which we discussed in Chapter 7), in which a physical symptom has correlated with low-calibrating dramas and traumas that have come into our lives and get stuck in our bodies. As we have learned, that energy will linger and ultimately manifest as a physical symptom unless we address the issue and release the energy.

We've already talked about how you can hold your own energetic state regardless of where your partner is vibrating, but this is much harder to do during sex, as your partner's energy is not just around you but figuratively and literally *in* you.

A Little Discussion on Casual Sex

There's nothing wrong with casual sex. It can be exciting and fun and releasing. But it's not Quantum Sex. You can't connect on a spiritual level with someone you just met, especially if you are both knee-deep in cocktails and barely remember each other's names. If you want connective, restorative, erotic sex that is filled with intention and love, then casual sex isn't going to be your best bet.

Any time you are intimate with another person, you absorb some of their energy and they absorb some of yours. If you have sex with positive, loving, uplifting people, that wonderful energy is absorbed and uplifts you. If you have sex with negative, pessimistic, unstable, depressive people, that energy may leave you feeling uneasy and disconnected. Keep in mind, too, that if the person you are sleeping with also sleeps with a variety of people, he or she absorbs those people's energy. As with sexually transmitted diseases, when you have sex with someone, you are having sex with everyone they have had sex with–and taking in that energy as well.

This is where I try to counsel women about casual sex. Yes, we are all aware of the risk of STDs, and some of us even know about the emotional risk of casual sex (in which sex, especially good sex, releases a flood of oxytocin, the attachment chemical, in our brains and bonds us to our partner even if we don't want to be). Casual sex isn't a bad thing, but there are some emotional and physical risks that come with it. Now I add energetic risk to the list as well.

What I call the "energy hangover" of sex is not just an emotional aftereffect; I believe it can actually leave your partner's energy inside of you, especially if you're receiving your partner's body into yours.

I experienced this phenomenon with a patient of mine, Mikayla. She had a long and painful history. Her first sexual experience was when an older cousin molested her, and from there she had a string of bad boyfriends and worse breakups. Her worst experience was when her doctor told her that she had chlamydia. It was then she discovered that her husband was a sex addict and had been cheating on her for years. They got a divorce and Mikayla moved on, or so she thought. She even met a wonderful man and got engaged. But something was wrong. Sex hurt.

"It feels like an ache. Or a sharp pain," she said. "A burning. Or an itching."

I was confused. Her symptoms didn't seem connected to any physical issue. In fact, she had been to six doctors who all told her that there was nothing wrong. Mikayla also said she felt the pain even when she wasn't having sex.

"Like a toothache," she said. "A painful cramp here and there."

"What do you think it is?" I asked her.

"I don't know," she said. "I think my ex-husband left behind bacteria and gave me some kind of disease that hasn't been discovered yet. What do you think?"

Since we'd exhausted all physical and medical options, I considered another path. "I think perhaps your ex left behind something, but I don't think it was physical," I said. "I think he left behind energy that is causing you both physical and emotional pain. I think the same is true of the family member who molested you as a child, and all the horrible experiences you had since. You are carrying around all of this pain, and you are carrying it in your most intimate and precious space."

"Dr. Berman, are you telling me I am carrying emotional pain in my pocketbook?" she said. "Is that even possible?"

"I believe it is," I said. "And I believe we can help you release that pain."

Mikayla seemed a bit skeptical about the idea that she was carrying pain in her "pocketbook," as she called it. But she was willing to hear what I had to say. I told her about the concept of energetic hangovers, how we exchange energy during sex and sometimes that energy can be left behind, most especially in cases of emotional or physical trauma. I sent Mikayla to an energy healer I knew, who gave her some meditations and visualizations to help her move this energy out of her body. They worked with crystals, and Mikayla even began pleasuring herself with a rose quartz dildo that the energy healer gave her! Rose quartz is believed to carry the vibration of love and to help absorb negative energy. Over time, Mikayla noticed that the pain was present less and less. She was able to enjoy sex with her new fiancé, and she stopped obsessing over STDs. She began having orgasms with her partner and no longer dreaded intimacy.

Ultimately, it is impossible to say what exactly helped Mikayla (talking through her issues, the crystals, the visualization . . . the dildo!). But in the end she did stop having painful sex. "Thanks for fixing my pocketbook," she said to me in our last session. "I never knew it could hold so much. But now it is holding good things—positive energy, unconditional love, acceptance, creativity."

"Sounds like a busy pocketbook!" I said, laughing.

"Oh, she's very busy," she said. "Just ask my fiancé!"

Sex itself builds sexual energy. I think there are physical and relationship reasons for that. In a long-term relationship, if you are really committing yourself to Quantum Love and practicing the techniques we have discussed in this chapter and elsewhere in this book, you're going to have fabulous sexual energy inside you. Sexual energy inside you, and between you and your partner, is something that you want to take care of, harness, and put to work in your relationship. It is dynamic, flowing and changing, expanding and contracting always. And it is powerful and creative. Quantum Sex is a physical manifestation of your powerful sexual energy that unifies you and your partner in an intense and intensely positive way. It is a benefit of and a step deeper into Quantum Love.

A THANK-YOU NOTE

Dearest Reader,

If you have read this book, you now know that because we have come into each other's orbits in this way, we are vibrating in the same field. That makes you not just my reader, but also my cosmic companion. And I want you to know the deep well of gratitude I feel that you stayed open enough and curious enough to come on this journey with me. Thank you for showing up in my vibrational field (or for manifesting me!) and for your willingness to dive headfirst into the never-ending ocean of Quantum Love.

I have written eight other books on the most intimate aspects of human existence: love and sexuality. And yet, this book has been the most intimate for *me*, because it has been the most personal. *Quantum Love* wasn't born out of intellectual curiosity and a desire to heal others, like the books I've written in the past. This book was born out of my own personal struggles and self-discovery.

I feel so lucky to be able to say that for more than 25 years I've found tremendous success and satisfaction in helping individuals and couples learn to love and be loved better. I have always felt blessed to have discovered a career that brings me so much fulfillment and joy, one that in turn brings joy, passion, love, and laughter to others. Essentially, I mended broken hearts for a living for more than two decades. What's cooler than that? But I had no idea that there was so much more to be discovered until I found Quantum Love through my own AFGE.

In her memoir *On Extended Wings,* the poet Diane Ackerman writes, "I don't want to get to the end of my life and find that I just lived the length of it. I want to live the width of it as well." Four years ago I wouldn't have been able to tell you how much wider and deeper my personal and professional life could become through living in and working with Quantum Love. I am filled with such excitement knowing that my journey into the applications of Quantum Love in my life and my patients' lives is just beginning.

When your next AFGE comes, and it will, I encourage you to use it to not only grow your own soul, but to also grow your relationship with your partner. Hold on to your center. Hold on to love. Use your AFGE to grow together. And, in that "dark night of the soul," I hope that you can find the courage to move into your emotions instead of running from them, staying conscious of your energy and your power to create a new reality, even (and most especially) in your darkest days. I am living proof that it is possible, and I think the very fact that you picked up and read this book is a sign that you are more than ready to embrace Quantum Love in your life and through your next AFGE (or your current one).

In her book *The Fear Cure,* Lissa Rankin describes what she calls the four courage-cultivating truths:

1. Uncertainty is the gateway to possibility.
2. Loss is natural and can lead to growth.
3. It's a purposeful universe.
4. We are all one.

I believe that we can take each of these beautiful axioms a step further by applying our quantum lens and the lessons of this book:

1. *Anything is possible.* The quantum field is nothing but pure potential, ready to be shaped by our energy and intention. You have the power to create any reality you choose by getting clear on what

you want and harnessing the powerful, beautiful, immutable energy within you.

2. *Loss or pain comes into your life for a reason.* The things that come into your life are drawn to you by your own soul's desire, and no matter how painful, each of them is a lesson your essential self desired. You may not understand the reasons in the moment, but you can have faith that it is for your benefit.
3. *Every experience serves you.* The universe will give you everything you ask for (whether you are conscious of it or not), and you will draw teachers and mirrors into your life that will reflect some powerful, and even painful, truths back to you. There will be no greater teacher in your life than your partner.
4. *We are all one.* Yes, I left this one the same. It is, I believe, the Quantum Truth at the core of everything we have discussed in this book—and, indeed, at the very core of our existence. We are all so intimately connected at a fundamental level that we will find comfort, support, gifts, lessons, and of course love—everything we need—through our connection with others. I truly believe that we are here in our human forms for this very purpose.

These truths remind us that there is wisdom in our experiences. Our struggles urge us to ask, "What can this teach me?" These truths remind us that everything that happens to us serves us. Our challenges inspire us to consider, "How is this *for* me?" These truths remind us that our reality is pure potential. They lead us to clarity on the key question "What do I *really* want?" These truths remind us that we are all energy, boundless and limitless, indestructible and immutable, connected to everything in the universe.

If you had asked the old me, "Dr. Berman, why are we here on this earth?" I would have fumbled for an answer. I might have spoken of evolution, of our biological drive to procreate, or I might even have confessed the obvious: *I have no idea.*

But now I have an answer to this ageless question. I believe we are here on this planet in human form to love and be loved better. We are here to become lovesmiths: to master the art of loving and to live love into existence every single day.

I thank you for allowing me to share my discoveries with you. It is my sincerest wish that you feel a new level of awareness in yourself and with your partner, and that you've already started to practice some of the tools and techniques you have discovered here. It is my hope that you are able to use Quantum Love and the lessons you've learned here as a source of comfort, support, and reassurance, as a way to move out of your fear and into the love you so deserve.

As you continue on this journey, remember: Your boundaries are your quest. You are on this earth in this body not only to find love, but to find and break down the boundaries you have built *against* love. In doing so, I believe you will transform not only yourself and your relationship, but the very world itself.

APPENDIX

Chapter 3: Discover Your Energy Profile

The Quantum Love Quiz

Think about your general attitudes and behaviors over the past three months as you answer each of the questions that follow on a scale of 1 to 4, "Never" to "Always." Circle the number that best applies to you. Remember, you don't need to be in a relationship to take this quiz. In fact, building Quantum Love in yourself will attract a wonderful mate into your reality. You may answer the questions with regard to a past relationship or just your general view on relationships.

Once you have answered each question in the section, add up your numbers and divide the total by 5 to determine your Quantum Love score for each area of your relationship. Each section's scores will show you which area you are vibrating from on the Quantum Lovemap. Your scores will be between 1 and 4 for each section.

You may find that you are vibrating at different frequencies in different areas of your relationship. For example, you might be vibrating from ego frequency (To Me) in security and from home frequency (By Me) in your sex life but not in your sense of worthiness. That is totally okay. In fact, I have found in my work with hundreds of couples that this will often be the case.

Once you have your scores for each section on the quiz below, go to page 336 and consider where you are on the Quantum Lovemap. There are four quadrants in the Quantum Lovemap that correspond to your score of 1 to 4 on each section. The first and second quadrants are two phases of ego frequency and To Me. The third and fourth quadrants are in home frequency or Quantum Love: the third quadrant represents By Me energy and the fourth Through Me energy.

Feel free to go to www.drlauraberman.com/quantumlove to find an electronic version of the Quantum Love Quiz and the Quantum Lovemap.

The Quantum Love Quiz

Sense of Security in My Relationship	Never	Sometimes	Often	Always
I feel secure in my relationship.	1	2	3	4
It is very easy for me to be present with my partner.	1	2	3	4
I find it easy to get attached to my lover(s) in a healthy way.	1	2	3	4
I feel I have enough power in my relationship.	1	2	3	4
I find it easy to open my heart and be vulnerable in my relationship.	1	2	3	4
Add up your score and divide by 5 (round up if necessary)	Security Score:			

Sexual Energy in My Relationship	Never	Sometimes	Often	Always
I prefer spontaneity to predictability in the bedroom.	1	2	3	4
I embrace my impulses and desires.	1	2	3	4
I feel comfortable exploring new sexual avenues.	1	2	3	4

I enjoy being sexual with my partner.	1	2	3	4
I am comfortable expressing myself sexually.	1	2	3	4
Add up your score and divide by 5 (round up if necessary)	Sexual Score:			

My Sense of Love-Worthiness	**Never**	**Sometimes**	**Often**	**Always**
I feel deserving of love by an available and committed partner.	1	2	3	4
I am comfortable being the object of my partner's love and desire.	1	2	3	4
I feel confident my partner won't leave me or cheat on me.	1	2	3	4
I deserve as much respect as I give in my relationship.	1	2	3	4
My partner and I share similar goals for our relationship over the long term.	1	2	3	4
Add up your score and divide by 5 (round up if necessary)	Worthiness Score:			

Openheartedness in My Relationship	**Never**	**Sometimes**	**Often**	**Always**
It comes easily to me to trust and open up to my partner.	1	2	3	4
I am comfortable with emotional intimacy.	1	2	3	4
I enjoy connection rather than keeping my partner at a distance.	1	2	3	4
When we argue I find it easy to be sensitive to my partner's pain.	1	2	3	4
I find it easy to be emotionally generous with my partner.	1	2	3	4
Add up your score and divide by 5 (round up if necessary)	Openheartedness Score:			

Self-Expression in My Relationship	**Never**	**Sometimes**	**Often**	**Always**
I am comfortable expressing my needs to my partner.	1	2	3	4
When necessary, I can be assertive about my needs.	1	2	3	4
I communicate well with my partner, balancing talking and listening.	1	2	3	4
I am confident and comfortable when telling my partner a difficult truth.	1	2	3	4
If I am unhappy about something, I will speak up about it.	1	2	3	4
Add up your score and divide by 5 (round up if necessary)	Self-Expression Score:			

Intuition in My Relationship	**Never**	**Sometimes**	**Often**	**Always**
I love to dream about the future with my partner.	1	2	3	4
I am aware of what I want in my relationship.	1	2	3	4
I am intuitively aware of what my partner needs without having to ask.	1	2	3	4
I can sense when my partner is troubled, lying, in danger, etc.	1	2	3	4
I know the mood my partner is in the moment he (or she) walks in the room.	1	2	3	4
Add up your score and divide by 5 (round up if necessary)	Intuition Score:			

My Relationship as Part of a Bigger Plan	Never	Sometimes	Often	Always
I understand both my partner and I are part of a higher power.	1	2	3	4
I trust my intuition in my relationship.	1	2	3	4
I believe my partner is my greatest teacher.	1	2	3	4
I recognize the gifts/lessons in the struggles we have together.	1	2	3	4
I am aware that our relationship is part of a much bigger plan.	1	2	3	4
Add up your score and divide by 5 (round up if necessary)	Bigger Plan Score:			

The EHFI Quiz

Below is a series of questions asking about key domains in your relationship. I have found in the years I have worked with couples that many of us feel wonderful in certain domains and not in others. This should give you a clear picture, if you don't have an idea already, of where your greatest areas of growth toward Quantum Love are to be found.

For each question, mark the Quantum Lovemap. Here's how it works. Remember, the EHFI is shaped like this:

There are three points on the EHFI. The left end of the infinity symbol indicates where you are your most pessimistic. The right end is where you are most optimistic, and exactly in the center is your point of transition (the feeling state from which you will likely be shifting from pessimism to optimism or vice versa). You can draw your EHFI on the questionnaire below by just marking where you are most pessimistic and optimistic and drawing the EHFI on top of that, or you can use the Quantum Lovemap below and mark each domain (or the domains you most want to work on) there. Feel free to go to www.drlauraberman.com/quantumlove to find an electronic version.

Keep in mind that you don't have to currently be in a relationship to take this quiz. Just think about the last significant relationship you had, or answer in a general sense according to how you typically feel in relationships.

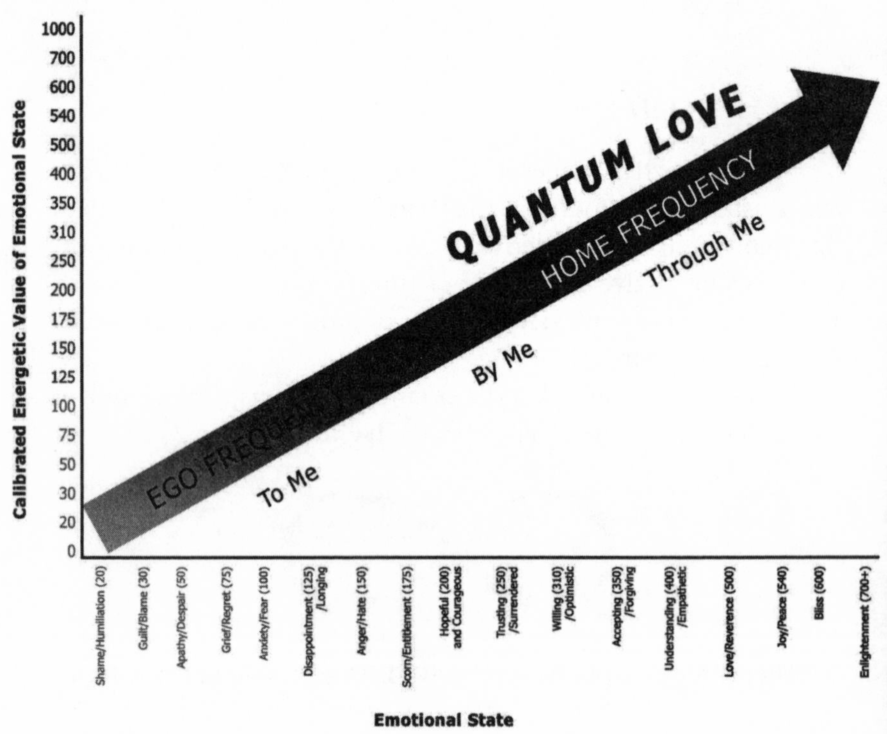

The Quantum Lovemap

Partnership

When I think of working out logistics, respecting each other's feelings, working together . . .

At my worst moments I feel (left end point of EHFI):

Shame	Guilt	Apathy	Regret	Fear	Longing	Anger	Scorn	Hopeful	Trusting	Optimistic	Accepting	Empathetic	Love	Joy	Bliss	Enlightened
20	30	50	75	100	125	150	175	200	250	310	350	400	500	540	600	700+

At my most optimistic I feel (right end point of EHFI):

Shame	Guilt	Apathy	Regret	Fear	Longing	Anger	Scorn	Hopeful	Trusting	Optimistic	Accepting	Empathetic	Love	Joy	Bliss	Enlightened
20	30	50	75	100	125	150	175	200	250	310	350	400	500	540	600	700+

What's the point of transition (exactly in the middle of the two points)?

Vision

When I think about how aligned we are in our vision of the future, parenting styles, etc. . . .

At my worst moments I feel (left end point of EHFI):

Shame	Guilt	Apathy	Regret	Fear	Longing	Anger	Scorn	Hopeful	Trusting	Optimistic	Accepting	Empathetic	Love	Joy	Bliss	Enlightened
20	30	50	75	100	125	150	175	200	250	310	350	400	500	540	600	700+

At my most optimistic I feel (right end point of EHFI):

Shame	Guilt	Apathy	Regret	Fear	Longing	Anger	Scorn	Hopeful	Trusting	Optimistic	Accepting	Empathetic	Love	Joy	Bliss	Enlightened
20	30	50	75	100	125	150	175	200	250	310	350	400	500	540	600	700+

What's the point of transition (exactly in the middle of the two points)?

Alliance

When I think about the two of us as allies and feeling like we're on the same team . . .

At my worst moments I feel (left end point of EHFI):

Shame	Guilt	Apathy	Regret	Fear	Longing	Anger	Scorn	Hopeful	Trusting	Optimistic	Accepting	Empathetic	Love	Joy	Bliss	Enlightened
20	30	50	75	100	125	150	175	200	250	310	350	400	500	540	600	700+

At my most optimistic I feel (right end point of EHFI):

Shame	Guilt	Apathy	Regret	Fear	Longing	Anger	Scorn	Hopeful	Trusting	Optimistic	Accepting	Empathetic	Love	Joy	Bliss	Enlightened
20	30	50	75	100	125	150	175	200	250	310	350	400	500	540	600	700+

What's the point of transition (exactly in the middle of the two points)?

Sex Life

When I think about the frequency and quality of our sexual connection . . .

At my worst moments I feel (left end point of EHFI):

Shame	Guilt	Apathy	Regret	Fear	Longing	Anger	Scorn	Hopeful	Trusting	Optimistic	Accepting	Empathetic	Love	Joy	Bliss	Enlightened
20	30	50	75	100	125	150	175	200	250	310	350	400	500	540	600	700+

At my most optimistic I feel (right end point of EHFI):

Shame	Guilt	Apathy	Regret	Fear	Longing	Anger	Scorn	Hopeful	Trusting	Optimistic	Accepting	Empathetic	Love	Joy	Bliss	Enlightened
20	30	50	75	100	125	150	175	200	250	310	350	400	500	540	600	700+

What's the point of transition (exactly in the middle of the two points)?

Communication

When I think about how we express ourselves, our level of respect and openness . . .

At my worst moments I feel (left end point of EHFI):

Shame	Guilt	Apathy	Regret	Fear	Longing	Anger	Scorn	Hopeful	Trusting	Optimistic	Accepting	Empathetic	Love	Joy	Bliss	Enlightened
20	30	50	75	100	125	150	175	200	250	310	350	400	500	540	600	700+

At my most optimistic I feel (right end point of EHFI):

Shame	Guilt	Apathy	Regret	Fear	Longing	Anger	Scorn	Hopeful	Trusting	Optimistic	Accepting	Empathetic	Love	Joy	Bliss	Enlightened
20	30	50	75	100	125	150	175	200	250	310	350	400	500	540	600	700+

What's the point of transition (exactly in the middle of the two points)?

Trust

When I think about the level of trust and support I feel with my partner . . .

At my worst moments I feel (left end point of EHFI):

Shame	Guilt	Apathy	Regret	Fear	Longing	Anger	Scorn	Hopeful	Trusting	Optimistic	Accepting	Empathetic	Love	Joy	Bliss	Enlightened
20	30	50	75	100	125	150	175	200	250	310	350	400	500	540	600	700+

At my most optimistic I feel (right end point of EHFI):

Shame	Guilt	Apathy	Regret	Fear	Longing	Anger	Scorn	Hopeful	Trusting	Optimistic	Accepting	Empathetic	Love	Joy	Bliss	Enlightened
20	30	50	75	100	125	150	175	200	250	310	350	400	500	540	600	700+

What's the point of transition (exactly in the middle of the two points)?

Fun/Joy

When I think about the level of fun and joy I feel with my partner . . .

At my worst moments I feel (left end point of EHFI):

Shame	Guilt	Apathy	Regret	Fear	Longing	Anger	Scorn	Hopeful	Trusting	Optimistic	Accepting	Empathetic	Love	Joy	Bliss	Enlightened
20	30	50	75	100	125	150	175	200	250	310	350	400	500	540	600	700+

At my most optimistic I feel (right end point of EHFI):

Shame	Guilt	Apathy	Regret	Fear	Longing	Anger	Scorn	Hopeful	Trusting	Optimistic	Accepting	Empathetic	Love	Joy	Bliss	Enlightened
20	30	50	75	100	125	150	175	200	250	310	350	400	500	540	600	700+

What's the point of transition (exactly in the middle of the two points)?

Emotional Connection

When I think about the emotional connection and closeness between us . . .

At my worst moments I feel (left end point of EHFI):

Shame	Guilt	Apathy	Regret	Fear	Longing	Anger	Scorn	Hopeful	Trusting	Optimistic	Accepting	Empathetic	Love	Joy	Bliss	Enlightened
20	30	50	75	100	125	150	175	200	250	310	350	400	500	540	600	700+

At my most optimistic I feel (right end point of EHFI):

Shame	Guilt	Apathy	Regret	Fear	Longing	Anger	Scorn	Hopeful	Trusting	Optimistic	Accepting	Empathetic	Love	Joy	Bliss	Enlightened
20	30	50	75	100	125	150	175	200	250	310	350	400	500	540	600	700+

What's the point of transition (exactly in the middle of the two points)?

Power

When I think about the balance of power in our relationship . . .

At my worst moments I feel (left end point of EHFI):

Shame	Guilt	Apathy	Regret	Fear	Longing	Anger	Scorn	Hopeful	Trusting	Optimistic	Accepting	Empathetic	Love	Joy	Bliss	Enlightened
20	30	50	75	100	125	150	175	200	250	310	350	400	500	540	600	700+

At my most optimistic I feel (right end point of EHFI):

Shame	Guilt	Apathy	Regret	Fear	Longing	Anger	Scorn	Hopeful	Trusting	Optimistic	Accepting	Empathetic	Love	Joy	Bliss	Enlightened
20	30	50	75	100	125	150	175	200	250	310	350	400	500	540	600	700+

What's the point of transition (exactly in the middle of the two points)?

Chapter 6: Commitment #2—I Will Get Clear on What I Want out of Love

Expanded List of Core Desired Relationship Feelings

What are yours? Feel free to add your own! Visit www.drlauraberman.com/quantumlove for an electronic version and more on Core Desired Relationship Feelings and your Quantum Love Goals.

Connected	Turned On	In Alignment	Supported
Joyful	Playful	Comforted	Encouraged
Cherished	Appreciated	Free	Calm
Trusted	Delighted	Seen and Heard	Passionate
Open	Protected	Tender	Attached To
Affectionate	Beloved	Esteemed	Liked
Intimate	Faithful	At Ease	United
Strong	Chosen	Adorable	Attractive
Flirtatious	Amiable	Loyal	Recognized
Delighted	Soothed	Frisky	Invigorated
Amorous	Prioritized	Tranquil	Sexy
Respected	Spirited	Satisfied	Fulfilled
Enthusiastic	Sensuous	Sultry	Lively
Accepted	Honest	Excited	Spontaneous

Plot Out Your Quantum Love Goals

First, what are the five Quantum Love Goals you chose? You can list them here if you wish.

In my relationship, I want to feel:

1. ______________________________
2. ______________________________
3. ______________________________
4. ______________________________
5. ______________________________

Now, to determine where you are in your Quantum Love Goals, do the following steps for each of your five core desired relationship feelings:

1. Answer each of the three questions (on the following pages) pertaining to how you feel in your relationship with regard to each core desired relationship feeling.
2. Find your EHFI for each of your core desired relationship feelings and plot it on the Quantum Lovemap. This will give you a clear picture of where you are and how far you have to go until your core desired feeling is a true reality for you.
3. Remember that the way you plot your EHFI is by thinking about how you feel at your least optimistic (the left end of the infinity symbol) and your most optimistic (right end of the infinity symbol). The midpoint between the two is the middle of the infinity symbol and your point of transition.
4. If you don't want to plot your EHFI, you can simply choose a point on the Quantum Lovemap to describe how you feel right now, or lately, and work from there.

Core Desired Relationship Feeling #1:

I want to feel ____

Question 1: When I am at my most pessimistic, I feel

____

Question 2: When I am at my most optimistic, I feel

____

Question 3: Today (lately), I feel

____

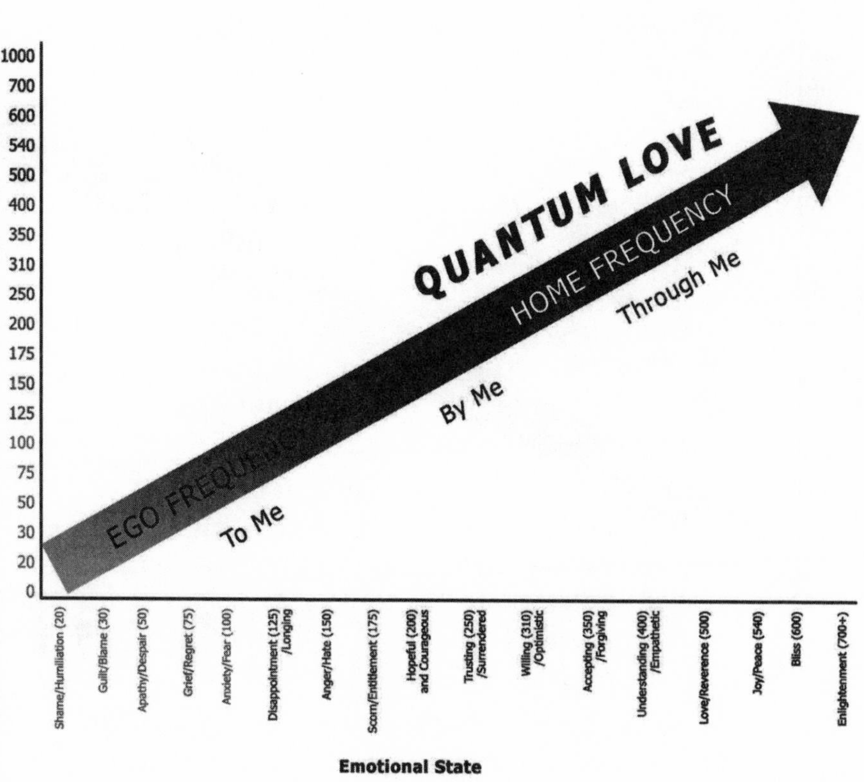

Core Desired Relationship Feeling #2:

I want to feel ______________________________

Question 1: When I am at my most pessimistic, I feel

____

Question 2: When I am at my most optimistic, I feel

____

Question 3: Today (lately), I feel

____

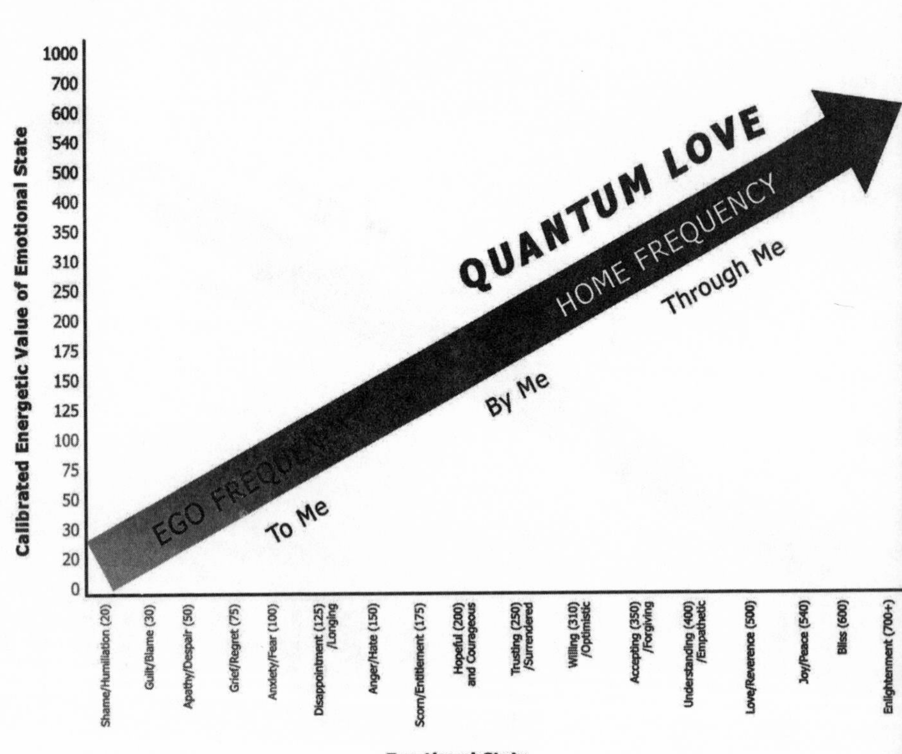

Core Desired Relationship Feeling #3:

I want to feel ______________________________

Question 1: When I am at my most pessimistic, I feel

____

Question 2: When I am at my most optimistic, I feel

____

Question 3: Today (lately), I feel

____

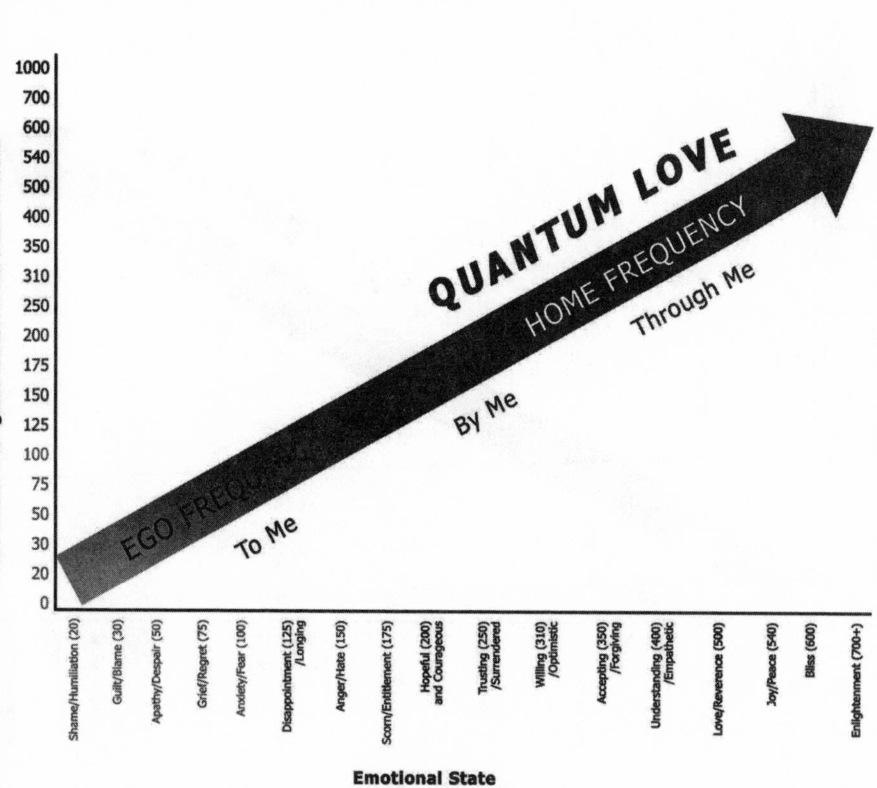

Core Desired Relationship Feeling #4:

I want to feel ______________________________

Question 1: When I am at my most pessimistic, I feel

____

Question 2: When I am at my most optimistic, I feel

____

Question 3: Today (lately), I feel

____

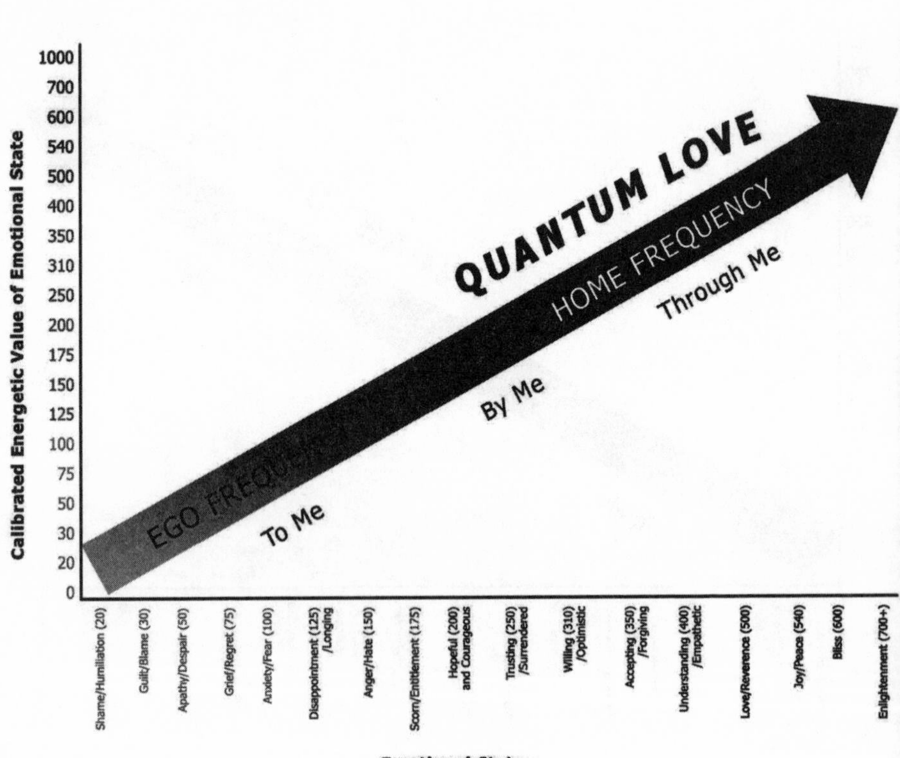

Core Desired Relationship Feeling #5:

I want to feel ______________________________________

Question 1: When I am at my most pessimistic, I feel

____

Question 2: When I am at my most optimistic, I feel

____

Question 3: Today (lately), I feel

____

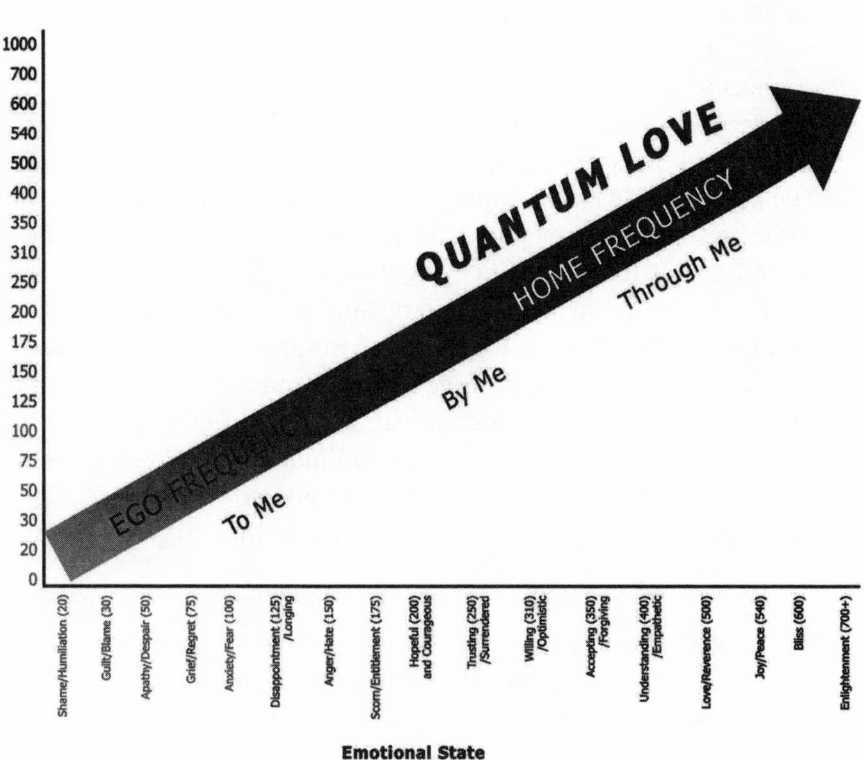

Chapter 8: Commitment #3—I Will Take Responsibility for My Body's Energy

Grace Points Exercise

A great immediate connection comes from stimulating your grace points to activate your body's meridians. Meridians are energy pathways that connect hundreds of tiny reservoirs of electromagnetic and more subtle energies along the surface of the skin. Known in Chinese medicine as acupuncture points, theses dots or "hot spots" can be stimulated with needles or physical pressure to release and redistribute energy. As you will see below, these different points are thought to activate the meridians in the body that connect to the heart.

Here is an exercise used by transformational coach Marci Shimoff and created by Edward Conmey of Peace Path that I have adapted. The key is to hold a loving intention to connect to your highest self while pressing three key points. Many healers claim that it is highly powerful for activating your crown chakra.

Point 1 is the main grace point (middle of the palm). This is thought to release contracted energy so insights are clearly received and to anchor you in a positive frame of mind. Point 2 (slightly to the right of the center of the palm) releases unmoving, stuck energy (usually in the form of fear and judgments). Point 3 (web between thumb and forefinger) is about ancestry, releasing judgment and beliefs that have been passed down through generations.

1. Ground yourself.
2. Press the first point for 10 to 15 seconds while you take some deep breaths. Invite in grace and surrender and state the intention to open up to the guidance of your higher self.
3. Repeat while pressing each of the other two points.

I AM Meditation

If your throat chakra is out of balance, it may be worthwhile to consider the words and the messages you are speaking to yourself and others. Words carry power and energetic frequency through sound as well as the energy of the thoughts and emotions the words create in our mind and body. As Wayne Dyer wrote, over the course of our lives we have become conditioned to think and speak in the language of "I'm not"—not good enough, not thin enough, not lovable. "I'm not" is the language of our worthiness-killing beliefs.

This is also where the powerful words "I AM" come in. This is discussed in great detail in Dyer's work, especially his book *Wishes Fulfilled,* which is a great read if you want to become a Master Manifester. I also recommend his *I AM Wishes Fulfilled* meditation tapes, in which he set the vibrational tone of the words "I AM" to music. He discovered these divine sounds as he was doing research on his book.

Now it's time to shift your mind-set from "I'm not" to "I AM."

1. Sit in a comfortable place and make sure you have a pen and paper or something you can use to take a few notes.
2. Ground yourself and open your heart.
3. Think about something you want to create more of in your life. A great idea is to start with one of your core desired relationship feelings. Choose one to work on now.
4. I want you to consider and try on what it would really feel like inside you if that core desired relationship experience you long for was a reality. It may help to imagine a scene or instance, even if it's fabricated, in which you had that experience. If your core desired relationship feeling is to be "playful," what kind of playful situation or circumstance can you imagine that would include your partner? Maybe you would be wrestling on the bed together, or simply cuddling on the couch sharing a deep belly laugh. Get creative—the more detail, the better!

5. Now get yourself into the feeling state of that desire by seeing yourself, *in the scene,* in first person. Employ all your senses as if you are experiencing it all in the here and now.
6. Now it's time to move into the "I AM." From this coherent, master manifesting state of being, think back to the scene you just imagined. As you look at yourself in the scene, describe yourself with a free-flowing list of sentences that start with the words, "I AM." Don't judge or edit yourself. Don't think about what's realistic or what "fits." Just let it all flow through you and write the words down as they come to you. Come up with as many sentences as you can.
7. It may help to close your eyes again, go back to the scene as you take some deep breaths, saying out loud, "I AM!" Then open your eyes and write down whatever comes to mind.
8. Once you have the list of sentences, read them out loud to yourself. Recite them as you look into your own eyes in the mirror. Scream them from the rooftops. And regularly pull that list out and move yourself into the feeling state of those words in your body. You know how to do that now.
9. Treat this like a meditation, and when you are done, simply move on and let it go. You have now activated the quantum field toward greater Quantum Love in the form of your core desired relationship feelings. That feeling and experience is already here for you; you just can't yet perceive it with your five senses. But it is coming your way soon! Now you just have to look for it and notice it in your reality.
10. Do this for as many of your inventoried list of sentences and core desired relationship feelings as you wish—or with anything else you want to manifest as a reality in your life.

Taoist Meditation: Inner Smile Meditation

I also love to use the Taoist Inner Smile meditation to send positive energy into different parts of my body. This simple meditation feels absolutely wonderful in mind and body! Go to www.drlauraberman.com/quantumlove to listen to a guided Inner Smile meditation.

1. Begin by grounding yourself. Sit on a chair with both your feet on the floor, close your eyes, and feel your connection to the earth. Take some deep breaths, ground yourself, and open your heart.
2. Create a source of smiling energy in your mind. This can be an image of your own smiling face, or of someone or something you love and respect, or any memory of a time when you felt deeply at peace, perhaps feeling sunshine, being by the ocean, or walking in a forest. Get a sense of that energy, a feeling of it. Sometimes I just imagine the shape of a smile in my mind.
3. Once you have that sense, imagine the *energy* of that joyful, smiling face, there, three feet in front of you.
4. Become aware of the midpoint between your eyebrows through which you will draw this abundant smiling energy in front of and around you. Let your forehead relax; as the smiling energy accumulates at mid-eyebrow, it will eventually overflow into your body.
5. Smile into your eyes. Feel the joyful energy shine into them. Now send the energy down to your neck, moving down to the collarbone. Your entire throat and shoulders are bathed in smiling light.
6. Smile into your chest, your heart, ribs, intestines, all your organs, your uterus (if you have one), your pelvis, your legs, arms, all over your body. Smile into them in the same way that you just smiled into

your eyes, until every organ and every cell of your body that you can think of is bathed in the light of a loving smile.

Chapter 10: Commitment #4—I Will Realize When I Am Stuck and Shift from Brain to Mind

Mindfulness Meditation

Below are two mindfulness meditations created by my friend and mindfulness coach Annmarie Chereso. One is for transforming fear to love; the other is for living from a place of love. Go to www.drlauraberman.com/quantumlove to hear an audio version of these meditations by Annmarie.

Fear to Love Meditation

So often we want to resist our fears, reject them, or push them away. In this meditation, we're going to practice loving our fears. Can you really love your fear? Can you be with your fear? Can you hold your fear like a tiny, scared baby who doesn't know what to do? Can you find empathy and compassion for this fear? Can you honor the fear without pushing it away or rejecting it?

1. Sit upright and find a comfortable position. Allow your spine to be relaxed, your neck to be loose, your head to rest gently on the top of your neck. Check in with your shoulders to see if they are tense and tight or relaxed and gently resting. Check in with your fingers and your toes. Are your fingers clenched, or are they gently resting in your lap? Are your toes and your feet comfortable and relaxed? Are you finding tension there? Our body is such a great guide if we just pay attention.

2. Now notice your breath. You can take an inventory: Is my breathing fast or slow? Is my breath full, or is it short and shallow? For a moment, follow the pace of your breath to the count of four. Breathe in (1, 2, 3, 4) and out (1, 2, 3, 4).
3. I now invite you to recall a time in your life when you felt afraid. Maybe you were scared of getting hurt or hurting someone else; scared of being in a relationship with someone or being *out* of a relationship with someone; maybe you were scared of failing at a job or of taking a risk. See if, in this moment, you can check in and find a time when you were afraid.
4. Notice if your breath is still, at the same rhythm as it was a second ago, or if it has changed. Just pay attention.
5. Once you locate that fear, that experience you had, take notice of where it lives in your body. For some of us, fears show up in our stomach, in tightness or butterflies. Or maybe it's in your shoulders or your back; maybe it's all in your head. In this moment, just notice: "Where does my fear live?"
6. As you feel that fear in the present moment, take note of your heart. Where is your heart in relation to your fear? Is your fear in your heart? Is it away from your heart? And as you begin to sink into your heart, I want you to imagine the light that exists within your heart shining down on to your fear. Imagine the warm rays of your heart's light and your love radiating to your fear.
7. Look at your fear lovingly. You might imagine your fear like a crying baby. You might want the crying and the noise to stop, but you don't push the baby away; you hold the baby closer. You cradle the baby. You care for and love that baby. See if you would be willing to love your fear in the same way. We don't have to give in to

our fears. We don't have to agree with our fears. We can just love them and appreciate them for what they are.

8. For this moment, imagine this fear living inside, embodying part of who you are, and continue to make the light from your heart shine brighter. It shines so bright that it is surrounding the fear and holding it up. It shines so bright that the fear begins to melt. Imagine the fear melting all around you like warm butter on pancakes. It starts at the top of your head and melts all the way down your shoulders and back, caressing every cell in your body. What is it like to melt your fear with love?
9. You may feel your fear start to come back. That's okay. Imagine yourself giving this fear a big hug, welcoming it. This time, invite it into your heart. Have it take a seat and be with you there. Lean over and touch the fear and look deeply into it. Get curious. "Fear, what do you want? How can I help?"
10. All the while, your love is expanding and growing and holding your fear in loving presence. There's nothing wrong, nothing to be rejected, nothing to turn away. Are you willing to be that much love?

Living from Love Meditation

1. Imagine yourself sitting in the center of a circle. Call to mind a few people whom you love deeply, surrounding you in this circle at arm's length. If you were to stretch your arms out, the tips of your fingers might just about touch them.
2. Now imagine another group of people sitting behind the first group at about the same distance. And surrounding them is another group. And so on, into infinity, like the ripples or rings of a pebble dropped into a pond.

3. As you're sitting in the center of this ring, I invite you to locate your beating heart right in the center of you. Perhaps you're willing to occupy your heart in this now moment. Maybe you feel or notice your heartbeat, just as you notice the pace and rhythm of your breath. Perhaps you even notice inside your heart a bright, intense light, as bright as the sun. And with each heartbeat, this light shines even brighter. And with each breath, you can imagine this light filling your heart up completely and fully. As you sit and occupy your heart, you actually become this light.
4. Notice this light expanding into every cell of your body. Imagine this light energy continuing to expand beyond your cells. In this moment, imagine this light expanding so brightly and so intensely that it reaches the first ring of people surrounding you.
5. With each breath, you inhale love and light. With each exhale, this light and love expands to those in your inner circle. You might even notice the light expanding out like the rays of the sun reaching down to earth. You might notice as the light reaches that first circle of people surrounding you that their light is reaching beyond them to the next layer of people. And the next layer. And the next layer, into infinity.
6. You might also notice as you breathe in that the rhythm of your breath is aligned with the rings of those around you. With each breath, your beating heart is sending the light from you into beyond. See if in this moment you can see the whole group rising up, breathing in, and your breath falling down like the waves of the ocean.
7. As you notice this light expanding out and beyond, take a moment to come back inward to the source of that light and love, the source that began within your own heart. In this now moment, are you willing

> to accept the infinite power of the love that exists within you, because of you, and through you? You are the source of this love, and the power belongs to you. Would you be willing to step into that power in each and every moment? Would you be willing to live from the light within your own heart? Would you be willing to live and expand in that power and that love to those around you? Would you be willing to be that much love in each and every moment?

Loving-Kindness Meditation

There are a few ways to practice loving-kindness meditation: with visualization, reflection, or an auditory practice. The auditory practice is probably the simplest, as it is merely the act of repeating a mantra (even "loving-kindness" will work) to yourself while thinking about your partner and sending love and good vibes to him in your mind. You can also visualize the other person sitting across from you and smile at him or feel joy in his direction.

The reflection practice is probably my favorite, however. Reflect on everything you love about the other person—her personality traits, acts of kindness, or the gifts she brings into the world. Dissolve the physical barrier between you and this person, remembering that you are one at a quantum level. Her positive traits and acts of kindness are shared with you and yours with her. Move into the feeling state of these positive things: how does it feel to give and receive these kindnesses? Then, with the understanding that you are one and the same, make a positive statement about yourself.

These three practices can be used all together (for instance, you can use visualization to help you enter into the feeling state, and then the positive reflective statement you make can become part of your auditory practice), or you can pick a favorite. The next step is to take your loving-kindness meditation out of the house! Bring your loving energy to work, to school, to your dinner table, even to the Starbucks where you like to grab an afternoon pick-me-up.

Send a quick "sending you love" message to a friend, or call your partner in the middle of the day just to say something nice.

When it comes to the energy of loving-kindness, the more you give, the more you receive. And as far as your frequency is concerned, it's By Me and Through Me all the way!

Loving-Kindness Guided Meditation

In this meditation, allow yourself to switch from the usual mode of doing to a mode of non-doing. Simply be. As your body becomes still, bring your attention to the fact that you are breathing. And become aware of the movement of your breath as it comes into your body and as it leaves. You don't have to change anything about your breath. Simply notice and observe it. Feel it flowing in and filling your belly as you breathe in . . . and notice how the belly falls back against the back as you breathe out. You are completely present and need to be nowhere but here. Right now. Right here.

If a distracting thought arises, acknowledge it. Say to yourself, "Thought." Don't do anything but return to breathing. Now bring to mind someone for whom you have deep feelings of love. See that person in your mind's eye and notice the feelings that arise in your body. Notice any sensations that arise: A bubbling in the chest area? A smile on your face? A warmth flowing through you? Just feel whatever you notice and breathe into it.

Now, holding on to the feelings in your body, let go of the picture of this person in your imagination. Bring yourself to mind now, and see if you can extend the love you have in your body to yourself. And as you do, say these words to yourself or out loud:

May I be happy
May I be healthy
May I ride the waves of my life
May I live in peace
No matter what I am given

Notice the feelings that arise, and let them be as you look within yourself, filling yourself with love. Imagine filling every cell in your body with beautiful light in whatever color feels right to you.

When you are ready, imagine sending that same light to someone who supports you, who has always been on your side. See that person in your mind and imagine the same light that is filling your body shooting out of your heart and through the quantum field to that person. As you do, say these words to yourself or out loud:

May you be happy
May you be healthy
May you ride the waves of your life
May you live in peace
No matter what you are given

Once your feelings flow easily to a loved one, turn your attention now to someone with whom you have difficulty. Maybe not someone who gives you tremendous trouble, but someone who makes you feel irritated or annoyed. As you take deep breaths, send that same light out of your heart toward that person. Imagine him or her bathed in your heartlight. As you keep this person in awareness, say out loud or to yourself:

May you be happy
May you be healthy
May you ride the waves of your life
May you live in peace
No matter what you are given

Notice the sensations and feelings that arise within you. Don't judge them or try to change them; just let them be. Now bring to mind the broader community of which you are a part. You might imagine your family, neighbors, colleagues—whoever you want. Now imagine bathing those people in your heartlight, saying these words:

May we be happy
May we be healthy
May we ride the waves of our lives
May we live in peace
No matter what we are given

Notice the sensations and feelings that arise within you. Sit with them for a few moments until you are ready to end the practice.

Go to www.drlauraberman.com/quantumlove to listen to an audio version of a guided loving-kindness meditation.

QUANTUM LOVE RESOURCES

Reading List

Chapter 1: What Is Quantum Love, Anyway?

Finding Your Own North Star: Claiming the Life You Were Meant to Live, by Martha Beck (Harmony, 2002)

Frequency: The Power of Personal Vibration, by Penney Peirce (Atria Books, 2009)

The Secret, by Rhonda Byrne (Atria Books/Beyond Words, 2006)

The Untethered Soul: The Journey Beyond Yourself, by Michael Singer (New Harbinger Publications, 2007)

Chapter 2: Meet Your Inner Quantum Physicist

E-Squared: Nine Do-It-Yourself Energy Experiments That Prove Your Thoughts Create Your Reality, by Pam Grout (Hay House, 2013)

Chapter 3: Discover Your Energy Profile

The 15 Commitments of Conscious Leadership: A New Paradigm for Sustainable Success, by Jim Dethmer, Diana Chapman, and Kaley Warner Klemp (Dethmer, Chapman & Klemp, 2015)

Many Lives, Many Masters: The True Story of a Prominent Psychiatrist, His Young Patient, and the Past-Life Therapy That Changed Both Their Lives, by Brian L. Weiss (Simon & Schuster, 2012)

My Stroke of Insight: A Brain Scientist's Personal Journey, by Jill Bolte Taylor, Ph.D. (Viking, 2008)

Power vs. Force: The Hidden Determinants of Human Behavior, by David R. Hawkins, M.D., Ph.D. (Hay House, 2002)

You Are the Placebo: Making Your Mind Matter, by Dr. Joe Dispenza (Hay House, 2014)

Chapter 4: Commitment #1—I Will Take Responsibility for the Energy I Bring into My Relationship

Life Unlocked: 7 Revolutionary Lessons to Overcome Fear, by Srinivasan S. Pillay (Rodale, 2010)

Chapter 5: Falling in Love versus Quantum Love

The 5 Love Languages: The Secret to Love That Lasts, by Gary Chapman (Northfield, 2015)

Conversations with God: An Uncommon Dialogue: Book 1, by Neale Donald Walsch (Hampton Roads Publishing, 1995)

The Divine Matrix: Bridging Time, Space, Miracles, and Belief, by Gregg Braden (Hay House, 2008)

Chapter 6: Commitment #2—I Will Get Clear on What I Want out of Love

The Fire Starter Sessions: A Soulful Practical Guide to Creating Success on Your Own Terms, by Danielle LaPorte (Crown Archetype, 2012)

Walking Between the Worlds: The Science of Compassion, by Gregg Braden (Radio Bookstore Press, 1997)

Chapter 7: Your Body Is an Energy Powerhouse

Finding Your Way in a Wild New World: Reclaim Your True Nature to Create the Life You Want, by Martha Beck (Free, 2012)

Heal Your Body, by Louise Hay (Hay House, 1984)

Chapter 8: Commitment #3—I Will Take Responsibility for My Body's Energy

The Blood Sugar Solution 10-Day Detox Diet, by Mark Hyman, M.D. (Little, Brown, 2014)

The Beauty Detox Solution, by Kimberly Snyder (Harlequin, 2011)

Crazy Sexy Cancer Tips, by Kris Carr (Globe Pequot Press, 2007)

The Daniel Plan, by Rick Warren, Daniel Amen, and Mark Hyman (Zondervan, 2013)

Energy Medicine: Balancing Your Body's Energy for Optimal Health, Joy and Vitality, by Donna Eden (Jeremy P. Tarcher, 2008)

Wishes Fulfilled, by Dr. Wayne W. Dyer (Hay House, 2013)

Chapter 9: Retrain Your Brain So Your Mind Can Work

How Quantum Physicists Build New Beliefs, by Greg Kuhn (CreateSpace Independent Publishing Platform, 2013)

Molecules of Emotion, by Candace Pert (Simon & Schuster, 1999)

A Return to Love, by Marianne Williamson (HarperOne, 1996)

Why Quantum Physicists Do Not Fail: Learn the Secrets of Achieving Almost Anything Your Heart Desires, by Greg Kuhn (CreateSpace Independent Publishing Platform, 2013)

Chapter 10: Commitment #4—I Will Realize When I Am Stuck and Shift from Brain to Mind

It's Not Him, It's You!: How to Take Charge of Your Life and Create the Love and Intimacy You Deserve, by Laura Berman, Ph.D. (Dorling Kindersley Ltd., 2011)

Loving What Is: Four Questions That Can Change Your Life, by Byron Katie (Harmony, 2002)

The Rise of Superman: Decoding the Science of Ultimate Human Performance, by Steven Kotler (New Harvest, 2014)

Chapter 11: Quantum Sex

The Book of Love: Every Couple's Guide to Emotional and Sexual Intimacy, by Laura Berman, Ph.D. (Dorling Kindersley Ltd., 2013)

The Fear Cure: Cultivating Courage as Medicine for the Body, Mind, and Soul, by Lissa Rankin, M.D. (Hay House, 2015)

Loving Sex: The Book of Joy and Passion, by Laura Berman, Ph.D. (Dorling Kindersley Ltd., 2011)

The Passion Prescription: 10 Weeks to Your Best Sex Ever, by Laura Berman, Ph.D. (Hachette, 2013)

Real Sex for Real Women, by Laura Berman, Ph.D. (Dorling Kindersley Ltd., 2011)

Slow Sex: The Art and Craft of Female Orgasm, by Nicole Daedone (Grand Central Life and Style, 2012)

Other Resources

Websites

American Association of Sexuality Educators, Counselors and Therapists
www.aasect.org
A website that can help you find a sex therapist near you.

Chakras
www.healer.ch/bmsarticle.html
Learn more about your chakras and how to use your body's feedback.

The Chopra Center
www.chopra.com/ccl/guided-meditations
Free guided meditations, as well as products and programs to enhance well-being in body, mind, and spirit.

Co-Dependents Anonymous (CoDA)
www.coda.org
Get assistance and support in treating codependence.

The Law of Attraction
www.abraham-hicks.com
Read more on the teachings of the spiritual guides known as Abraham.

OneTaste
www.onetaste.us
Learn about the practice of Orgasmic Meditation.

Quantum Love
www.drlauraberman.com/quantumlove
Here you will find more Quantum Love interactive material, including guided meditations.

Transcendental Meditation
www.tm.org
Find out more about TM and how to locate classes and teachers.

UCLA Mindful Awareness Resource Center
www.marc.ucla.edu
Free guided meditations; information on mindfulness practice and research.

National Domestic Violence Hotline

www.thehotline.org
800-799-SAFE (7233)
800-787-3224 (TTY)
Offering anonymous and confidential help, 24/7.

Healers, Coaches, and Experts

Martha Beck, life coach
www.marthabeck.com

Diana Chapman, life coach
www.dianachapman.com

Annmarie Chereso, mindfulness coach
www.projectmindfulness.net

Marla Henderson, wellness guide and intuitive healer
www.haniawellbeing.tumblr.com

Susan Hyman, intuitive strategist and leadership coach
www.susanhyman.com

Jackie Lesser, life coach, creator of the wHolyShift
www.THEwHolyShift.com

Robert Ohotto, intuitive life strategist
www.ohotto.com

Srinivasan Pillay, psychiatrist, expert on fear
www.srinipillay.com

Therese Rowley, intuitive healer
www.thereserowley.com

Kimberly Snyder, nutritionist
www.kimberlysynder.com

NOTES

Chapter 2: Meet Your Inner Quantum Physicist

1. Greg Kuhn, *Why Quantum Physicists Do Not Fail: Learn the Secrets of Achieving Almost Anything Your Heart Desires* (Charleston, SC: CreateSpace Independent Publishing Platform, 2013).
2. Pam Grout, *E-Squared: Nine Do-It-Yourself Energy Experiments That Prove Your Thoughts Create Your Reality* (Carlsbad, CA: Hay House, 2013).
3. Todd L. Richards, Leila Kozak, Clark Johnson, and Leanna J. Standish, "Replicable Functional Magnetic Resonance Imaging Evidence of Correlated Brain Signals Between Physically and Sensory Isolated Subjects," *Journal of Alternative and Complementary Medicine* 11, no. 6 (2005):955–963.
4. E. Schrödinger, "Die gegenwärtige Situation in der Quantenmechanik," *Naturwissenschaften* 23 (1935): 807–812; 823–828; 844–849. Discussion by A. Einstein, B. Podolsky, and N. Rosen, *Physical Review* 47 (1935):777.
5. Andrew Robinson, *The Last Man Who Knew Everything* (New York: Pi Press, 2006).
6. To see these crystals, go to the Bioenergy Healing & Beyond YouTube channel at https://www.youtube.com/watch?v=tAvzsjcBtx8.
7. Karl H. Pribram, "Holonomic Brain Theory in Imaging and Object Perception," *Acta Psychologica* 63, no. 2 (1986):175–210.

Chapter 3: Discover Your Energy Profile

1. Martha Anderson, "Kinesiology, a Tool of Consciousness—How to Tell Truth from Falsehood," *Natural News,* January 21, 2012.
2. J. Diamond, *BK—Behavioral Kinesiology: How to Activate Your Thymus and Increase Your Life Energy* (New York: Harper & Row, 1979).
3. David R. Hawkins, *Power vs. Force: The Hidden Determinants of Human Behavior* (Carlsbad, CA: Hay House, 2013).
4. Michael Singer, *The Untethered Soul: The Journey Beyond Yourself* (Oakland, CA: New Harbinger Publications/Noetic Books, 2007).

Chapter 5: Falling in Love versus Quantum Love

1. John Money, *Lovemaps: Clinical Concepts of Sexual/Erotic Health and Pathology* (New York: Irvington Publishers, 1993).
2. G. N. Fuller and P. C. Burger, "Nervus terminalis (Cranial Nerve Zero) in the Adult Human," *Clinical Neuropathology* 9, no. 6 (November 1990):279–283.
3. C. Wedekind et al., "MHC-Dependent Mate Preferences in Humans," *Proceedings of the Royal Society of London B* 260, no. 1359 (June 1995):245–249; C. Ober et al., "HLA and Mate Choice in Humans," *American Journal of Human Genetics* 61 (1997):497–504.
4. Gregg Braden, *The Divine Matrix: Bridging Time, Space, Miracles, and Belief* (Carlsbad, CA: Hay House, 2007).
5. Helen Fisher, A. Aron, and L. L. Brown, "Romantic Love: An fMRI Study of a Neural Mechanism for Mate Choice," *The Journal of Comparative Neurology* 493, no. 1 (2005):58–62.
6. Salynn Boyles, "Romantic Love Affects Your Brain Like a Drug," *WebMD Health News*, October 13, 2010.
7. Hongwen Song et al., "Love-Related Changes in the Brain: A Resting-State Functional Magnetic Resonance Imaging Study," *Frontiers in Human Neuroscience* 9 (2015).
8. Martin Sommer et al., "Mechanisms of Human Motor Cortex Facilitation Induced by Subthreshold 5-Hz Repetitive Transcranial Magnetic Stimulation," *Journal of Neurophysiology* 109, no. 12 (2013):3060–3066.
9. Deepak Chopra, "The 7 Spiritual Laws of Love," *Care 2*, August 2012. http://www.care2.com/greenliving/the-7-spiritual-laws-of-love.html.
10. John M. Gottman and Julie Schwartz Gottman, "The Empirical Basis of Gottman Couples Therapy," distributed under license by The Gottman Institute, Inc. (2013). https://www.gottman.com/wp-content/uploads/EmpiricalBasis-Update3.pdf.
11. John M. Gottman et al., "Predicting Marital Happiness and Stability from Newlywed Interactions," *Journal of Marriage and the Family* 60, no. 1 (1998):5–22.

Chapter 7: Your Body Is an Energy Powerhouse

1. Elizabeth C. D. Gullette et al., "Effects of Mental Stress on Myocardial Ischemia," *Journal of the American Medical Association* 277, no. 19 (May 1997):1521–1526.
2. G. Rein, M. Atkinson, and Rollin McCraty, "The Physiological and Psychological Effects of Compassion and Anger," *Journal of Advancement in Medicine* 8, no. 2 (1995).
3. Shaoni Bhattacharya, "Brain Study Links Negative Emotions and Lowered Immunity," *New Scientist*, September 2, 2003. http://www.newscientist.com/

article/dn4116-brain-study-links-negative-emotions-and-lowered-immunity.html#.VTj6OmTBzGc.

4. Katharine Gammon, "Why Loneliness Can Be Deadly," *LiveScience,* March 2, 2012. http://www.livescience.com/18800-loneliness-health-problems.html.
5. John M. Gottman and Robert W. Levenson, "The Social Psychophysiology of Marriage," in P. Noller and M. A. Fitzpatrick eds, *Perspectives on Marital Interaction* (Philadelphia: Multilingual Matters, 1988).
6. Gottman et al., "Predicting Marital Happiness and Stability from Newlywed Interactions."
7. S. A. McLeod, "What Is the Stress Response?" (2010), retrieved from www.simplypsychology.org/stress-biology.html.
8. Gottman and Levenson, "The Social Psychophysiology of Marriage."
9. Lewis Madison Terman et al., *Psychological Factors in Marital Happiness* (New York: McGraw-Hill, 1938).
10. Rollin McCraty et al., "The Coherent Heart: Heart-Brain Interactions, Psychophysiological Coherence, and the Emergence of System-Wide Order," *Integral Review* 5, no. 2 (2009):10–115.
11. Rollin McCraty and Mike Atkinson, "Influence of Afferent Cardiovascular Input on Cognitive Performance and Alpha Activity [abst.]," *Proceedings of the Annual Meeting of the Pavlovian Society*, 1999.
12. Rollin McCraty, Mike Atkinson, and William A. Tiller, "Influence of Afferent Cardiovascular Input on Cognitive Performance and Alpha Activity," *Proceedings of the Tenth International Montreux Congress on Stress,* 1999.
13. Lauri Nummenmaa et al., "Bodily Maps of Emotions," *Proceedings of the National Academy of Sciences of the United States of America* 111, no. 2 (2013):645–651. doi: 10.1073/pnas.1321664111.

Chapter 8: Commitment #3—I Will Take Responsibility for My Body's Energy

1. Harvard Medical School, "Relaxation Techniques: Breath Control Helps Quell Errant Stress Response," *Harvard Health Publications*, January 26, 2015; web April 23, 2015. http://www.health.harvard.edu/mind-and-mood/relaxation-techniques-breath-control-helps-quell-errant-stress-response.
2. Swami Shivapremananda, *Yoga for Stress Relief* (New York: Random House, 1997).
3. Thomas Campbell II, *The China Study: The Most Comprehensive Study of Nutrition Ever Conducted and the Startling Implications for Diet, Weight Loss and Long-Term Health* (Dallas: BenBella Books, 2004).
4. Susan Yanovski, "Sugar and Fat: Cravings and Aversions," *Journal of Nutrition* 133, no. 3 (2003):835S–837S.
5. Audrey Ensminger, *Food for Health: A Nutrition Encyclopedia* (Clovis, CA: Pegus Press, 1986).

Chapter 9: Retrain Your Brain So Your Mind Can Work

1. K. R. Scherer, A. Schorr, and T. Johnstone, *Appraisal Processes in Emotion: Theory, Methods, Research* (New York: Oxford University Press, 2001); L. F. Barrett et al., "The Experience of Emotion," *Annual Review of Psychology* 58 (2007):373–403.
2. J. A. Dusek et al., "Stress Management versus Lifestyle Modification on Systolic Hypertension and Medication Elimination: A Randomized Trial," *Journal of Alternative and Complementary Medicine* 14, no. 2 (2008):129–38.
3. B. Alan Wallace, *The Attention Revolution: Unlocking the Power of the Focused Mind* (Boston: Wisdom Publications, 2006).
4. Phillip Cohen, "Mental Gymnastics Increase Bicep Strength," *New Scientist*, November 21, 2001; G. Yue and K. J. Cole, "Strength Increases from the Motor Program: Comparison of Training with Maximal Voluntary and Imagined Muscle Contractions," *Journal of Neurophysiology* 67, no. 5 (1992):1114–1123.
5. R. A. Emmons and M. E. McCullough, "Counting Blessings versus Burdens: An Experimental Investigation of Gratitude and Subjective Well-Being in Daily Life," *Personality & Social Psychology* 88 (2003):377–389.

Chapter 10: Commitment #4—I Will Realize When I Am Stuck and Shift from Brain to Mind

1. Ferris Jabr, "Why Your Brain Needs More Downtime," *Scientific American*, October 15, 2013. http://www.scientificamerican.com/article/mental-downtime/.
2. Bridget Murray, "Finding the Peace within Us," *Monitor on Psychology* 33, no. 7 (July/August 2002):56.
3. Tenzin Gyatso, "The Monk in the Lab," *The New York Times*, April 26, 2003.
4. Alex Korb, "Yoga: Changing the Brain's Stressful Habits," *Psychology Today*, September 7, 2011. https://www.psychologytoday.com/blog/prefrontal-nudity/201109/yoga-changing-the-brains-stressful-habits.

Chapter 11: Quantum Sex

1. Cindy M. Meston and David M. Buss, "Why Humans Have Sex," *Archives of Sexual Behavior* 36, no. 4 (2007):477–507.
2. Chip Walter, "Affairs of the Lips," *Scientific American Mind* 19, no. 1 (2008):24–29.

ACKNOWLEDGMENTS

I am filled with such gratitude for the love and support that surrounds me. First of all, thank you to Hay House for taking a chance on what was a new direction for me and believing in the Quantum Love message. I hope I do you proud! Anne Barthel, you are a wonderful and thoughtful editor. Thank you for your talents, patience, and focus. Ann Maynard, thank you for your brilliance and ability to articulate the most complicated ideas with poetry! Bridget Sharkey, you are so gifted. Thank you for your guidance, edits, and ever-present speediness! To my manager at 2 Market Media, Steve Carlis, thank you for your drive, creativity, and vision. A special shout-out goes to Martha Beck, who set me on the path that would change my life with her time, compassion, and suggestion to just write one thing that was true every day.

To my Forum sisters: Munisha Bhatia, Elyse Klein, Lucy Moog, Michele Sakheim-Wein, Carter Sharfstein, and Karen Zucker. You have been my rocks, my cheerleaders and growth partners, always there holding me in love. To my fellow Fire Starters, Kathy Bresler, Annmarie Chereso, Lisa Carter, Susan Hyman, Elizabeth Kilbourne, Andrea Kaufman, and Cookie Weber, I am filled with gratitude that I manifested each of you into my universe. Each of you has been my teacher, inspiring me and shoring me up through my leap into Quantum Love.

I am so lucky to have many soul siblings in my life: Marla Henderson, who's been my spiritual muse and companion as long as I can remember; Randy Wilder, whose unconditional love and irreverence are irreplaceable; and Robert Ohotto, intuitive extraordinaire, thank you for telling me to land my plane! Special mention goes out to my other soul siblings who have unwaveringly supported and cheered me on: Laura Coe, Elizabeth Evans, Jennifer Gilbert, Thea Goodman, Niamh King, Elise Paschen, and Dana Weinstein.

To my father, Irwin Berman, thank you for loving me so deeply and challenging me to love myself. Thank you to Gail Rose for restoring generous love to my father's life and sharing it with the rest of us. To my mother, Linda Berman, and my grandmothers, Teal Friedman and Jean Berman, no longer on this plane, you are with me and within me every day. To my honorary mother, Sandra Flowers, you are love personified, teaching me so much about trust and faith.

To my children, Ethan, Sammy, and Jackson, you are my greatest blessings. Thank you for your generous agreement to allow so much of your story told, and for opening your hearts to Quantum Love in our home (albeit with occasional eye rolls). And to my beloved Sam Chapman, my husband and my greatest teacher, you are the best Quantum Lover a girl could hope for. Thank you for your willingness to continually stretch and grow alongside me.

ABOUT THE AUTHOR

Laura Berman, Ph.D., is a world-renowned educator and therapist in the area of love, sex, and relationships. She is the founder and director of the Berman Institute in Chicago, which specializes in helping couples learn to resolve conflict, come together in crises, and grow their emotional and physical intimacy to new heights. She is assistant clinical professor of psychiatry and obstetrics/gynecology at the Feinberg School of Medicine at Northwestern University. Considered a thought leader in her field, Dr. Berman is a *New York Times* best-selling author of many books on love, sex, and relationships and host of the nationally syndicated radio show *Uncovered Radio with Dr. Laura Berman.* She has appeared in the pages of nearly every major U.S. magazine and newspaper, as well as on most television talk and news shows. Dr. Berman serves on the advisory board for *The Dr. Oz Show* and is the most frequent guest on *Steve Harvey.* She lives in Chicago with her husband, three sons, and dog.

Website: www.drlauraberman.com

Hay House Titles of Related Interest

YOU CAN HEAL YOUR LIFE, the *movie,*
starring Louise Hay & Friends
(available as a 1-DVD program and an expanded 2-DVD set)
Watch the trailer at: www.LouiseHayMovie.com

THE SHIFT, the *movie,*
starring Dr. Wayne W. Dyer
(available as a 1-DVD program and an expanded 2-DVD set)
Watch the trailer at: www.DyerMovie.com

CONSCIOUS LOVING EVER AFTER: How to Create Thriving Relationships at Midlife and Beyond, by Gay Hendricks, Ph.D., and Kathlyn Hendricks, Ph.D.

HOW TO LOVE YOURSELF (AND SOMETIMES OTHER PEOPLE): Spiritual Advice for Modern Relationships, by Lodro Rinzler and Meggan Watterson

LOVEABILITY: Knowing How to Love and Be Loved, by Robert Holden, Ph.D.

REWIRE YOUR BRAIN FOR LOVE: Creating Vibrant Relationships Using the Science of Mindfulness, by Marsha Lucas, Ph.D.

All of the above are available at your local bookstore, or may be ordered by contacting Hay House (see next page).